Heroes of the Nations

EDITED BY

H. W. C. Davis

FACTA DUCIS VIVENT, OPEROSAQUE
GLORIA RERUM——OVID, IN LIVIAM, 265.
THE HERO'S DEEDS AND HARD-WON
FAME SHALL LIVE

CANUTE THE GREAT

CANUTE AND EMMA
(The King and Queen are presenting a golden cross to Winchester
Abbey, New Minster.)
From a miniature reproduced in *Liber Vitæ* (Birch).

CANUTE THE GREAT

995 (circ)–1035

AND THE RISE OF DANISH IMPERIALISM DURING THE VIKING AGE

BY

LAURENCE MARCELLUS LARSON, Ph.D.

ASSOCIATE PROFESSOR OF HISTORY IN THE UNIVERSITY OF ILLINOIS

G. P. PUTNAM'S SONS

NEW YORK AND LONDON

The Knickerbocker Press

1912

The Knickerbocker Press, New York

To

MY WIFE

LILLIAN MAY LARSON

FOREWORD

TOWARD the close of the eighth century, there appeared in the waters of Western Europe the strange dragon fleets of the Northmen, the "heathen," or the vikings, as they called themselves, and for more than two hundred years the shores of the West and the Southwest lived in constant dread of pillage and piracy. The viking invasions have always been of interest to the student of the Middle Ages; but only recently have historians begun to fathom the full significance of the movement. The British Isles were preeminently the field of viking activities. English historians, however, have usually found nothing in the invasions but two successive waves of destruction. As an eminent writer has tersely stated it,—the Dane contributed nothing to English civilisation, for he had nothing to contribute.

On the other hand, Scandinavian students, who naturally took great pride in the valorous deeds of their ancestors, once viewed the western lands chiefly as a field that offered unusual opportunities for the development of the dormant energies of the Northern race. That Christian civilisation could not fail to react on the heathen mind was clearly seen; but this phase of the problem was not emphasised; the importance of western influences was minimised.

Serious study of the viking age in its broader aspects began about fifty years ago with the researches of Gudbrand Vigfusson, a young Icelandic scholar, much of whose work was carried on in England. Vigfusson's work was parallelled by the far more thorough researches of the eminent Norwegian philologist, Sophus Bugge. These investigators both came to the same general conclusion: that Old Norse culture, especially on the literary side, shows permeating traces of Celtic and Anglo-Saxon elements; that the Eddic literature was not an entirely native product, but was largely built up in the viking colonies in Britain from borrowed materials.

Some years earlier, the Danish antiquarian, J. J. A. Worsaae, had begun to study the "memorials" of Norse and Danish occupation in Britain, and had found that the islands in places were overlaid with traces of Scandinavian conquest in the form of place names. Later Worsaae's countryman, Dr. J. C. H. R. Steenstrup, carried the research into the institutional field, and showed in his masterly work, *Normannerne* (1876–1882), that the institutional development among the Anglo-Saxons in the tenth and eleventh centuries was largely a matter of adapting and assimilating Scandinavian elements.

Studies that embodied such differing viewpoints could not fail to call forth much discussion, some of which went to the point of bitterness. Recently there has been a reaction from the extreme position assumed by Professor Bugge and his followers; but quite generally Norse scholars are coming to take the position that both Sophus Bugge and Johannes Steenstrup have been correct in their main contentions; the most prominent representative of this view is Professor Alexander Bugge. Where two vigorous peoples representing differing types or different stages of civilisation come into more than temporary contact, the reciprocal influences will of necessity be continued and profound.

The viking movement had, therefore, its aspects of growth and development as well as of destruction. The best representative of the age and the movement, when considered from both these viewpoints, is Canute the Great, King of England, Denmark, and Norway. Canute began as a pirate and developed into a statesman. He was carried to victory by the very forces that had so long subsisted on devastation; when the victory was achieved, they discovered, perhaps to their amazement, that their favourite occupation was gone. Canute had inherited the imperialistic ambitions of his dynasty, and piracy and empire are mutually exclusive terms.

It is scarcely necessary to say anything further in justification of a biographical study of such an

eminent leader, one of the few men whom the
world has called "the Great." But to write a
true biography of any great secular character of
mediæval times is a difficult, often impossible, task.
The great men of modern times have revealed
their inner selves in their confidential letters;
their kinsmen, friends, and intimate associates
have left their appreciations in the form of ad-
dresses or memoirs. Materials of such a character
are not abundant in the mediæval sources. But
this fact need not deter us from the attempt. It
is at least possible to trace the public career of the
subject chosen, to measure his influence on the
events of his day, and to determine the importance
of his work for future ages. And occasionally
the sources may permit a glimpse into the private
life of the subject which will help us to understand
him as a man.

The present study has presented many difficulties. Canute lived in an age when there was but
little writing done in the North, though the granite
of the runic monument possesses the virtue of
durability. There is an occasional mention of
Canute in the Continental chronicles of the time;
but the chief contemporary sources are the
Anglo-Saxon Chronicle, the *Encomium Emmæ*,
and the praise lays of the Norse and Icelandic
scalds. The *Chronicle* was written by a patriotic
Englishman who naturally regarded the Danes
with a strong aversion. The *Encomium*, on the
other hand, seems to be the product of an alien

clerk, whose chief purpose was to glorify his patroness, Queen Emma, and her family. The lays of the scalds are largely made up of flattering phrases, though among them are woven in allusions to historic facts that are of great value.

The Anglo-Norman historians and the later monastic annalists in England have not very much to add to our information about Canute; but in their accounts they are likely to go to the other extreme from the *Chronicle*. Too often the monkish writers measured excellence by the value of gifts to churches and monasteries, and Canute had learned the value of donations properly timed and placed.

Adam of Bremen wrote a generation later than Canute's day, but, as he got his information from Canute's kinsmen at the Danish court, his notices of Northern affairs are generally reliable. There is no Danish history before the close of the twelfth century, when Saxo wrote the *Acts of the Danes*. It is evident that Saxo had access to a mass of sources both written and of the saga type. The world is grateful to the Danish clerk for preserving so much of this material; but sound, critical treatment (of which Saxo was probably incapable) would have enhanced the value of his work.

The twelfth century is also the age of the sagas. These are of uneven merit and most of them are of slight value for present purposes. However, the sources on which these are in a measure based, the fragments of contemporary verse that are extant and much that has not survived, have been woven into a history, the equal of which for artistic treatment, critical standards, and true historical spirit will be difficult to find in any other mediæval literature. Wherever possible, therefore, reference has been made in this study to Snorre's *Kings' Sagas*, commonly known as "Heimskringla," in preference to other saga sources.

In the materials afforded by archæology, the Northern countries are peculiarly rich, though, for the purposes of this study, these have their only value on the side of culture. An exception must be made of the runic monuments (which need not necessarily be classed with archæological materials), as these often assist in building up the narrative. More important, perhaps, is the fact that these inscriptions frequently help us to settle disputed points and to determine the accuracy of accounts that are not contemporary.

One of the chief problems has been where to begin the narrative. To begin in the conventional way with childhood, education, and the rest is not practicable when the place and the year of birth are unknown and the forms and influences of early training are matters of inference and conjecture. At the same time it was found impossible to separate the man from his time, from the great activities that were going on in the lands about the North Sea, and from the purposes of the dynasty that he belonged to. Before it is possible to give an intelligent account of how Canute led the viking movement to successful conquest, some account must be given of the movement itself. The first chapter and a part of the second consequently have to deal with matters introductory to and preparatory for Canute's personal career, which began in 1012.

In the writing of proper names the author has planned to use modern forms whenever such exist; he has therefore written Canute, though his preference is for the original form Cnut. King Ethelred's by-name, "Redeless," has been translated "Ill-counselled," which is slightly nearer the original meaning than "unready"; "uncounselled" would scarcely come nearer, as the original seems rather to imply inability to distinguish good from bad counsel.

In the preparation of the study assistance has been received from many sources; especially is the author under obligation to the libraries of the Universities of Illinois, Chicago, Wisconsin, and Iowa, and of Harvard University; he is also indebted to his colleagues Dean E. B. Greene, Professor G. S. Ford, and Professor G. T. Flom, of the University of Illinois, for assistance in the form of critical reading of the manuscript.

L. M. L.

CHAMPAIGN, Ill., 1911.

CONTENTS

ILLUSTRATIONS

CANUTE THE GREAT

CHAPTER I

THE HERITAGE OF CANUTE THE GREAT

AMONG the many gigantic though somewhat shadowy personalities of the viking age, two stand forth with undisputed pre-eminence: Rolf the founder of Normandy and Canute the Emperor of the North. Both were sea-kings; each represents the culmination and the close of a great migratory movement,—Rolf of the earlier viking period, Canute of its later and more restricted phase. The early history of each is uncertain and obscure; both come suddenly forth upon the stage of action, eager and trained for conquest. Rolf is said to have been the outlawed son of a Norse earl; Canute was the younger son of a Danish king: neither had the promise of sovereignty or of landed inheritance. Still, in the end, both became rulers of important states—the pirate became a constructive statesman. The work of Rolf as founder of Normandy was perhaps the more enduring; but far more brilliant was the career of Canute.

Few great conquerors have had a less promising future. In the early years of the eleventh century, he seems to have been serving a military apprenticeship in a viking fraternity on the Pomeranian coast, preparatory, no doubt, to the profession of a sea-king, the usual career of Northern princes who were not seniors in birth. His only tangible inheritance seems to have been the prestige of royal blood which meant so much when the chief called for recruits.

But it was not the will of the Norns that Canute should live and die a common pirate, like his grand-uncle Canute, for instance, who fought and fell in Ireland[1]: his heritage was to be greater than what had fallen to any of his dynasty, more than the throne of his ancestors, which was also to be his. In a vague way he inherited the widening ambitions of the Northern peoples who were once more engaged in a fierce attack on the West. To him fell also the ancient claim of the Danish kingdom to the hegemony of the North. But more specifically Canute inherited the extensive plans, the restless dreams, the imperialistic policy, and the ancient feuds of the Knytling dynasty.[2] Canute's career is the history of Danish imperial-

[1] Saxo Grammaticus, *Gesta Danorum*, 321.
[2] The saga writers call the members of the Danish dynasty the Knytlings, from its foremost representative Canute (Knut).

ism carried to a swift realisation. What had proved a task too great for his forbears Canute in a great measure achieved. In England and in Norway, in Sleswick and in Wendland, he carried the plans of his dynasty to a successful issue. It will, therefore, be necessary to sketch with some care the background of Canute's career and to trace to their origins the threads of policy that Canute took up and wove into the web of empire. Some of these can be followed back at least three generations to the reign of Gorm in the beginning of the tenth century.

In that century Denmark was easily the greatest *10th Cert.* power in the North. From the Scanian frontiers to the confines of modern Sleswick it extended over "belts" and islands, closing completely the entrance to the Baltic. There were Danish outposts on the Slavic shores of modern Prussia; the larger part of Norway came for some years to be a vassal state under the great earl, Hakon the Bad; the Wick, which comprised the shores of the great inlet that is now known as the Christiania Firth, was regarded as a component part of the Danish monarchy, though in fact the obedience rendered anywhere in Norway was very slight.

In the legendary age a famous dynasty known as the Shieldings appears to have ruled over Danes and Jutes. The family took its name from a mythical ancestor, King Shield, whose coming to the Daneland is told in the opening lines of the Old English epic *Beowulf*. The Shieldings were

worthy descendants of their splendid progenitor:
they possessed in full measure the royal virtues
of valour, courage, and munificent hospitality.
How far their exploits are to be regarded as historic is a problem that does not concern us at
present; though it seems likely that the Danish
foreworld is not without its historic realities.

Whether the kings of Denmark in the tenth
century were of Shielding ancestry is a matter of
doubt; the probabilities are that they sprang from
a different stem.   The century opened with Gorm
the Aged, the great-grandfather of Canute, on the
throne of Shield, ruling all the traditional regions
of Denmark,—Scania, the Isles, and Jutland—
but apparently residing at Jelling near the south-
east corner of the peninsula, not far from the
Saxon frontier.   Tradition remembers him as a
tall and stately man, but a dull and indolent king,
wanting in all the elements of greatness.[1]   In this
case, however, tradition is not to be trusted.
Though we have little real knowledge of Danish
history in Gorm's day, it is evident that his reign
was a notable one.   At the close of the ninth
century, the monarchy seems to have faced
dissolution; the sources tell of rebellious vassals,
of a rival kingdom in South Jutland, of German
interference in other parts of the Jutish peninsula.[2]
Gorm's great task and achievement were to reunite
the realm and to secure the old frontiers.

[1] Saxo, *Gesta Danorum*, 318.
[2] Wimmer, *De danske Runemindesmærker*, I., ii., 71–72.

Though legend has not dealt kindly with the King himself, it has honoured the memory of his masterful Queen. Thyra was clearly a superior woman. Her nationality is unknown, but it seems likely that she was of Danish blood, the daughter of an earl in the Holstein country.[1] To this day she is known as Thyra Daneboot (Danes' defence) —a term that first appears on the memorial stone that her husband raised at Jelling soon after her death. In those days Henry the Fowler ruled in Germany and showed hostile designs on Jutland. In 934, he attacked the viking chiefs in South Jutland and reduced their state to the position of a vassal realm. Apparently he also encouraged them to seek compensation in Gorm's kingdom. To protect the peninsula from these dangers a wall was built across its neck between the Schley inlet and the Treene River. This was the celebrated Danework, fragments of which can still be seen. In this undertaking the Queen was evidently the moving force and spirit. Three years, it is said, were required to complete Thyra's great fortification. The material character of the Queen's achievement doubtless did much to preserve a fame that was highly deserved; at the same time, it may have suggested comparisons that were not to the advantage of her less fortunate consort. The Danework, however, proved only a temporary frontier; a century later Thyra's great descendant Canute pushed the boundary

[1] *Danmarks Riges Historie*, i., 293.

to the Eider River and the border problem found
a fairly permanent solution.

In the Shielding age, the favourite seat of royalty
was at Lethra (Leire) in Zealand, at the head of
Roeskild Firth. Here, no doubt, was located
the famous hall Heorot, of which we read in
Beowulf. There were also king's garths elsewhere; the one at Jelling has already been mentioned as the residence of Gorm and Thyra. After
the Queen's death her husband raised at Jelling,
after heathen fashion, a high mound in her honour,
on the top of which a rock was placed with a brief
runic inscription:

Gorm the king raised this stone in memory of
Thyra his wife, Denmark's defence.[1]

The runologist Ludvig Wimmer believes that the
inscription on the older Jelling stone dates from
the period 935–940; a later date is scarcely probable. The Queen evidently did not long survive
the famous "defence."

A generation later, perhaps about the year 980,
Harold Bluetooth, Gorm's son and successor,
raised another mound at Jelling, this one, apparently, in honour of his father. The two mounds stand
about two hundred feet apart; at present each is
about sixty feet high, though the original height
must have been considerably greater. Midway
between them the King placed a large rock as a
monument to both his parents, which in addition

[1] Wimmer, *De danske Runemindesmærker*, I., ii., 15.

THE OLDER JELLING STONE, A

THE OLDER JELLING STONE, B

to its runic dedication bears a peculiar blending of Christian symbols and heathen ornamentation. The inscription is also more elaborate than that on the lesser stone:

Harold the king ordered this memorial to be raised in honour of Gorm his father and Thyra his mother, the Harold who won all Denmark and Norway and made the Danes Christians.[1]

In one sense the larger stone is King Harold's own memorial. It is to be observed that the inscription credits the King with three notable achievements: the unification of Denmark, the conquest of Norway, and the introduction of Christianity. The allusion to the winning of Denmark doubtless refers to the suppression of revolts, perhaps more specifically to the annihilation of the viking realm and dynasty south of the Danework (about 950).[2] In his attitude toward his southern neighbours Harold continued the policy of Gorm and Thyra: wars for defence rather than for territorial conquest.

It is said that King Harold became a Christian (about 960) as the result of a successful appeal to the judgment of God by a zealous clerk named Poppo. The heated iron (or iron gauntlet, as Saxo has it) was carried the required distance, but Poppo's hand sustained no injury. Whatever be the truth about Poppo's ordeal, it seems evident

[1] Wimmer, *De danske Runemindesmærker*, I., ii., 28–29.
[2] *Ibid.*, 72.

that some such test was actually made, as the
earliest account of it, that of Widukind of Corvey,
was written not more than a decade after the
event.[1]   The importance of the ordeal is manifest:
up to this time the faith had made but small headway in the Northern countries.   With the conversion of a king, however, a new situation was
created: Christianity still had to continue its
warfare against the old gods, but signs of victory
were multiplying.   One of the first fruits of Harold
Bluetooth's conversion was the Church of the
Holy Trinity, built at Roeskild by royal command,[2]
—a church that long held an honoured place in
the Danish establishment.   In various ways the
history of this church closely touches that of the ·
dynasty itself: here the bones of the founder were
laid; here, too, his ungrateful son Sweyn found
quiet for his restless spirit; and it was in this
church where Harold's grandson, Canute the
Great, stained and violated sanctuary by ordering
the murder of Ulf, his sister's husband.

In the wider activities of the tenth century,
Harold Bluetooth played a large and important
part.   About the time he accepted Christianity,
he visited the Slavic regions on the south Baltic
coasts and established his authority over the lands
about the mouth of the Oder River.   Here he
founded the stronghold of Jomburg, the earls and

[1] *Danmarks Riges Historie*, i., 335–336.   Saxo, *Gesta Danorum*,
338.   Saxo places the ordeal in the reign of Harold's successor.
[2] Adamus, *Gesta Hammenburgensis Ecclesiæ Pontificum*, ii., c.26.

THE LARGER SÖNDER VISSING STONE

THE LATER JELLING STONE, A

garrisons of which played an important part in Northern history for more than two generations. The object of this expansion into Wendland was no doubt principally to secure the Slavic trade which was of considerable importance and which had interested the Danes for more than two centuries.[1] As the Wendish tribes had practically no cities or recognised markets, the new establishment on the banks of the Oder soon grew to be of great commercial as well as of military importance.

During the same period Harold's attention was turned to Norway where a difficult situation had arisen. Harold Fairhair, the founder of the Norse monarchy, left the sovereignty to his son Eric (later named Bloodax); but the jealousies of Eric's many brothers combined with his own cruel regime soon called forth a reaction in favour of a younger brother, Hakon the Good, whose youth had been spent under Christian influences at the English court. King Hakon was an excellent ruler, but the raids of his nephews, the sons of Eric, caused a great deal of confusion. The young exiles finally found a friend in Harold Bluetooth who even adopted one of them, Harold Grayfell, as his own son.[2]

The fostering of Harold Grayfell had important consequences continuing for two generations till the invasion of Norway by Canute the Great. With a force largely recruited in Denmark, the

---

[1] *Danmarks Riges Historie*, i., 322–324.
[2] Snorre, *Saga of Hakon the Good*, cc. 3, 4, 5, 10.

sons of Eric attacked Norway and came upon King Hakon on the island of Stord where a battle was fought in which the King fell (961). But the men who had slain their royal kinsman found it difficult to secure recognition as kings: the result of the battle was that Norway was broken up into a number of petty kingdoms and earldoms, each aiming at practical independence.

A few years later there appeared at the Danish court a young, handsome, talented chief, the famous Earl Hakon whose father, Sigurd, earl in the Throndelaw, the sons of Eric had treacherously slain. The King of Denmark had finally discovered that his foster-son was anything but an obedient vassal, and doubtless rejoiced in an opportunity to interfere in Norwegian affairs. Harold Grayfell was lured down into Jutland and slain. With a large fleet the Danish King then proceeded to Norway. The whole country submitted: the southern shores from the Naze eastward were added to the Danish crown; the Throndelaw and the regions to the north were apparently granted to Earl Hakon in full sovereignty; the rest was created into an earldom which he was to govern as vassal of the King of Denmark.[1]

A decade passed without serious difficulties between vassal and overlord, when events on the German border brought demands on the earl's fidelity to which the proud Norseman would not

[1] Snorre, *Olaf Trygvesson's Saga*, c. 15. See also Munch, *Det norske Folks Historie*, I., ii., 53.

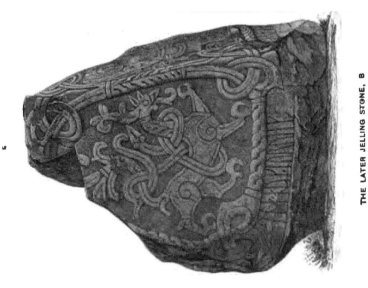

THE LATER JELLING STONE, B

THE LATER JELLING STONE, C

submit. It seems probable that King Harold in a vague way had recognised the overlordship of the Emperor; at any rate, in 973, when the great Otto was celebrating his last Easter at Quedlingburg, the Danish King sent embassies and gifts.[1] A few weeks later the Emperor died and almost immediately war broke out between Danes and Saxons.

Hostilities soon ceased, but the terms of peace are said to have included a promise on Harold's part to introduce the Christian faith among his Norwegian subjects. Earl Hakon had come to assist his overlord; he was known to be a zealous heathen; but King Harold seized him and forced him to receive baptism. The earl felt the humiliation keenly and as soon as he had left Denmark he repudiated the Danish connection and for a number of years ruled in Norway as an independent sovereign.[2] King Harold made an attempt to restore his power but with small success. However, the claim to Norway was not surrendered; it was successfully revived by Harold's son Sweyn and later still by his grandson Canute.

Earl Hakon's revolt probably dates from 974 or 975; King Harold's raid along the Norse coasts must have followed within the next few years. The succeeding decade is memorable for two notable expeditions, the one directed against King Eric of Sweden, the second against Hakon of

[1] Thietmar, *Chronicon*, ii., c. 20.
[2] Snorre, *Olaf Trygvesson's Saga*, cc. 24, 26–28.

Norway. In neither of these ventures was Harold directly interested; both were undertaken by the vikings of Jom, though probably with the Danish King's approval and support. The Jomvikings were in the service of Denmark and the defeat that they suffered in both instances had important results for future history. The exact dates cannot be determined; but the battles must have been fought during the period 980-986.

In those days the command at Jomburg was held by Styrbjörn, a nephew of the Swedish King. Harold Bluetooth is said to have given him the earl's title and his daughter Thyra to wife; but this did not satisfy the ambitious prince, whose desire was to succeed his uncle in Sweden. Having induced his father-in-law to permit an expedition, he sailed to Uppland with a strong force. The battle was joined on the banks of the Fyris River where King Eric won a complete victory. From that day he was known as Eric the Victorious.[1]

Styrbjörn fell in the battle and Sigvaldi, the son of a Scanian earl, succeeded to the command at Jomburg. In some way he was induced to attack the Norwegian earl. Late in the year the fleet from the Oder stole northwards along the Norse coast hoping to catch the earl unawares. But Hakon's son Eric had learned what the vikings were planning and a strong fleet carefully hid in Hjörunga Bay lay ready to welcome the invader.

The encounter at Hjörunga Bay is one of the

[1] *Danmarks Riges Historie*, i., 340-341.

most famous battles in Old Norse history.   During
the fight, says the saga, Earl Hakon landed and
sacrificed his young son Erling to the gods.   The
divine powers promptly responded: a terrific
hailstorm that struck the Danes in their faces
helped to turn the tide of battle, and soon Sigvaldi
was in swift flight southwards.[1]

As to the date of the battle we have no certain
knowledge; but Munch places it, for apparently
good reasons, in 986.   Saxo is probably correct in
surmising that the expedition was inspired by
King Harold.[2]   As to the significance of the two
defeats of the Jomvikings, there can be but one
opinion: northward expansion of Danish power
had received a decisive check; Danish ambition
must find other fields.

The closing years of Harold's life were embit-
tered by rebellious movements in which his son
Sweyn took a leading part.   It is not possible
from the conflicting accounts that have come down
to us to determine just why the Danes showed such
restlessness at this time.   It has been thought
that the revolts represented a heathen reaction
against the new faith, or a nationalistic protest
against German influences; these factors may
have entered in, but it is more likely that a general
dissatisfaction with Harold's rule caused by the
ill success of his operations against Germans,
Swedes, and Norwegians was at the bottom of the

[1] Snorre, *Olaf Trygvesson's Saga*, cc. 35–52.
[2] *Gesta Danorum*, 327.

hostilities. The virile personality of the young prince was doubtless also a factor. To later writers his conduct recalled the career of Absalom; but in this instance disobedience and rebellion had the victory. Forces were collected on both sides; battles were fought both on land and on sea. Finally during a truce, the aged King was wounded by an arrow, shot, according to saga, from the bow of Toki, the foster-father of Sweyn. Faithful henchmen carried the dying King across the sea to Jomburg where he expired on All Saints' Day (November 1), probably in 986, the year of the defeat at Hjörunga Bay. His remains were carried to Roeskild and interred in the Church of the Holy Trinity.[1]

Of Harold's family not much is known. According to Adam of Bremen his queen was named Gunhild, a name that points to Scandinavian ancestry.[2] Saxo speaks of a Queen Gyrith, the sister of Styrbjörn.[3] On a runic monument at Sönder Vissing, not far from the garth at Jelling, we read that

> Tova raised this memorial,
> Mistiwi's daughter,
> In memory of her mother,
> Harold the Good
> Gorm's son's wife.[4]

Tova might be a Danish name, but Mistiwi seems clearly Slavic. It may be that Harold was thrice

---

[1] Adamus, *Gesta*, ii., c. 26. Saxo, *Gesta*, 332.
[2] *Gesta*, ii., cc. 3, 26.   [3] *Gesta*, 325.
[4] Wimmer, *De danske Runemindesmærker*, I., ii., 78 ff.

married; it is also possible that Tova in baptism received the name Gunhild. Gyrith was most likely the wife of his old age. The question is important as it concerns the ancestry of Canute the Great. If Tova was Canute's grandmother (as she probably was) three of his grandparents were of Slavic blood.

Of Harold's children four are known to history. His daughter Thyra has already been mentioned as the wife of the ill-fated Styrbjörn. Another daughter, Gunhild, was the wife of an Anglo-Danish chief, the ealdorman Pallig. Two sons are also mentioned, Sweyn and Hakon. Of these Sweyn, as the successor to the kingship, is the more important.

The accession of Sweyn Forkbeard to the Danish throne marks an era in the history of Denmark. Harold Bluetooth had not been a weak king: he had enlarged his territories; he had promoted the cause of the Christian faith; he had striven for order and organised life. But his efforts in this direction had brought him into collision with a set of forces that believed in the old order of things. In Harold's old age the Danish viking spirit had awakened to new life; soon the dragons were sailing the seas as of old. With a king of the Shielding type now in the high-seat at Roeskild, these lawless though energetic elements found not only further freedom but royal favour and leadership.

It would seem that the time had come to wipe

away the stain that had come upon the Danish
arms at Hjörunga Bay; but no immediate move
was made in that direction. Earl Hakon was
still too strong, and for a decade longer he enjoyed
undisputed possession of the Norwegian sovereignty. Sweyn did not forget the claims of his
dynasty, but he bided his time. Furthermore,
this same decade saw larger plans developing at
the Danish court. Norway was indeed desirable,
but as a field of wider activities it gave no great
promise. Such a field, however, seemed to be
in sight: the British Isles with their numerous
kingdoms, their large Scandinavian colonies, and
their consequent lack of unifying interests seemed
to offer opportunities that the restless Dane could
not afford to neglect.

The three Scandinavian kingdoms did not
comprise the entire North: in many respects,
greater Scandinavia was fully as important as the
home lands. It is not necessary for present purposes to follow the eastward stream of colonisation
that transformed the Slavic East and laid the
foundations of the Russian monarchy. The
southward movement of the Danes into the
regions about the mouth of the Oder will be discussed more in detail later. The story of Sweyn
and Canute is far more concerned with colonising
movements and colonial foundations in the West.
Without the preparatory work of two centuries,
Canute's conquest of the Anglo-Saxon kingdom
would have been impossible.

The same generation that saw the consolidation of the Norse tribes into the Norwegian kingdom also saw the colonisation of the Faroe Islands and Iceland. A century later Norsemen were building homes on the bleak shores of Greenland. Less than a generation later, in the year 1000, Vineland was reached by Leif the Lucky.[1] Earlier still, perhaps a century or more before the Icelandic migration, the Northmen had begun to occupy parts of the British Isles. The ships that first sought and reached North Britain probably sailed from two folklands (or shires) in South-western Norway, Hordaland and Rogaland, the territories about the modern ports of Bergen and Stavanger. Due west from the former city lie the Shetland Islands; in the same direction from Stavanger are the Orkneys. It has been conjectured that the earliest Scandinavian settlements in these parts were made on the shores of Pentland

---

[1] The American shores were evidently too far distant for successful colonisation; but the visits to the far West clearly did not cease with the journeys of Leif and his associates. Vineland is mentioned in a runic monument from the eleventh century which records an expedition to the West that seems to have ended disastrously:

"They came out [upon the ocean] and over wide stretches [of land] and in need of dry clothes for changes and of food toward Vineland and over icy wastes in the wilderness. Evil may deprive one of good fortune so that death comes early."

This inscription, which is the earliest document that mentions the New World, was found at Hönen in South-eastern Norway. The original has been lost, but copies are extant. The translation is from Bugge's rendering into modern Norse. (*Norges Historie*, I., ii., 285.)

2

Firth, on the Orkneys and on the coast of Caithness.
Thence the journey went along the north-western
coast of Scotland to the Hebrides group, across
the narrow straits to Ireland, and down to the
Isle of Man.[1]

The Emerald Isle attracted the sea-kings and
the period of pillage was soon followed by an age
of settlement. The earliest Norse colony in
Ireland seems to have been founded about 826,
on the banks of the Liffey, where the city of Dublin
grew up a little later, and for centuries remained
the centre of Norse power and influence on the
island. Other settlements were established at
various points on the east coast, notably at Wick-
low, Wexford, and Waterford, which names show
clearly their Norse origin. About 860 a stronghold was built at Cork.[2]

Toward the close of the eighth century the
vikings appeared in large numbers on the coasts
of Northern England. Two generations later
they had destroyed three of the four English
kingdoms and were organising the Danelaw on
their ruins. Still later Rolf appeared with his
host of Northmen in the Seine Valley and founded
the Norman duchy.

[1] Bugge, *Vikingerne*, i., 135 ff.

[2] "All along the Irish coast from Belfast to Dublin and Limerick there still remains an unbroken series of Norse place names,
principally the names of firths, islands, reefs, and headlands,
which show that at such points the fairway has been named by
Northmen." *Norges Historie*, I., ii., 87; see also pp. 73-76.
(Bugge.)

It must not be assumed that in these colonies
the population was exclusively Scandinavian.
The native elements persisted and seem, as a rule,
to have lived on fairly good terms with the invaders.   It is likely that wherever these energetic
Northerners settled they became the dominant
social force; but no feeling of contempt or aloof-
ness appears to have been felt on either side after
the races had learned to know each other.   Inter-
marriage was frequent, not only between Dane
and Angle, but between Celt and Norseman as
well.   In time the alien was wholly absorbed into
the native population; but in the process the
victorious element underwent a profound trans-
formation which extended to social conventions
as well as to race.[1]

The largest of these colonies was the Danelaw, a
series of Danish and Norse settlements extending
from the Thames to the north of England.   According to an English writer of the twelfth century,
it comprised York and fourteen shires to the south.[2]
The area controlled was evidently considerably

---

[1] Of this process and its results Normandy furnishes the best
illustration.   The population of Rollo's duchy soon came to be a
mixture of races with French as the chief element, though in
some sections, as the Cotentin and the Bessin, the inhabitants
clung to their Scandinavian speech and customs for a long time.
Steenstrup, *Normannerne*, i., 175–179.

[2] Simeon of Durham, *Opera Omnia*, ii., 393.   The area
varied at different periods; but the earlier Danelaw seems to have
comprised fifteen shires.   See Steenstrup, *Normannerne*, iv.,
36–37.

larger than the region actually settled; and in some of the shires the Scandinavian population was probably not numerous. Five cities in the Danelaw enjoyed a peculiar pre-eminence. These were Lincoln, Nottingham, Derby, Leicester, and Stamford. It has been conjectured that these were garrison towns held and organised with a view to securing the obedience of the surrounding country.[1] If this be correct, we should infer that the population beyond the walls was largely Anglian. The Five Boroughs seem to have had a common organisation of a republican type: they formed "the first federation of boroughs known in this island, and in fact the earliest federation of towns known outside of Italy."[2] Part of the Danelaw must have contained a large Scandinavian element, especially the shires of Lincoln and York.[3] There were also Danish and Norwegian settlements in England outside the Danelaw in

---

[1] Steenstrup, *Normannerne*, iv., 40–43.

[2] *Saga Book of the Viking Club*, VI., i., 23 (Bugge). See also Collingwood, *Scandinavian Britain*, 109. The federation was later enlarged till it included Seven Boroughs. *Anglo-Saxon Chronicle*, 1015.

[3] The Danish antiquarian Worsaae found more than four hundred Norse place names in Yorkshire alone. While his list cannot be regarded as final, it will probably be found to be fairly correct. The subject of English place names has not yet been fully investigated. Recent studies are those by F. M. Stenton, *The Place Names of Berkshire* (Reading, 1911), H C. Wyld and T. O. Hirst, *The Place Names of Lancashire* (London, 1911), and F. W. Moorman, *The Place Names of the West Riding of Yorkshire* (Leeds, 1910).

its narrower sense: in the north-western shires and in the Severn Valley, perhaps as high up as Worcestershire.[1]

Danish power in England seems to have centered about the ancient city of York. It would be more nearly correct to speak of Northumbria in the ninth and tenth centuries as a Norse than as a Danish colony; but the Angles made no such distinction. The population must also have contained a large English element. A native ecclesiastic who wrote toward the close of the tenth century speaks with enthusiasm of the wealth and grandeur of York.

The city rejoices in a multitude of inhabitants; not fewer than 30,000 men and women (children and youths not counted) are numbered in this city. It is also filled with the riches of merchants who come from everywhere, especially from the Danish nation.[2]

In some respects the Danelaw is the most important fact in the history of the Anglo-Saxon monarchy: it was the rock on which Old English nationality foundered. By the middle of the tenth century, Saxon England was practically confined to the country south of the Thames River and the western half of the Midlands, a comparatively small area surrounded by Scandinavian and Celtic settlements. If this fact is fully appreciated, there should be little difficulty in

[1] Steenstrup, *Normannerne*, iii., 228.
[2] *Historians of the Church of York*, i., 454.

the western rulers an opportunity to regain much
that had been lost.   In England the expansion
of Wessex which had begun in the days of Alfred
was continued under his successors, until in
Edgar's day one lord was recognised from the
Channel to the Forth.   But with Edgar died both
majesty and peace.   About 980 the viking spirit
was reawakened in the North.   The raven banner
reappeared in the western seas, and soon the
annals of the West began to recount their direful
tales.   Among all the chiefs of this new age, one
stands forth pre-eminent, Sweyn with the Forked
Beard, whose remarkable achievement it was to
enlist all this lawless energy for a definite purpose,
the conquest of Wessex.

In 979 Ethelred the Ill-counselled was crowned
king of England and began his long disastrous
reign.   If we may trust the Abingdon chronicler,
who, as a monk, should be truthful, England was
duly warned of the sorrows to come.   For "in
that same year blood-red clouds resembling fire
were frequently seen; usually they appeared at
midnight hanging like moving pillars painted
upon the sky."   The King was a mere boy of ten
summers; later writers could tell us that signs of
degeneracy were discovered in the prince as early
as the day of his baptism.   On some of his contemporaries, however, he seems to have made a
favourable impression.   We cannot depend much
on the praises of a Norse scald who sang in the
King's presence; but perhaps we can trust the

English writer who describes him as a youth of "elegant manners, handsome features, and comely appearance."[1]

That Ethelred proved an incompetent king is beyond dispute. Still, it is doubtful whether any ruler with capabilities less than those of an Alfred could have saved England in the early years of the eleventh century. For Ethelred had succeeded to a perilous inheritance. In the new territorial additions to Wessex there were two chief elements, neither of which was distinctly pro-Saxon: the Dane or the half-Danish colonist was naturally hostile to the Saxon regime; his Anglian neighbour recalled the former independence of his region as Mercia, East Anglia, or Northumbria, and was weak in his loyalty to the southern dynasty. The spirit of particularism asserted itself repeatedly, for it seems unlikely that the many revolts in the tenth century were Danish uprisings merely.

It seems possible that Ethelred's government might have been able to maintain itself after a fashion and perhaps would have satisfied the demands of the age, had it not been that vast hostile forces were just then released in the North. These attacked Wessex from two directions: fleets from the Irish Sea ravaged the South-west; vikings from the East entered the Channel and plundered the southern shores. It is likely that in the advance-guard of the renewed piracy,

---

[1] *Historians of the Church of York*, i., 455. For a fragment of a lay in praise of Ethelred see *Corpus Poeticum Boreale*, ii., 111.

Sweyn Forkbeard was a prominent leader. We have seen that during the last years of Harold's reign, there were trouble and ill-feeling between father and son. These years, it seems, the undutiful prince spent in exile and piratical raids. As the Baltic would scarcely be a safe refuge under the circumstances, we may assume that those seven years were spent in the West.[1]

In the second year of Ethelred's reign the incursions began: "the great chief Behemoth rose against him with all his companions and engines of war."[2] In that year Chester was plundered by the Norsemen; Thanet and Southampton were devastated by the Danes. The troubles at Chester are of slight significance; they were doubtless merely the continuation of desultory warfare in the upper Irish Sea. But the attack on Southampton, the port of the capital city of Winchester, was ominous: though clearly a private undertaking it was significant in revealing the weakness of English resistance. The vikings probably wintered among their countrymen on the shores of the Irish Sea, for South-western England was again visited and harried during the two succeeding years.

For a few years (983–986) there was a lull in the

[1] Saxo gives the period as seven years (*Gesta*, 337). But his account is confused and unreliable; seven must be taken as a round number. Still, the period between the renewal of the raids in England and Sweyn's accession covers nearly seven years.

[2] *Historians of the Church of York*, i., 455.

operations against England. The energies of the
North were employed elsewhere: this was evidently the period of Styrbjörn's invasion of Sweden
and Sigvaldi's attack on Norway with the desperate battles of Fyris River and Hjörunga Bay.
But, in 986, viking ships in great numbers appeared
in the Irish Sea.[1] Two years later a fleet visited
Devon and entered Bristol Channel. It is probable that Norman ships took part in this raid;
at any rate the Danes sold English plunder in
Normandy.

In 991, the attack entered upon a new phase.
Earlier the country had suffered from raids in
which no great number of vikings had taken part
in any instance; now they came in armies and the
attack became almost an invasion. That year a
fierce battle was fought near Maldon[2] in Essex
where one of the chief leaders of the vikings was
an exiled Norwegian prince, Olaf Trygvesson, who
four years later restored the Norwegian throne.
It is likely, therefore, that the host was not
exclusively Danish but gathered from the entire
North.

The fight at Maldon was a crushing defeat for
the English and consternation ruled in the councils
of the irresolute King. Siric, the Archbishop of

[1] Steenstrup, *Normannerne*, iii., 221.
[2] The English were led by the East Anglian ealdorman Byrhtnoth, whose valour and death are told in what is perhaps the
finest poem in Old English literature. See Grein-Wülker,
Bibliothek der angelsächsischen Poesie, i., 358–373.

Canterbury, and two ealdormen were sent as an embassy to the viking camp to sue for peace. A treaty was agreed to which seems to imply that the host was to be permitted to remain in East Anglia for an undefined time. The vikings promised to defend England against any other piratical bands, thus virtually becoming mercenaries for the time being. In return Ethelred agreed to pay a heavy tribute and to furnish provisions "the while that they remain among us."[1] Thus began the Danegeld which seems to have developed into a permanent tax in the reign of Canute.

The next year King Ethelred collected a fleet in the Thames in the hope of entrapping his new allies; but treason was abroad in England and the plan failed.[2] The following year the pirates appeared in the Humber country; here, too, the English defence melted away. After relating the flight of the Anglian leaders, Florence of Worcester adds significantly, "because they were Danes on the paternal side."[3]

The next year (994) King Sweyn of Denmark joined the fleet of Olaf and his associates and new purposes began to appear. Instead of seeking

[1] For the treaty see Liebermann, *Gesetze der Angelsachsen*, i., 220–225.

[2] *Anglo-Saxon Chronicle*, 992, 993. As the betrayer, Alfric, had a part in the treaty-making of the year before, he may have looked on the new plans as dishonourable.

[3] *Chronicon*, i., 150–151.

promiscuous plunder, the invaders attempted to reduce cities and strongholds. Once more the English sued for peace on the basis of tribute.[1] Sweyn evidently returned to Denmark where his presence seems to have been sorely needed. For two years England enjoyed comparative peace. The energies of the North found other employment: we read of raids on the Welsh coast and of piratical expeditions into Saxony; interesting events also occurred in the home lands. To these years belong the revolt of the Norsemen against Earl Hakon, and perhaps also the invasion of Denmark by Eric the Victorious.

Thirty years of power had developed tyrannical passions in the Norwegian Earl. According to the sagas he was cruel, treacherous, and licentious. Every year he became more overbearing and despotic; every year added to the total of discontent. Here was Sweyn Forkbeard's opportunity; but he had other irons in the fire, and the opportunity fell to another. About 995 a pretender to the Norse throne arrived from the West,— Olaf Trygvesson, the great-grandson of Harold Fairhair.

Our earliest reliable information as to Olaf's career comes from English sources; they tell of his operations in Britain in 991 and 994 and the circumstances indicate that the intervening years were also spent on these islands. While in England he was attracted to the Christian faith,

[1] *Anglo-Saxon Chronicle*, 994.

a fact that evidently came to be known to the English, for, in the negotiations of 994, particular attention was paid to the princely chieftain. An embassy was sent to him with Bishop Alphege as leading member, and the outcome was that Olaf came to visit King Ethelred at Andover, where he was formally admitted to the Christian communion, Ethelred acting as godfather.[1]

At Andover, Olaf promised never to come again to England "with unpeace"; the Chronicler adds that he kept his word. With the coming of spring he set out for Norway and never again saw England as friend or foe. We do not know what induced him at this time to take up the fight with Hakon the Bad; but doubtless it was in large measure due to urging on the part of the Church. For Olaf the Viking had become a zealous believer; when he landed in Norway he came provided with priests and all the other necessaries of Christian worship. It is not necessary to tell the story of the Earl's downfall,—how he was hounded into a pig-sty where he died at the hands of a thrall. Olaf was soon universally recognised as king and proceeded at once to carry out his great and difficult purpose: to christianise a strong and stubborn people (995).[2]

As to the second event, the invasion of Sweyn's dominions by the King of Sweden, we cannot be so

---

[1] Taranger, *Den angelsaksiske Kirkes Indflydelse paa den norske*, 125.

[2] Snorre, *Olaf Trygvesson's Saga*, cc. 47–50.

sure, as most of the accounts that have come down to us are late and difficult to harmonise.   Historians agree that, some time toward the close of his reign, King Eric sought revenge for the assistance that the Danish King had given his nephew Styrbjörn in his attempt to seize the Swedish throne. The invasion must have come after Sweyn's accession (986?) and before Eric's death, the date of which is variously given as 993, 995, 996.[1]   If Eric was still ruling in 994 when Sweyn was absent in England, it is extremely probable that he made use of a splendid opportunity to seize the lands of his enemy.   This would explain Sweyn's readiness to accept Ethelred's terms in the winter of 994–995.[2]

After the death of King Eric, new interests and new plans began to germinate in the fertile mind

[1] Steenstrup favours the earlier date (*Danmarks Riges Historie*, i., 371); Munch sees reasons for a later year (*Det norske Folks Historie*, I., ii., 102).

[2] That serious business was awaiting Sweyn in his own country is evident from two runic inscriptions that have been found in the Jutish borderland: the Heathby (or Vedelspang) Stone and the Danework Stone.   The former was raised by "Thorolf, Sweyn's housecarle" in memory of a companion " who died when brave men were besieging Heathby."   The second was raised by Sweyn himself " in memory of Skartha, his housecarle, who had fared west to England but now died at Heathby."   The expedition to the West may have been the one that Sweyn undertook in 994. One stone mentions the siege of Heathby, but Heathby was destroyed shortly before 1000.   The siege therefore probably dates from 995 or one of the following years; but whether the enemy was a part of Eric's forces cannot be determined.   For the inscriptions see Wimmer, *De danske Runemindesmærker*, I., ii., 113, 117.

of Sweyn the Viking. Late in life the Swedish
King seems to have married a young Swedish
woman who is known to history as Sigrid the
Haughty. Sigrid belonged to a family of great
wealth and prominence; her father Tosti was a
famous viking who had harvested his treasures on
an alien shore. Eric had not long been dead
before wooers in plenty came to seek the hand of the
rich dowager. So importunate did they become
that the Queen to get rid of them is said to have
set fire to the house where two of them slept. Olaf
Trygvesson was acceptable, but he imposed an
impossible condition: Sigrid must become a
Christian. When she finally refused to surrender
her faith, the King is said to have stricken her
in the face with his gauntlet. The proud Queen
never forgave him.

Soon afterwards Sigrid married Sweyn Forkbeard
who had dismissed his earlier consort, Queen
Gunhild, probably to make room for the Swedish
dowager. We do not know what motives prompt-
ed this act, but it was no doubt urged by state-
craft. In this way the wily Dane cemented an
alliance with a neighbouring state which had but
recently been hostile.[1]

The divorced Queen was a Polish princess of an
eminent Slavic family; she was the sister of
Boleslav Chrobri, the mighty Polish duke who
later assumed the royal title. When Gunhild
retired to her native Poland, she may have taken

[1] Snorre, *Olaf Trygvesson's Saga*, cc. 43, 60–61, 91.

with her a small boy who can at that time scarcely have been more than two or three years old, perhaps even younger. The boy was Canute, the King's younger son, though the one who finally succeeded to all his father's power and policies. The only information that we have of Canute's childhood comes from late and not very reliable sources: it is merely this, that he was not brought up at the Danish court, but was fostered by Thurkil the Tall, one of the chiefs at Jomburg and brother of Earl Sigvaldi.[1] The probabilities favour the accuracy of this report. It was customary in those days to place boys with foster-fathers; prominent nobles or even plain franklins received princes into their households and regarded the charge as an honoured trust. Perhaps, too, a royal child would be safer among the warriors of Jomburg than at the court of a stepmother who had employed such drastic means to get rid of undesirable wooers. The character of his early impressions and instruction can readily be imagined: Canute was trained for warfare.

When the young prince became king of England Thurkil was exalted to a position next to that of the ruler himself. After the old chief's death, Canute seems to have heaped high honours on Thurkil's son Harold in Denmark. We cannot be sure, but it seems likely that this favour is to be ascribed, in part, at least, to Canute's affection for his foster-father and his foster-brother.

[1] *Flateyarbok*, i., 203.

In those same years another important marriage was formed in Sweyn's household: the fugitive Eric, the son of Earl Hakon whose power was now wielded by the viking Olaf, had come to Denmark, where Sweyn Forkbeard received him kindly and gave him his daughter Gytha in marriage. Thus there was formed a hostile alliance against King Olaf with its directing centre at the Danish court. In addition to his own resources and those of his stepson in Sweden, Sweyn could now count on the assistance of the dissatisfied elements in Norway who looked to Eric as their natural leader.

It was not long before a pretext was found for an attack. Thyra, Sweyn's sister, the widow of Styrbjörn, had been married to Mieczislav, the Duke of Poland. In 992, she was widowed the second time. After a few years, perhaps in 998, Olaf Trygvesson made her queen of Norway. Later events would indicate that this. marriage, which Olaf seems to have contracted without consulting the bride's brother, was part of a plan to unite against Sweyn all the forces that were presumably hostile, — Poles, Jomvikings, and Norsemen.[1]

---

[1] Snorre tells us (*Olaf Trygvesson's Saga*, c. 92) that Thyra had fled from her husband, who is mistakenly called Boleslav, and had come as a fugitive to Olaf's court. So attractive did she prove to the sympathetic King that he promptly married her. The account is evidently largely fiction; there seems to have been a good understanding between Olaf and Boleslav when the Norse fleet came south in 1000. In the account given above I have followed Bugge (*Norges Historie*, I., ii., 271).

3

The saga writers, keenly alive to the influence
of human passion on the affairs of men, emphasise
Sigrid's hatred for Olaf and Thyra's anxiety to
secure certain possessions of hers in Wendland as
important causes of the war that followed.   Each
is said to have egged her husband to the venture,
though little urging can have been needed in
either case.   In the summer of 1000, a large and
splendid Norwegian fleet appeared in the Baltic.
In his negotiations with Poles and Jomvikings,
Olaf was apparently successful: Sigvaldi joined the
expedition and Slavic ships were added to the
Norse armament.   Halldor the Unchristian tells us
that these took part in the battle that followed:
"The Wendish ships spread over the bay, and the
thin beaks gaped with iron mouths upon the
warriors."[1]

Sweyn's opportunity had come and it was not
permitted to pass. He mustered the Danish
forces and sent messages to his stepson in Sweden
and to his son-in-law Eric. Sigvaldi was also in
the alliance. Plans were made to ambush the
Norse King on his way northward. The confeder-
ates gathered their forces in the harbour of Swald,
a river mouth on the Pomeranian coast a little to
the west of the isle of Rügen. Sigvaldi's part was
to feign friendship for Olaf and to lead him into
the prepared trap. The plan was successfully
carried out. A small part of King Olaf's fleet
was lured into the harbour and attacked from all

[1] *Corpus Poeticum Boreale*, ii., 101 (Vigfusson's translation).

THE SJAELLE STONE
(Runic monument raised to Gyrth,
Earl Sigvaldi's brother.)

THE LARGER AARHUS STONE

sides. The fight was severe but numbers pre-
vailed. Olaf's own ship, the famous *Long Serpent*,
was boarded by Eric Hakonsson's men, and the
King in the face of sure capture leaped into the
Baltic.[1]

The victors had agreed to divide up Norway and
the agreement was carried out. Most of the coast
lands from the Naze northwards were given to
Earl Eric. The southern shores, the land from
the Naze eastwards, fell to King Sweyn. Seven
shires in the Throndhjem country and a single
shire in the extreme Southeast were assigned to the
Swedish King; but only the last-mentioned shire
was joined directly to Sweden; the northern
regions were given as a fief to Eric's younger
brother Sweyn who had married the Swede-
king's daughter. Similarly Sweyn Forkbeard
enfeoffed his son-in-law Eric, but the larger part
he kept as his own direct possession.[2]

The battle of Swald was of great importance to
the policies of the Knytlings. The rival Norse
kingdom was destroyed. Once more the Danish
King had almost complete control of both shores
of the waterways leading into the Baltic. Danish

---

[1] The chief authorities on the battle of Swald are Snorre and
Adam of Bremen. There seems also to be an allusion to the
fight in an inscription on a runic monument, the Aarhus Stone,
which was raised by four men, presumably warriors, in memory
of a comrade "who died on the sea to the eastward when the
kings were fighting." Wimmer, *De danske Runemindesmærker*,
I., ii., 133.

[2] *Norges Historie*, I., ii., 285–286.

hegemony in the North was a recognised fact. But all of Norway was not yet a Danish possession —that ambition was not realised before the reign of Canute. And England was still unconquered.

DANISH COINS FROM THE REIGN OF
CANUTE, MINTED AT ODENSE,
VIBORG, HEATHBY.

CHAPTER II

1003–1013

DURING the five years of rivalry between Olaf and Sweyn (995–1000), England had enjoyed comparative peace. Incursions, indeed, began again in 997; but these were clearly of the earlier type, not invasions like the movements led by Olaf and Sweyn. Who the leaders were at this time we do not know; but the Northern kings were in those years giving and taking in marriage and busily plotting each other's destruction, so we conclude that the undertakings continued to be of the private sort, led, perhaps, by Norse chiefs who had found life in Norway uncongenial after King Olaf had begun to persecute the heathen worshippers.

The English had now come to realise the importance of the upper Irish Sea as a rendezvous for all forms of piratical bands; and the need of aggressive warfare at this point was clearly seen. Accordingly, in the year 1000, Ethelred collected a fleet and an army and harried the Norse settle-

ments in Cumberland and on the Isle of Man.
The time was opportune for a movement of this
sort, as no reinforcements from the North could be
expected that year. The expedition, however,
accomplished nothing of importance; for the fleet
that Ethelred had hoped to intercept did not
return to the western waters but sailed to Normandy.[1] Ethelred was angry with Duke Richard
of Normandy for sheltering his enemies, and proceeded to attack his duchy with his usual ill success.[2]

Nevertheless, the hostilities terminated favourably for Ethelred, as the Norman duke offered
his beaten enemy not only peace, but alliance.
Recent events in the North may have caused
Richard to reflect. The diplomacy of Sweyn,
culminating in the partition of Norway, had made
Denmark a state of great importance. Sweyn's
designs on England were probably suspected;
at any rate, Normandy for the moment seemed
willing to support England. In early spring, 1002,
the bond was further strengthened by a marriage
between Ethelred and Duke Richard's sister
Emma, who later married her husband's enemy,
the Danish Canute. That same year England
was once more rid of the enemy through the payment of Danegeld.[3]

The prospects for continued peace in England
were probably better in 1002 than in any other

[1] *Anglo-Saxon Chronicle*, 1000.
[2] William of Jumièges, *Historia Normannorum*, v., c. 4.
[3] *Anglo-Saxon Chronicle*, 1002.

year since the accession of Ethelred. But toward
the end of the year, all that gold and diplomacy
had built up was ruined by a royal order, the
stupidity of which was equalled only by its criminality. On Saint Brice's Day (November 13),
the English rose, not to battle but to murder.
It had been planned on that date to rid the country of all its Danish inhabitants. How extensive
the territory was that was thus stained with blood,
we are not informed; but such an order could
not have been carried out in the Danelaw. In
justification of his act, Ethelred pleaded that he
had heard of a Danish conspiracy, directed not
only against his own life, but against the lives of
the English nobility as well.

It is likely that, when England bought peace
earlier in the year, a number of the vikings remained in the land, intending, perhaps, to settle
permanently; such arrangements were by no means
unusual. The massacre of Saint Brice's may,
therefore, have had for its object the extermination
of the raiders that came in 1001. But these were
not the only ones slain: among the victims were
Gunhild, King Sweyn's sister, and her husband,
the ealdorman Pallig.[1] It is probable that Pallig,
though a Saxon official, was a Dane living among
the Danes in some Scandinavian settlement in
South-western England.[2] We are told that

[1] Richard of Cirencester, *Speculum Historiale*, ii., 147–148.
[2] As there seems to have been a Danish settlement in the Severn
Valley, it seems probable that Pallig's home was in that region.

Ethelred had treated him well, had given him lands and honours; but he did not remain faithful to his lord; only the year before, when the vikings were in Devon, he joined them with a number of ships. Pallig no doubt deserved the punishment of a traitor, but it would have been politic in his case to show mercy. If he was, as has been conjectured from the form of his name, connected with the family of Palna Toki, the famous Danish archer and legendary organiser of the Jomburg fraternity, he was bound to Sweyn by double ties, for Palna Toki was Sweyn's reputed foster-father.[1]

Sweyn Forkbeard at once prepared to take revenge for the death of his kinsfolk. The next year (1003), his sails were seen from the cliffs of the Channel shore. But before proceeding to the attack, he seems to have visited his Norman friend, Duke Richard the Good. For some reason, displeasure, perhaps, at the shedding of noble Scandinavian blood on Saint Brice's Day, the duke was ready to repudiate his alliance with his

---

[1] The story of Palna Toki is told in various sagas, particularly *Jómsvíkingasaga.* Of his exploits in archery Saxo has an account in his tenth book. Having once boasted that no apple was too small for his arrow to find, he was surprised by an order from the King that he should shoot an arrow from his son's head. The archer was reluctant to display his skill in this fashion, but the shot was successful. It is also told that Palna Toki had provided himself with additional arrows which he had intended for the King in case the first had stricken the child. Saxo wrote a century before the time of the supposed Tell episode.

English brother-in-law.   The two worthies reached
the agreement that Normandy should be an open
market for English plunder and a refuge for the
sick and wounded in the Danish host.[1]   Evidently
Sweyn was planning an extended campaign.

Having thus secured himself against attacks
from the rear, Sweyn proceeded to Exeter, which
was delivered into his hands by its faithless Norman commander Hugo.[2]   In the surrender of
Exeter, we should probably see the first fruit of
the new Danish-Norman understanding.   From
this city the Danes carried destruction into the
southern shires.   The following year (1004), East
Anglia was made to suffer.   Ulfketel, the earl of
the region, was not prepared to fight and made
peace with Sweyn; but the Danes did not long
observe the truce.   After they had treacherously
attacked Thetford, the earl gathered his forces and
tried to intercept Sweyn's marauding bands on
their way back to the ships; but though the East
Anglians fought furiously, the Danes escaped.
The opposition that Sweyn met in the half-Danish
East Anglia seems to have checked his operations.
The next year he left the land.[3]

The forces of evil seemed finally to have spent
their strength, for the years 1007 and 1008 were
on the whole comparatively peaceful.   Those
same years show considerable energy on the part

[1] William of Jumièges, *Historia Normannorum*, v., c. 7.
[2] *Anglo-Saxon Chronicle*, 1003.
[3] *Ibid.*, 1004–1005.

of the English: in the Pentecostal season, May,
1008, the King met his "wise men" at Eanham,
and a long legislative enactment saw the light.[1]
It was hoped that by extensive and thorough-
going reforms the national vigour might be restored.　Among other things provisions were made
for an extensive naval establishment, based on a
contribution that grew into the ship money of later
fame.　A large number of ships were actually assembled; but the treacherous spirit and the jealous
conduct of some of the English nobles soon ruined
the efficiency of the fleet; the new navy went to
pieces at a moment when its service was most sorely
needed.　For in that year, 1009, a most formidable enemy appeared in the Channel: the vikings of
Jom had left their stronghold on the Oder and were
soon to re-establish themselves on the Thames.[2]

For about two decades Sigvaldi ruled at Jomburg; but after the battle of Swald he disappears
from the sagas: all that we learn is that he was
slain on some expedition to England.　Perhaps he
was one of the victims of Saint Brice's (1002); or
he may have perished in one of the later raids.　His
death must, however, be dated earlier than 1009; for
in that year his brother Thurkil came to England,
we are told, to take revenge for a slain brother.[3]

[1] Liebermann, *Gesetze der Angelsachsen*, i., 246–256.

[2] *Anglo-Saxon Chronicle*, 1009.

[3] *Encomium Emmæ*, i., c. 2.　It is barely possible that the
brother was Gyrth, whose name appears on a runic monument
(Wimmer, *De danske Runemindesmærker*, I., ii., 138 ff.).　But
in the absence of information to the contrary we shall have to

Thurkil's fleet appeared at Sandwich in July.
Associated with the tall Dane was a short, thick-
set Norwegian, Olaf the Stout, a young viking
of royal blood who later won renown as the missionary King of Norway and fell in war against Canute
the Great. In August came a second fleet, under
the leadership of Eglaf and Heming, Thurkil's
brother. The fleets joined at Thanet; this time
nearly all the southern counties had to suffer.
The host wintered on the lower Thames and during
the winter months plundered the valley up as far
as Oxford. Ethelred tried to cut off its retreat
but failed.[1]

During the Lenten weeks the vikings refitted
their ships, and on April 9, 1010, they set sail for
East Anglia. Ulfketel was still in control of that
region and had made preparations to meet the
invader. On May 5, the Danes met the native
levies at Ringmere in the southern part of Norfolk.
The fight was sharp, with final victory for the sea-
kings. The English sources attribute the outcome
to the treasonable behaviour of Thurkil Mareshead,
who was evidently a Dane in Ulfketel's service.
The Norse scalds ascribe the result to the valour
of Olaf the Stout, who here won the "sword-
moot" for the seventh time.[2]

---

assume that Gyrth was buried where his monument was placed
and was therefore not the brother who fell in England.

[1] Florence of Worcester, *Chronicon*, i., 160–161.

[2] *Ibid.*, 160–163. Snorre, *Saga of Saint Olaf*, c. 14. Storm
in his translation of Snorre (Christiania, 1900) locates Ringmere
in East Wretham, Norfolk, (p. 239).

During the remaining months of the year and all through the following summer, the vikings rode almost unresisted through Southern England, plundering everywhere. Finally the King and the "wise men" began to negotiate for peace on the usual basis. But so often had Danegelds been levied that it was becoming difficult to collect the money and the payment was not so prompt as the vikings desired. In their anger they laid siege to Canterbury, and, after a close investment of twenty days, by the assistance of an English priest were enabled to seize the city. Many important citizens were held for ransom, among them the Archbishop Alphege, who remained a prisoner for nearly six months. His confinement cannot have been severe; the Prelate was interested in the spiritual welfare of the Scandinavian pirates, and seems to have begun a mission among his keepers. But he forbade the payment of a ransom, and after a drunken orgy the exasperated Danes proceeded to pelt him to death with the bones of their feast. Thrym, a Dane whom he had confirmed the day before, gave him the mercy stroke.[1]

During the closing days of the archbishop's life, an assembly of the magnates in London had succeeded in raising the tribute agreed upon, 48,000 pounds. Not merely were the invaders bought off,—they were induced to enter Ethelred's service as mercenaries; there must have been

[1] *Anglo-Saxon Chronicle*, 1011. Florence of Worcester, *Chronicon*, i., 163–165.

reasons why it would be inadvisable to return to
Jomburg. The English King now had an army
of some four thousand or perhaps five thousand
men, a splendid force of professional warriors led
by the renowned viking Thurkil the Tall. According to William of Malmesbury, they were quartered
in East Anglia,[1] which seems plausible, as Wessex
must have been thoroughly pillaged by 1012.

When the year 1013 opened, there were reasons
to hope that the miseries of England were past.
For a whole generation the sea-kings had infested
the Channel and the Irish Sea, scourging the
shores of Southern Britain almost every year.
Large sums of money had been paid out in the
form of Danegeld, 137,000 pounds silver, but to
little purpose: the enemy returned each year as
voracious as ever. Now, however, the pirate had
undertaken to defend the land. The presence of
Danish mercenaries was doubtless an inconveni-
ence, but this would be temporary only. It was
to be expected that, as in the days of Alfred, the
enemy would settle down as an occupant of the
soil, and in time become a subject instead of a
mercenary soldier.

But just at this moment, an invasion of a far
more serious nature was being prepared in Denmark. In the councils of Roeskild Sweyn Forkbeard was asking his henchmen what they thought
of renewing the attack on England. The question
suggested the answer: to the King's delight favour-

[1] *Gesta Regum*, i., 207.

able replies came from all. It is said that Sweyn
consulted his son Canute with the rest; and the
eager youth strongly urged the undertaking.[1]
This is the earliest act on Canute's part that any
historian has recorded. In 1012, he was perhaps
seventeen years old; he had reached the age when
a Scandinavian prince should have entered upon an
active career. His great rival of years to come,
Olaf the Stout, who can have been only two years
older than Canute, had already sailed the dragon
for six or seven years. It is likely that the young
Dane had also experienced the thrills of viking life,
but on this matter the sagas are silent. But it is
easy to see why Canute should favour the proposed venture: as a younger son he could not hope
for the Danish crown. The conquest of England
might mean not only fame and plundered wealth,
but perhaps a realm to govern as well.

The considerations that moved the King to
renew the attempts at conquest were no doubt
various; but the deciding factor was evidently the
defection of Thurkil and the Jomvikings. An
ecclesiastic who later wrote a eulogy on Queen
Emma and her family discusses the situation in
this wise:

Thurkil, they said, the chief of your forces, O King,
departed with your permission that he might take
revenge for a brother who had been slain there, and
led with him a large part of your host. Now that he

---

[1] *Encomium Emmæ*, i., c. 3.

rejoices in victory and in the possession of the southern part of the country, he prefers to remain there as an exile and a friend of the English whom he has conquered by your hand, to returning with the host in submission to you and ascribing the victory to yourself. And now we are defrauded of our companions and of forty ships which he sailed to England laden with the best warriors of Denmark.[1]

So the advice was to seize the English kingdom as well as the Danish deserter. No great difficulty was anticipated, as Thurkil's men would probably soon desert to the old standards.

The customs of the Northmen demanded that an undertaking of this order should first be approved by the public assembly, and the Encomiast tells us that Sweyn at once proceeded to summon the freemen. Couriers were sent in every direction, and at the proper time the men appeared, each with his weapons as the law required. When the heralds announced the nature of the proposed undertaking—not a mere raid with plunder in view but the conquest of an important nation—the host gave immediate approval.

In many respects the time was exceedingly favourable for the contemplated venture. A large part of England was disposed to be friendly; the remainder was weak from continued pillage. Denmark was strong and aggressive, eager to follow the leadership of her warlike king. Sweyn's

[1] *Encomium Emmæ*, i., c. 2.

older son, Harold, had now reached manhood, and could with comparative safety be left in control of the kingdom. Denmark's neighbours in the North were friendly: Sweyn's vassal and son-in-law controlled the larger part of Norway; his stepson, Olaf, ruled in Sweden. Nor was anything to be feared from the old enemies to the south. The restless vikings of Jom were in England. The lord of Poland was engaged in a life-and-death struggle with the Empire. The Saxon dynasty, which had naturally had Northern interests, no longer dominated Germany; a Bavarian, Henry II., now sat on the throne of the Ottos. In the very year of Sweyn's invasion of England, the German King journeyed to Italy to settle one of the numberless disputes that the Roman see was involved in during the tenth and eleventh centuries. He remained in Italy till the next year (1014), when the victorious Pope rewarded him with the imperial crown.

Something in the form of a regency was provided for the Danish realm during Sweyn's absence. Harold seems to have received royal authority without the royal title. Associated with him were a few trusted magnates who were to give "sage advice," but also, it seems, to watch over the interests of the absent monarch.[1] A part of the host was left in Denmark; but the greater part of the available forces evidently accompanied the King to England.

[1] *Encomium Emmæ*, i., c. 3.

About midsummer (1013), the fleet was ready
to sail. The Encomiast, who had evidently seen
Danish ships, gives a glowing description of the
armament, which apart from rhetorical exaggeration probably gives a fairly accurate picture of an
eleventh-century viking fleet of the more preten-
tious type. He notes particularly the ornamentation along the sides of the ships, bright and varied
in colours; the vanes at the tops of the masts in the
forms of birds or of dragons with fiery nostrils; and
the figureheads at the prows: carved figures of
men, red with gold or white with silver, or of bulls
with necks erect, or of dolphins, centaurs, or other
beasts. The royal ship was, of course, splendid
above all the rest.[1]

The customary route of the Danish vikings
followed the Frisian coast to the south-eastern
part of England, the shires of Kent and Sussex.
Ordinarily, the fleets would continue the journey
down the Channel, plundering the shore lands and
sending out larger parties to harry the interior.
Sweyn had developed a different plan: Wessex was
to be attacked from the old Danelaw. Following
the ancient route, his ships appeared at Sandwich
on the Kentish coast early in August. Sandwich
was at this time a place of considerable importance,
being the chief port in Southern England.[2] Here
Sweyn and Canute remained for a few days, but
soon the fleet turned swiftly northwards up the
eastern coast to the Humber. Sweyn entered

[1] *Encomium Emmæ*, i., c. 4.   [2] *Ibid.*, i., c. 5.

4

and sailed up this river till he came to the mouth
of the Trent, which stream he ascended as far as
Gainsborough. Here his men disembarked and
preparations were made for the war.

Sweyn had evidently counted on a friendly
reception in the Scandinavian settlements of the
Danelaw, and he was not disappointed. Recruits
appeared and his forces increased materially.
Uhtred, the earl of Northumbria, who was probably of Norse ancestry, soon found it to his advantage to do homage to the invader. Sweyn's
lordship was also accepted by "the folk of Lindsey,
and afterwards by the folk in the Five Boroughs,
and very soon by all the host north of Watling
Street, and hostages were given by every shire."[1]
In addition to hostages, Sweyn demanded horses
and provisions for the host.

The summer was probably past before Sweyn
was ready to proceed against Ethelred. But
finally, some time in September or a little later,
having concluded all the necessary preliminaries,
he gave the ships and the hostages into the keeping
of his son Canute, and led his mounted army southward across the Midlands with Winchester, the
residence city of the English kings, as the objec-
tive point. So long as he was still within the
Danelaw, Sweyn permitted no pillaging; but
"as soon as he had crossed Watling Street, he
worked as great evil as a hostile force was able."
The Thames was crossed at Oxford, which city

[1] *Anglo-Saxon Chronicle*, 1013.

THE TULSTORP STONE
(Runic monument showing viking ship ornamented with beasts' heads.)

promptly submitted and gave hostages. Winchester, too, seems to have yielded without a struggle. From the capital Sweyn proceeded eastward to London, where he met the first effective resistance.

In London was King Ethelred supported by Thurkil the Tall and his viking bands. It seems that Olaf the Stout had entered the English service with Thurkil the year before, and did valiant service in defence of the city; the story given by Snorre of the destruction of London Bridge apparently belongs to the siege of 1013 rather than to that of 1009. Sweyn approached the city from the south, seized Southwark, and tried to enter London by way of the bridge, which the Danes had taken and fortified. It is said that Olaf the Stout undertook to destroy the bridge. He covered his ships with wattle-work of various sorts, willow roots, supple trees, and other things that might be twisted or woven; and thus protected from missiles that might be hurled down from above, the ships passed up the stream to the bridge, the supports of which Olaf and his men proceeded to pull down. The whole structure crashed into the river and with it went a large number of Sweyn's men,[1] who drowned, says the Chronicler, "because they neglected the bridge."

[1] Snorre, *Saga of Saint Olaf*, cc. 12–13. The story in the saga has the appearance of genuineness and is based on the contemporary verses of Ottar the Swart. Snorre's chronology, however, is much confused.

Sweyn soon realised that a continued siege would be useless: the season was advancing; the resistance of the citizens was too stubborn and strong. For the fourth time the heroic men of London had the satisfaction of seeing a Danish force break camp and depart with a defeated purpose: the first time in 991; then again in 994 when Sweyn and Olaf Trygvesson laid siege to it; the third time in 1009, when Thurkil the Tall and Olaf the Stout were the besiegers; now once more in 1013. The feeling that the city was impregnable was doubtless a factor in the stubborn determination with which the townsmen repelled the repeated attacks of the Danish invaders, though at this time the skill and valour of the viking mercenaries were an important part of the resistance.

Leaving London unconquered, Sweyn marched up the Thames Valley to Wallingford, where he crossed to the south bank, and continued his progress westward to Bath. Nowhere, it seems, did he meet any mentionable opposition. To Bath came the magnates of the south-western shires led by Ethelmer who was apparently ealdorman of Devon; they took the oaths that the conqueror prescribed and gave the required hostages. From Bath, Sweyn returned to his camp at Gainsborough; it was time to prepare for winter. Tribute and provisions were demanded and doubtless collected, and the host went into winter quarters on the banks of the Trent. "And all the nation had him

[Sweyn] for full king; and later the borough-men
of London submitted to him and gave hostages;
for they feared that he would destroy them."[1]

The submission of London probably did not
come before Ethelred's cowardly behaviour had
ruined the hopes of the patriots: he had fled the
land. Earlier in the year (in August, according
to one authority)[2] Queen Emma, accompanied
by the abbot of Peterborough, had crossed the
Channel, and sought the court of her brother, the
Norman duke. Whether she went to seek military aid or merely a refuge cannot be determined;
but the early departure and the fact that she was
not accompanied by her children would indicate
that her purpose was to enlist her brother's interest in Ethelred's cause. Assistance, however, was
not forthcoming; but Emma remained in Richard's
duchy and a little later was joined by her two sons,
Edward and Alfred, who came accompanied by
two English ecclesiastics. Ethelred, meanwhile,
continued some weeks longer with Thurkil's fleet;
but toward the close of December we find him on
the Isle of Wight, where he celebrated Christmas.
In January, he joined his family in Normandy.
Duke Richard gave him an honourable reception;
but as he was having serious trouble with another
brother-in-law, Count Odo of Chartres, he was
probably unable to give much material assistance
to the fugitive from England.

[1] *Anglo-Saxon Chronicle,* 1013.
[2] William of Malmesbury, *Gesta Regum,* i., 209.

Ethelred's flight must have left Thurkil and the Jomvikings in a somewhat embarrassing position. They had undertaken to serve the King and defend his country; but now Ethelred had deserted the kingdom, and his subjects had accepted the rule of the invader. In January, however, the sea is an unpleasant highway, so there was nothing for the tall chief to do but to remain faithful and insist on the terms of the contract. While Sweyn was calling for silver and supplies to be brought to Gainsborough, Thurkil seems to have been issuing similar demands from Greenwich. No doubt his men were also able to eke out their winter supplies by occasional plundering: "they harried the land as often as they wished."[1]

Then suddenly an event occurred that created an entirely new situation. On February 3, 1014, scarcely a month after Ethelred's departure from Wight, the Danish conqueror died. As to his manner of death, the Chronicle has nothing to say; but later historians appear to be better informed. The Encomiast, who was indeed Sweyn's contemporary, gives an account of a very edifying death: when Sweyn felt that the end of all things was approaching, he called Canute to his side and impressed upon him the necessity of following and supporting the Christian faith.[2] The Anglo-Norman historians have an even more wonderful story to relate: in the midst of a throng

---

[1] *Anglo-Saxon Chronicle*, 1013.
[2] *Encomium Emmæ*, i., c. 5; see also Saxo, *Gesta*, 342.

of his henchmen and courtiers, the mighty viking fell, pierced by the dart of Saint Edmund. Sweyn alone saw the saint; he screamed for help; at the close of the day he expired. It seems that a dispute was on at the time over a contribution that King Sweyn had levied on the monks who guarded Saint Edmund's shrine.[1] The suddenness of the King's death was therefore easily explained: the offended saint slew him.

If it is difficult to credit the legend that traces the King's death to an act of impiety, it is also hard to believe that he died in the odour of sanctity. Sweyn was a Christian, but his religion was of the passive type. He is said to have built a few churches, and he also appears to have promoted missionary efforts to some extent[2]; but the Church evidently regarded him as rather lukewarm in his religious professions. The see of Hamburg-Bremen, which was charged with the conversion of the Northern peoples, did not find him an active friend; though in this case his hostility may have been due to his dislike for all things that were called German.

Sweyn's virtues were of the viking type: he was a lover of action, of conquest, and of the sea. At times he was fierce, cruel, and vindictive; but these passions were tempered by cunning, shrewdness, and a love for diplomatic methods that were not common among the sea-kings. He seems to have

[1] *Memorials of Saint Edmund's Abbey*, i., 34 ff.
[2] Adamus, *Gesta*, ii., c. 39.

formed alliances readily, and appears even to have attracted his opponents. His career, too, was that of a viking. Twice he was taken by the Jomvikings, but his faithful subjects promptly ransomed him. Once the King of Sweden, Eric the Victorious, conquered his kingdom and sent him into temporary exile. Twice as a king he led incursions into England in which he gained only the sea-king's reward of plunder and tribute. But in time fortune veered about; his third expedition to Britain was eminently successful, and when Sweyn died, he was king not only of Denmark but also of England, and overlord of the larger part of Norway besides.

As to his personality, we have only the slight information implied in his nickname. Forkbeard means the divided beard. But the evident popularity that he enjoyed both in the host and in the nation would indicate that he possessed an attractive personality. That Sweyn appreciated the loyalty of his men is evident from the runic monument that he raised to his housecarle Skartha who had shared in the English warfare.[1]

By his first wife, the Polish princess who was renamed Gunhild, Sweyn had several children, of whom history makes prominent mention of three: Harold, Canute, and Gytha, who was married to Earl Eric of Norway. In the Hyde *Register* there is mention of another daughter,

[1] Wimmer, *De danske Runemindesmærker*, I., ii., 117.

Santslaue, "sister of King Canute,"[1] who may have been born of the same marriage, as her name is evidently Slavic. His second wife, Sigrid the Haughty, seems to have had daughters only. Of these only one appears prominently in the annals of the time—Estrid, the wife of Ulf the Earl, the mother of a long line of Danish kings.

At the time of his death Sweyn is thought to have been about fifty-four years old and had ruled Denmark nearly thirty years. His body was taken to York for interment, but it did not remain there long. The English did not cherish Sweyn's memory, and seemed determined to find and dishonour his remains. Certain women—English women, it appears—rescued the corpse and brought it to Roeskild some time during the following summer (1014)[2], where it was interred in the Church of the Holy Trinity, which also sheltered the bones of Sweyn's father whom he had wronged so bitterly thirty years before.

---

[1] *Liber Vitæ*, 58. Steenstrup suggests that the name may be Slavic and calls attention to the Slavic form Svantoslava (*Venderne og de Danske*, 64–65).

[2] *Encomium Emmæ*, ii., c. 3. The rescue and removal of Sweyn's remains by English women is asserted by the contemporary German chronicler Thietmar (*Chronicon*, vii., c. 26).

CHAPTER III

1014–1016

THE death of Sweyn was the signal for important movements throughout the entire North. Forces that had been held in rein by his mighty personality were once more free to act. In Denmark, his older son Harold succeeded at once to the full kingship. Three years later a national ruler re-established the Norwegian throne. But in England the results were most immediate and most evident: the national spirit rose with a bound and for three years more the struggle with the invader continued.

The host at Gainsborough promptly recognised the leadership of Canute and proclaimed him king. This, however, gave him no valid claim to the Saxon crown; England was, in theory at least, an elective monarchy, and not till the assembly of the magnates had accepted him could he rightfully claim the royal title. The Danish pretender was young and untried—he was probably not yet twenty years old. He must, however, have had

58

some training in matters of government as well as in warfare: that his great father trusted him is evident from the fact that he left him in charge of the camp and fleet at Gainsborough, when Sweyn set out on his march into Wessex. Doubtless the Danes surmised that the youthful chief possessed abilities of a rare sort; but the English evidently regarded him as a mere boy whose pretensions did not deserve serious attention.

During the winter months of 1014, the most prominent leader among the English was evidently Thurkil, the master of the mercenary forces. It seems safe to infer that he had much to do with the events of those months, though we have nothing recorded. In some way the English lords were called into session; at this meeting preparations were made to recall the fugitive Ethelred. No lord could be dearer to them than their native ruler, the magnates are reported to have said; but they added significantly, "if he would deal more justly with them than formerly."[1] The lords who attended this gemot were probably the local leaders south of the Thames; that the chiefs of the Danelaw were in attendance is very unlikely.

Ethelred, however, was not willing to leave Normandy immediately. He first sent an embassy to England under the nominal leadership of his son Edward; these men were to negotiate further, and probably study the sentiment of the

[1] *Anglo-Saxon Chronicle,* 1014.

nation. Edward was a mere boy, ten or eleven
years old at the highest; but his presence was
important as evidence of the King's intentions.
The Prince brought friendly greetings and fair
promises: Ethelred would be a kind and devoted
king; all the requests of the magnates should be
granted; the past should be forgiven and forgotten. The English on their part pledged absolute
loyalty; and, to emphasise the covenant, the assembly outlawed all Danish claimants. Sweyn
had died in the early part of February; the negotiations were probably carried on in March;
Ethelred returned to England some time during
Lent, most likely in April, as the Lenten season
closed on the 25th of that month.

The moment to strike had surely come. Canute
was in England with a good army, but his forces
doubtless had decreased in numbers since the
landing in the previous August, and further
shrinkage was inevitable. On the other hand,
recruiting would be found difficult. The inevitable
break-up of Sweyn's empire in the North would
mean that the invader would be deprived of resources that were necessary to the success of the
venture. Nor could assistance be expected from
the Scandinavian colonies on the western shores of
Britain or about the Irish Sea. In the very days
when the reaction was being planned in England,
Celts and Norsemen were mustering their forces
for a great trial of strength on Irish soil. On
Good Friday (April 23), the battle of Clontarf

was fought on the shores of Dublin Bay.[1] The
Norsemen suffered an overwhelming defeat, the
significance of which, for English history, lies in
the fact that the viking forces of the West had now
been put on the defensive. Raids like those of
the early years of Ethelred's reign were now a
thing of the past.

Meanwhile, Canute had not been idle. For
aggressive movements the winter season was, of
course, not favourable; but preparations seem to
have been made looking toward offensive operations immediately after Easter. The men of
Lindsey, Danish colonists no doubt, had promised
horses and were apparently to share in a joint
expedition. But before Canute's arrangements
had all been made, Ethelred appeared in the north
country with a formidable host, and Canute was
compelled to retire to his ships. The men of
Lincoln were made to suffer for their readiness to
join in Canute's plans: Ethelred marched his men
into the Lindsey region, and pillage began.

It was hardly an English army that Ethelred
brought up to the Trent in May, 1014. Englishmen no doubt served in it; but its chief strength
was probably the mercenary contingent under
Thurkil's command, which, as we have seen, had
wintered at Greenwich. It was fortunate for
Ethelred that an organised force was at hand

[1] For a brief account of the Norse colonies in Ireland and the
events that culminated in the battle of Clontarf, seĕ *Norges
Historie*, I., ii., 292–310. (Bugge.)

on his return and ready for warfare. Its service, however, was expensive: that year another Dane-geld of 21,000 pounds was levied to pay Thurkil and his vikings for their assistance in driving Canute out of the land.[1]

But Thurkil was not the only great chief of the viking type that assisted in expelling the Danes: Olaf the Stout once more appears in Ethelred's service. It will be recalled that, in the siege of London the autumn before, he assisted vigorously in its defence. He seems to have left the English service shortly afterwards to assist in warfare on French soil. Duke Richard of Normandy was engaged in a controversy with his brother-in-law, Count Odo of Chartres, on the matter of his sister's dowry. In the warfare that ensued, Olaf, serving on the Norman side, ravaged the northern coast of Brittany and took the castle of Dol. This must have occurred late in the year 1013 or during the winter of 1013–1014. When, on the mediation of King Robert, peace was made between the warring brethren, Olaf returned to Rouen, where he was received with signal honours. It was probably on this occasion that the mighty Sea-king, on the urgent request of Archbishop Robert, accepted the Christian faith and received baptism. It is stated that many of his men were baptised at the same time.[2]

In Rouen, Olaf evidently met the fugitive

[1] *Anglo-Saxon Chronicle*, 1014.
[2] William of Jumièges, *Historia Normannorum*, v., cc. 11-12.

Ethelred; for when the King returned to England, Olaf accompanied him. Instead of coming as a returning exile, Ethelred appeared in his kingdom with ships and men. The Norse poets, who later sang in King Olaf's hall, magnified his viking exploits far beyond their real importance. In their view, Olaf was Ethelred's chief support. Snorre quotes the following lines from Ottar the Swart:

> Thou broughtst to land and landedst,
> King Ethelred, O Landward,
> Strengthened by might! That folk-friend
> Such wise of thee availèd.
>
> Hard was the meeting soothly,
> When Edmund's son thou broughtest
> Back to his land made peaceful,
> Which erst that kin-stem rulèd. [1]

The emergency was too great for Canute. With the generalship of experienced warriors like Thurkil and Olaf, supported by the resources of a roused people, he could not be expected to cope. Presently, he determined to flee the country. His men embarked, and the hostages given to his father (some of them at least) were also brought on board. The fleet sailed down the east coast to Sandwich, where an act of barbarity was committed for which there can be little justification. The hostages were mutilated—their hands, ears, and

[1] *Saga of Saint Olaf*, c. 13. (Translation by William Morris.)

noses were cut off—and landed. The men were
personal pledges given to Sweyn, but not to his son.
Canute, however, probably looked at the matter
in a different light; to him they may have seemed
a pledge given to the dynasty; terror must be
stricken into the hearts of the oath-breakers.
After disposing of the hostages, the young King
continued his journey to Denmark.

What Canute's plans were when he arrived in his
native land we do not know. According to the
Encomiast, he assured his surprised brother that
he had returned, not because of fear, but for love
of his brother, whose advice and assistance he
bespoke. But he requested more than this:
Harold, he thought, ought to share Denmark with
him; the two kings should then proceed with the
conquest of England; when that was accomplished,
there might be a new division of territory on the
basis of a kingdom for each. He proposed to spend
the succeeding winter in preparation for the joint
attack.[1]

The proposal to share the rule of Denmark
evidently did not appeal to King Harold; he is
represented as stoutly rejecting it. Denmark
was his, given to him by his father before he left
for England. He would assist Canute to win a
kingdom in Britain, but not a foot should he have
of Denmark. Realising the futility of insisting,
Canute promised to maintain silence as to his
supposed hereditary rights to Danish soil. He put

[1] *Encomium Emmæ*, ii., c. 2.

his trust in God, the good monk adds; and the Encomiast was perhaps not the only one who regarded Harold's early death as a providential event.

The problem of Norway was one that the brothers must have discussed, though we do not know what disposition they made of the Danish rights there. In addition to the overlordship over at least a part of Eric's earldom, Sweyn had had direct royal authority over the southern shores, though it is not believed that he exercised this authority very rigidly. There is a single circumstance that suggests that Norway was assigned to Canute: when the young prince called on his brother-in-law, Earl Eric, to assist him in England, the Norse ruler seems to have obeyed the summons without question.[1]

During the course of the year, the two brothers united in certain acts of a filial nature, one of which is worthy of particular notice. Together they proceeded to the Slavic coast, Poland most likely, where their mother, Queen Gunhild, was still in exile. After twenty years, she was restored to her honours at the Danish court. Sigrid the Haughty had evidently taken leave of earthly things; for peace and good-will continued between the Swedish and Danish courts, an impossible

---

[1] The conjecture of Norse historians that he left Norway because of disagreements with his brother Sweyn has little in its favour. Eric believed in peace, but scarcely to the point of expatriation.

condition with Sigrid in retirement and her old
rival in the high-seat. That same year the
brothers gave Christian burial to the remains of
their father Sweyn.[1]

We are told that Canute continued his preparations for a descent upon England; still, it may be
doubted whether he actually had serious hope of
conquering the country at that time. Then suddenly there occurred in England a series of events
that placed the fate of Ethelred in Canute's hands.

The saga that relates the exploits of the Jomvikings tells somewhat explicitly of an English
attack on two corps of "thingmen," as the Danish mercenaries were called in Northern speech,
the corps in London and Slesswick.[2] The latter
locality has not been identified, but it seems hardly
necessary to seek it far north of the Thames—
the saga locates it north of London. It is asserted
that the massacre was planned by Ulfketel, and
that in Slesswick it was thoroughly carried out:
from this we may infer that the place was in East
Anglia, or Ulfkellsland, as the scalds called it.
The garrisons, we are told, were located by Sweyn;
this is doubtless an error,—the corps were probably divisions of the viking forces in Ethelred's
service. No doubt there were other similar corps,
for Thurkil was apparently connected with neither
of the two.

---

[1] *Encomium Emmæ*, ii., cc. 2–3. The banishment of Gunhild
is also mentioned in Thietmar's *Chronicle* (vii., c. 28).

[2] *Jómsvíkingasaga*, cc. 50–52.

Canute was out of the country and no hostile
force was in sight.   There could then be small need
of retaining the thingmen who were furthermore a
source of expense, perhaps of danger.   As in 1002,
it was determined to fall upon them and slay them.
If it is true that Thurkil's men were originally
quartered in East Anglia,[1] we can readily understand why Ulfketel might take the lead in such an
undertaking.   In London, where resistance had
been so persistent and successful, the mercenaries
must have been regarded with strong aversion.
It was planned to strike during the Yule festivities
when the vikings would probably not be in the
best possible state of vigour and sobriety.   In
London armed men were smuggled into the
stronghold in waggons that were ostensibly laden
with merchandise for the midwinter market.   But
the corps was warned in time by a woman who
wished to save her lover Thord.   Eilif, who was
in command here, escaped to Denmark.   In
Slesswick, the plan succeeded, none escaping;
among the fallen was the chief, Heming, the
brother of Thurkil the Tall.   The attack is thought
to have been made some time during the early
part of January, 1015.[2]

It is evident that something of a serious nature
occurred in England in those days, and while
some of the details in the saga tale are probably
fictitious, in substance the account is perhaps

[1] William of Malmesbury, *Gesta Regum*, i., 207.
[2] *Danmarks Riges Historie*, i., 383.

correct. Heming disappears from the English sources, while Eilif is prominent in English politics for another decade. Most significant of all, a few weeks later Thurkil appears in Denmark to urge upon Canute the desirability of an immediate attack on England. He now had another brother to avenge. Thurkil's desertion of the English cause must have done much to stimulate Danish ambition. Help was secured from Olaf of Sweden. Eric, the Norse earl, was also summoned to the host. Great preparations must have gone forward in Denmark, for all writers agree that Canute's fleet, when it finally sailed, was immense in the number of ships. Thurkil's position in Denmark appears to have been a trifle uncertain at first. Canute could hardly be expected to give cordial greeting to a man who had recently sent him out of England in full flight; but after some discussion the two were reconciled, and Thurkil joined the expedition.[1]

In all the North there was none more famous for successful leadership in warfare than Earl Eric of Norway. He had fought in the battles of Hjörunga Bay and Swald; in both these encounters the highest honours were his. It is, therefore, not strange that Canute was anxious to have his assistance. Eric was no longer young and had no direct interest in the proposed venture; still, when the mandate came, he showed no reluctance, so far as we know. He called together the magnates

[1] *Encomium Emmæ*, ii., c. 3.

·of the realm and arranged for a division of his
earldom between his brother Sweyn and his young
son Hakon.[1] It need not be assumed that Eric
at this time made a final surrender of his own
rights; most likely it was the administration during
the period of his absence only that was provided
for in this way.

As Hakon was yet but a youth, Eric gave him a
guardian in his kinsman, the famous Thronder
chief, Einar Thongshaker. In his day, Einar was
the best archer in Norway; hence his nickname,
the one who makes the bow-thong tremble. He,
too, had fought at Swald, but on King Olaf's ship;
twice did his arrow seek Eric's life; the third time
he drew the bow it was struck by a hostile shaft,
and broke. "What broke?" asked the King.
"Norway from your hands," replied the confident
archer.[2] After Eric and his brother had become
rulers in Norway, they made peace with Einar,
married him to their sister, the generous Bergljot,
and endowed him greatly with lands and influence.
Of the three men to whom Norway was now
committed, he was clearly the ablest, if not of the
greatest consequence.

Turning again to England, we find a situation
developing that was anything but promising.
Some time during the first half of the year, a gemot
was summoned to meet at Oxford, near the border
of the Danelaw. Evidently an attempt was to be

[1] Snorre, *Saga of Saint Olaf*, c. 24.
[2] *Ibid.*, *Olaf Trygvesson's Saga*, c. 108.

made in the direction of a closer union between the
North and the South.   Among others who attended
were two Scandinavian nobles from the Seven
Boroughs, Sigeferth and Morcar.   So far as names
show the nationality of the bearers, they might
be either Angles or Northmen; but the name of
their father, Arngrim, is unmistakably Norse.
During the sessions of the gemot, the brothers
were accused of treason and slain in the house of
Eadric, the Mercian earl.[1]   The result was a riot;
the followers of the murdered men called for
revenge, but were repulsed and driven into the
tower of Saint Frideswide's Church, which the
English promptly burned.   Such a violation of
the right of sanctuary could not be overlooked
even in those impassioned times; and only through
penance on the part of the luckless King was the
stain removed.[2]

The sources are at one in laying the blame for
this trouble on Earl Eadric.   William of Malmesbury says that he desired the wealth of the two
Danes, and we find that Ethelred actually did
exact forfeiture.   But it may also be that Eadric
was endeavouring to extend and consolidate his
Mercian earldom; to do this he would have to
devise some method to deprive the Seven Boroughs
of their peculiarly independent position in the

[1] *Anglo-Saxon Chronicle*, 1015; Florence of Worcester, *Chronicon*, i., 170-171.   The Five Boroughs had by this time become
the Seven Boroughs.
[2] William of Malmesbury, *Gesta Regum*, i., 213.

Danelaw or Danish Mercia. Whatever his purpose, he seems to have had the approval of the
ill-counselled King.

Sigeferth's widow, Aldgyth, was taken as a prisoner to Malmesbury, where Edmund, Ethelred's
virile son, saw her and was attracted by her. But
Ethelred objected to his son's matrimonial plans;
the reasons are not recorded, but one of them, at
least, can be readily inferred: callous of heart as the
old King doubtless was, he probably did not enjoy
the thought of having in his household as daughter-
in-law a woman who could not help but be a
constant reminder of a deed that was treacherous,
stupid, and criminal. Passion, however, was
strong in Edmund Ironside; he married the widow
in spite of his father's veto; more than that, he
demanded her slain husband's forfeited official
position. Ethelred again refused, whereupon the
Prince proceeded to the Danish strongholds and
took possession.[1]

Edmund's act was that of a rebel; but in the
Danelaw it was probably regarded in large part as
proper vengeance. Thus fuel was added to the
old fire that burned in the hearts of Dane and
Saxon. The spirit of rebellion, so general in the
kingdom, had now appeared in the royal family
itself. Most significant of all, the Prince had
probably thwarted a great ambition: how much of
Mercia was under Eadric's control at this time
we do not know; but a man of the ealdorman's

[1] William of Malmesbury, *Gesta Regum*, i., 213.

type could scarcely be satisfied with anything less than the whole. And here was the King's son actually governing the strongholds of the earldom. Would he not in time supplant the low-born Eadric? We have in these transactions the most plausible explanation of Eadric's treachery a little later, when Canute was again in the land.

It was late in the summer,—some time between August 15th and September 8th, according to Florence of Worcester,—when Edmund appeared as claimant in the Danelaw. Those very same weeks must have seen the departure of Canute's fleet from Denmark. The expedition that now arrived in England was a most formidable one; statements vary as to the number of ships[1] and we know nothing as to the strength of the host; but it seems likely that twenty thousand men is not an extreme estimate. The entire North assisted in its make-up, though it may be that the Norse contingent under Earl Eric did not arrive till later in the year.[2] The distance to the earl's garth in the Thronder country was long; the Norwegian chiefs lived scattered and apart; a large force could, therefore, not be collected in haste.

Again the Encomiast seizes the opportunity to

[1] The Encomiast counts two hundred ships (*Encomium Emmæ*, ii., c. 4). The *Jómsvikingasaga* reports 960 (c. 52). Adam of Bremen puts the number at 1000 (*Gesta*, ii., c. 50). The Encomiast is doubtless nearest the truth.

[2] The *Knytlingasaga* seems to indicate that Eric came late (c. 13).

describe a Northern fleet. He mentions particularly the gleaming weapons of the warriors on
board; the flaming shields that hung along the
gunwales; the figureheads bright with silver and
gold—figures of lions, of men with threatening
faces, of fiery dragons, and of bulls with gilded
horns. And he asks who could look upon such an
armament and not fear the King at whose bidding
it came. The warriors, too, were carefully selected:

> Moreover, in the whole force there could be found
> no serf, no freedman, none of ignoble birth, none
> weak with old age. All were nobles, all vigorous with
> the strength of complete manhood, fit for all manner of
> battle, and so swift on foot that they despised the
> fleetness of cavalry. [1]

There is evidently some exaggeration here; the
numerous "nobles" were probably plain freemen;
still, it is clear that Canute led a valiant, well-
equipped host.

But Canute was not the only adventurer who
sailed in quest of kingship in 1015. While the
youthful Prince was mustering his fleet in the
straits of Denmark, Olaf the Stout was in Britain
preparing to sail for Norway on a similar errand—
to win a crown. But here all similarity ceases;
two merchant ships and fewer than two hundred
men made up the force that began the Norse
revolt. Still, Olaf Haroldsson, too, was successful

[1] *Encomium Emmæ*, ii., c. 4.

and bore the crown of Norway till he fell in war
with Canute in 1030.

After the expulsion of the Danes from England
the year before, Olaf seems to have returned to
piracy; there is some evidence that he took part
in an expedition of this sort along the coasts of
Gaul as far as Aquitaine.   On his return he seems
to have visited Normandy, where he may have
learned of Canute's intentions and preparations.
The probability is strong that he was also informed
of the part that Eric was to have in the venture,
for he seems carefully to have timed his departure so as to reach Norway just after the earl
had left the country to join Canute.   He first
sailed to England, stayed for a time in North-
umberland, where he made the necessary preparations, and thence proceeded to the west coast
of Norway.[1]

Fortune smiled on the bold adventurer.   Soon
after he had landed he learned that Hakon was
in the neighbourhood and set out to capture him.
In this he was successful: Olaf's ships were merchant ships, and the young unsuspecting earl
rowed into a sound where the enemy was waiting
for him and passed in between the supposed merchant vessels.   Olaf had stretched a rope from
ship to ship, and when the earl's boat was directly
between them, Olaf's men pulled the rope till
Hakon's boat capsized.   The young chief and a
few of his followers were saved.   Olaf gave him

[1] Snorre, *Saga of Saint Olaf*, cc. 28–29.

quarter on condition that he should leave Norway, surrender his rights to sovereignty, and swear never more to fight against his stout opponent. Hakon took the required oaths and was permitted to depart. He hastened to England and reported the matter to his uncle Canute. But the English campaign had only fairly begun, so Canute was in no position to interfere. Hakon remained long with Canute, and in time was invested with an English earldom.[1]

Meanwhile, the Danish fleet had arrived at Sandwich; but from Kent, Canute did not sail north to his former friends in the Humber lands; he reverted to the old viking practices of harrying the Southwest, Dorset, Wilts and Somerset.[2] Whether this was his original plan cannot be known: it may be that the news of Edmund's activity in the Danelaw was to some extent responsible for this move. It was now autumn of the year 1015; but if England hoped that the host would soon follow viking customs and retire into winter quarters, the country was doomed to bitter disappointment; for the enemy now had a leader who saw no need of rest, who struck in winter as well as in summer.

Canute also differed from earlier chiefs in his ideas of conduct on the battle-field. The viking band, as a development of the Teutonic comitatus, was naturally inspired with its ideas of honour and

[1] Snorre, *Saga of Saint Olaf*, cc. 30–31.
[2] *Anglo-Saxon Chronicle*, 1015.

valour. When the challenge to combat had been accepted, it was the duty of the warrior to conquer or perish with his leader; and it was the chief's duty to set an honourable example for his men. It was this spirit that animated King Olaf Trygvesson at Swald when his men urged the feasibility of flight before the battle had really begun. "Strike the sails," he commanded. "My men shall not think of flight; never have I fled from combat."[1]

The young Dane brought no such ideas to the campaign that he was now on the point of beginning. Being by race more a Slav than a Dane, it may be that he did not readily acquire Germanic ideas. His training with the Jomvikings, perhaps in his early youth, at least now in his British camp, where veterans from Jom were numerous and Thurkil the Tall was the chief warrior, ran counter to such notions. The Jomvikings would retreat, sometimes they would even take to flight, as we infer from a runic inscription that reads like a rebuke for cowardly retreat.[2]

---

[1] Snorre, *Olaf Trygvesson's Saga*, c. 102.

[2] The Hällestad Stone, raised in memory of Toki, Canute's granduncle, who fell in the battle of Fyris River:

"Askell raised this monument in memory of Toki, Gorm's son his beloved lord.

> He did not flee
> At Upsala.
> Henchmen have raised
> To their brother's memory

THE HÄLLESTAD STONE

To add to the difficulties of England, Ethelred was stricken with an illness that ended his life a few months later. The hope of England now lay in the rebellious Edmund, who was still in the North country. He and Eadric were both gathering forces in Mercia; but when they joined disagreements seem to have arisen; for soon the Earl again played the traitor, deserted the Etheling, and with "forty ships" repaired to Canute and joined his host.

In the language of the day, the term "ship" did not necessarily refer to an actual sea-going craft; it was often used as a rude form of reckoning military forces, somewhat less than one hundred men, perhaps. It has been thought that Eadric's deserters were the remnant of Ethelred's Danish mercenary force[1]; but it is unlikely that so many vikings still remained in the English service. The

---

> On the firm-built hill
> This rock with runes.
> To Gorm's son Toki
> They walked nearest."

Wimmer, *De danske Runemindesmærker*, I., ii. 86, ff.

[1] Thus Steenstrup (*Normannerne*, iii., 287–289) and Oman (*England before the Norman Conquest*, 577) on the authority of Florence of Worcester (*Chronicon*, i., 171) who speaks of these men as Danish warriors. But the contemporary writer of the *Chronicle* speaks of Eadric's forces as the "fyrd," a term which is always used for the native levy, "here" being the term used for alien troops.

On the theory of serious disagreements with Edmund, whose accession to the throne seemed imminent, Eadric's treason becomes perfectly intelligible. For a selfish, ambitious man like the earl, there was scarcely any other course to take.

chances are that they were Mercians, possibly
Danish Mercians. Wessex now gave up the fight,
accepted Canute as king, and provided horses for
the invading army.

It must have been about Christmas time when
Eadric marched his men down into the South to
join the Danes. A few days later the restless
Prince, with Eadric in his train, started northward,
crossed the Thames at Cricklade in Wiltshire,
and proceeded toward the Warwick country.
Edmund had apparently come south to meet him,
but the militia were an unwilling band. They
suddenly became sticklers for legal form and regularity, and refused to go on without the presence
of the King and the aid of London. As neither
was forthcoming, the English dispersed. Once
more the summons went abroad, and once more
the men insisted that the King must be in personal
command: let him come with what forces he could
muster. Ethelred came, but the hand of death
was upon him. Evidently the old King had
neither courage nor strength. Whispers of treason came to him: "that they who should be a
help to him intended to betray him"[1]; and he
suddenly deserted the army and returned to the
fastness of London.

The second attempt at resistance having failed,
Edmund left the South to its fate, and rode into
Northumbria to seek Earl Uhtred. No better
evidence can be found of the chaos that existed

[1] *Anglo-Saxon Chronicle,* 1016.

in England at the time. The Saxon South accepts the invader, while a prince of the house of Alfred is looking for aid in the half-Scandinavian regions beyond the Humber that had once so readily submitted to Sweyn Forkbeard. What agreements and promises were made are not known; but soon we have the strange spectacle of Edmund and his new ally harrying English lands, the Mercian counties of Stafford, Salop, and Chester. Doubtless the plan was to punish Eadric, but it was a plan that did not lead to a united England.

The punishment of the deserters was probably incidental; evidently the allies were on the march southward to check Canute. Here was an opportunity for the young Dane to show some generalship, and the opportunity was improved. Turning eastward into Bucks, he marched his army in a northeasterly direction toward the Fenlands, and thence northward through Lincoln and Nottingham toward York. When Earl Uhtred learned of this attack on his territories, he hastened back to Northumbria. But he was not in position to fight, and, therefore,

driven by necessity, he submitted, and all Northumbria with him, and gave hostages. Nevertheless, on the advice of Eadric, he was slain, and with him Thurkil, the son of Nafena. And after that the king made Eric earl of Northumbria with all the rights that Uhtred had.[1]

[1] *Anglo-Saxon Chronicle*, 1016.

The Chronicler seems to believe that Uhtred was slain soon ,after his submission, and it could not have been very much later. Simeon of Durham tells us that the Earl was slain by an enemy named Thurbrand[1]; but it seems clear that Canute approved the act and perhaps desired it. It is extremely probable that Uhtred was removed to make room for Eric. When young Hakon arrived as a fugitive, Eric doubtless realised that his Norwegian earldom was slipping away. All through the fall and winter Olaf had been travelling along the shores and up through the dales; wherever it was practicable he had summoned the peasantry to public assemblies and presented his case. His appeal was to national Norse pride and to the people's sense of loyalty to Harold Fairhair's dynasty. Almost everywhere the appeal was successful.

But the men who loved the old order were not willing to yield, without a struggle. While Canute was making his winter campaign from the Channel to York, both parties were active in Norway, Sweyn and Einar in the Throndelaw, Olaf in the South. All through Lent the fleets were gathering. Finally on Palm Sunday, March 25, 1016, the dragons encountered each other at the Nesses, near the mouth of the Christiania Firth. Neither force was great, though that of Sweyn and Einar was considerably larger than the pretender's host. It has been estimated that Olaf

[1] *Opera*, ii., 148.

had fewer than 2000 men, his opponents nearly twice as many. At the Nesses for the first time the cross figured prominently in Norwegian warfare: golden, red, or blue crosses adorned the shining shields of the kingsmen. After mass had been sung and the men had breakfasted, Olaf sailed out and made the attack. The outcome was long uncertain, but finally victory was with the King.[1]

From the Nesses Einar and Sweyn fled to Sweden. Here they were offered assistance and were planning an expedition against King Olaf for the following year, when Earl Sweyn suddenly died. As there was no one in Norway around whom the dissatisfied elements could rally, all attempts to dislodge the new King were given up for the time. Some of the defeated chiefs may have sought refuge with Canute; at any rate the news of the Nesses could not have been long in reaching the York country. As Eric had come to England at Canute's request, the Prince doubtless felt that he owed his brother-in-law some compensation. Furthermore, with the Norse earl in control at York, Canute could feel more secure as to Northumbrian loyalty. There thus existed in the spring of 1016 a double reason for removing Uhtred.

Another Northumbrian magnate, Thurkil the son of Nafna, is mentioned as sharing the strong earl's fate. Who Thurkil was is not known; but

[1] Snorre, *Saga of Saint Olaf*, cc. 46–51.

6

it is clear that he must have been a noble of
considerable prominence, as he would otherwise
hardly be known to a chronicler in Southern
England. His name gives evidence of Northern
blood; but thus far his identity has been a mystery,
and the following attempt at identification can
claim plausibility only. King Olaf Trygvesson
had a younger half-brother who was known to
the scalds as Thurkil Nefja or "Nosy." In the
expedition to Wendland in 1000, he commanded
the *Short Serpent*. At Swald he fought on King
Olaf's own ship, and was the last to leap over-
board when Eric and his men boarded and seized
it. Of him sang Hallfred Troublous-scald:

> Strong-souled Thurkil
> Saw the Crane and the Dragons
> Two float empty
> (Gladly had he grappled),
>
> Ere the arm-ring wearer,
> Mighty in warfare,
> Leaped into the sea, seeking
> Life by swimming.[1]

The inference is that he actually escaped, and it
seems possible that we find him again in England
after sixteen years. As all the rulers of the North
had conspired against Olaf, he would be compelled
to seek refuge in other lands, preferably in one of

---

[1] Snorre, *Olaf Trygvesson's Saga*, c. 111., *Corpus Poeticum
Boreale*, ii., 92

the Scandinavian colonies in the West.   But for
Thurkil now to serve loyally and peaceably under
the man who drove his brother to death and seized
his kingdom might be difficult; and he may therefore have been sacrificed to Eric's security.   The
statement that his father's name was Nafna
presents a difficulty; but the Chronicler may not
have been thoroughly informed on the subject
of Norse nicknames and may have mistaken the
by-name for the name of his father.

After the submission of Northumbria, Canute
returned to the South.   This time he carefully
avoided the Danelaw; evidently he wished that
his friends in Danish Mercia should suffer no
provocation to rise against him; the route, therefore, lay through the West.   The campaign was
swiftly carried through, for by Easter (April 1),
Canute was again with his ships.   Wessex and
Northumbria were now both pacified.   In the
Midlands there can have been but little active
hostility.   London alone showed the old determination to resist; here were Ethelred and Edmund
with a number of the English magnates.   Canute
immediately began preparations for a last descent
upon the stubborn city; but before his dragons
had actually left harbour, England had lost her
king.

April 23, 1016, Ethelred died.   To say anything
in real praise of the unfortunate King is impossible.   The patriotic monk who chronicled the
sad events of this doleful period can only say

that "he kept his realm with great trouble and suffering the while that he lived."[1]   Any striking abilities Ethelred cannot have possessed. He was easily influenced for evil—perhaps he was faithless.   But to lay all the blame for the downfall of England upon the incapable king would be missing the point.   The Old English monarchy was, after all, a frail kingdom.   The success of Edgar in reducing the Scandinavian colonies to unquestioned obedience was probably due in large part to his sterling qualities as king; but in still greater measure, perhaps, to the fact that, during his reign, the viking spirit was at its lowest ebb: consequently the stream of reinforcements having ceased to flow across the North Sea, the Anglo-Danes were forced to yield.   But now the situation was totally different.   In the early years of the eleventh century only statesmanship of the highest order could have saved the dynasty; but England had neither statesmen nor statesmanship in Ethelred's day.

[1] *Anglo-Saxon Chronicle*, 1016.

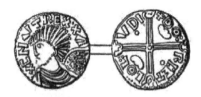

CHAPTER IV

THE STRUGGLE WITH EDMUND IRONSIDE

1016

THE Old English kingship was elective: on the death of a ruler, the great lords and the high officials of the Church, the "witan" or wise, would meet in formal assembly to select a successor. Usually the nearest male heir of the house of Alfred would be chosen; but circumstances might dictate a different selection, and in such cases the "wise men" seem to have possessed plenary powers. In the spring of 1016, however, a free choice was impossible; nearly the whole kingdom was pledged to the invader. In his camp were the Saxon hostages; and the great Dane had shown on an earlier occasion that he could be cruel when he thought a pledge was broken.

During the winter months the Danish fleet had apparently been moored at the old viking rendezvous, the Isle of Wight, or in some neighbouring harbour. In April, Canute was back from his march to York and was getting his ships in readiness for further operations, when the death of Ethelred checked his movements. With remarkable promptness the notables (perhaps those of Southern England only) came together at some point unknown, awarded the kingship to Canute, and proscribed all the descendants of Ethelred. This done, they adjourned to Southampton to give their pledges of loyalty. It was a body of great respectability that thus gathered to pay homage, containing, as it did, both laymen and churchmen, lords, bishops, and abbots. The election must have been held some time about the close of the month, for by the seventh of May, Canute was at Greenwich with his fleet.[1]

In London, too, an assembly had met and a king had been chosen. Edmund was in the city when his father died. The chiefs present, "all the witan who were in London and the citizens of London," as the Chronicler carefully puts it, at once proclaimed Edmund king. Thus both the peace party and the war party had acted. It is clear, however, that neither of these elections could lay any claim to legality; neither assembly could pretend to represent the entire kingdom; between the death of Ethelred in April and the accession of Canute at the following Christmas, England had no lawful ruler.

Canute at once proceeded to the siege of London. His plan was to isolate the city completely, to block the Thames both above and below the town, and to prevent all intercourse with the country to the north. To accomplish this invest-

[1] Florence of Worcester, *Chronicon*, i., 173.

ment, a canal was dug around London Bridge wide enough to permit the long but narrow viking ships to pass into the stream west of the city. On the north side a ditch was dug enclosing the entire town, "so that no man could come either in or out."[1] Vigorous efforts were made from time to time to storm the fortifications, "every morning the lady on the Thames bank sees the sword dyed in blood"[2]; but the townsmen held their own. The siege continued through the month of May and perhaps till late in June, when it seems to have been interrupted by disquieting news from the West.

On the approach of the fleet, or at least before the investment had become complete, Edmund left London. We are told that his departure was secret, which is probable, as it was surely to his interest to keep Canute in the dark as to his whereabouts. We do not know who directed the defence of London during his absence; a year or two later, Thietmar, the bishop of Merseburg, introduced into his *Chronicle* a confused account of these events, in which Queen Emma is made to play an important part in the resistance of 1016.[3] It may be that the Queen had returned with Ethelred, but it is doubtful. When Canute heard that his enemies were mustering in the South-west, he seems to have detached a part of his force and

[1] *Anglo-Saxon Chronicle*, 1016.
[2] *Corpus Poeticum Boreale*, ii., 108: the Lithsmen's Song.
[3] Book vii., c. 28.

sent it westward to look for Edmund. At Penselwood, near Gillingham in Dorset, the Danes came
upon the Saxon forces. Edmund's success in
raising the West had not been great; but, "trusting
in the help of God," he gave battle and won a
victory.[1] It is likely that the affair at Penselwood
was little more than a skirmish, for it seems to
have made small difference in the relative positions
of the contending forces. But it gave Edmund
what he sorely needed—the prestige of success.
A month later, battle was again joined at Sherstone,
a little farther to the north near Malmesbury in
the upper part of Wiltshire.

The encounter at Sherstone was a genuine
battle fiercely fought, one that lived long in the
memories of Englishmen. It occurred after the
feast of Saint John, probably in the early days of
July. The earlier sources do not mention Canute
in connection with this fight; with Eric he was
apparently continuing the siege of London. The
western campaign was evidently in Thurkil's
hands; the sources also mention three prominent
Englishmen, Eadric, Almar Darling, and Algar,
as fighting on the Danish side.[2] The Encomiast,
who speaks of a Danish victory at Sherstone,
gives the entire credit to Thurkil, whom he naively
describes as a fervent believer "continuously
sending up silent prayers to God for victory."[3]

---

[1] Florence of Worcester, *Chronicon*, i., 174.   [2] *Ibid.*, i., 175.
[3] *Encomium Emmæ*, ii., c. 6. See also Thietmar, *Chronicon*,
vii., c. 28.

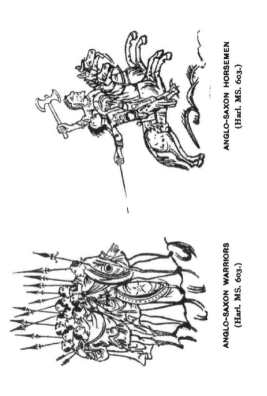

ANGLO-SAXON HORSEMEN
(Harl. MS. 603.)

ANGLO-SAXON WARRIORS
(Harl. MS. 603.)

Sherstone was at best a drawn battle, neither side claiming a victory. The Anglo-Norman historians, true to their habit of looking for some traitor on whom to blame the outcome, could not overlook Eadric; he is said to have picked up the head of a soldier who bore some resemblance to Edmund and thus to have deceived the Saxons into believing that their leader was dead.[1] The tale is obviously mythical; if Henry of Huntingdon is to be trusted, the trick was played again later in the year at Ashington.

After the encounter at Sherstone, Thurkil seems to have joined Canute before London; but his whole force did not return with him. Eadric once more had shifted his allegiance; he had made peace with Edmund and had joined him against the invader. Whatever his motives may have been, there can be no dispute as to the importance of his new move. Edmund's army was strengthened, as was doubtless his prestige in the Midlands. For the third time he had an army at his command, gathered, it seems, from the region north of the Thames. With this host he marched to the relief of London. On the appearance of this force, Canute found himself in a difficult situation: to maintain a siege and fight a vigorous foeman at the same time, required forces greater than those at the Dane's command. Prudence was Canute's greatest virtue, and he promptly raised the siege

[1] The story is first told by Florence of Worcester (*Chronicon*, i., 175).

and withdrew to his ships. Edmund seems to
have come up with his forces to Brentford, just
as the Danes were busy crossing to the south bank.
The enemy fled; but many of the English were
drowned "because of their own heedlessness, as
they rushed ahead of the main force to get at the
booty."[1] Evidently the whole Danish force had
not left London, as the fight at Brentford was two
days after the city had been relieved.

With the relief of London, the English seem to
have considered their duty done, and soon Edmund found himself once more without an army.[2]
It may, of course, be that the apparent lack of
patriotism was due to the necessities of the harvest
season, which must have arrived by this time.
The tireless Edmund next made a visit to Wessex
to raise the militia there. While he was seeking
recruits, the Danes returned to London, resumed
the siege, and attacked the city furiously by land
and sea, but as usual failed to take it.

---

[1] If the skirmishers who were seeking booty were in advance of
the rest and by a rally of the Danes were driven into the Thames,
the main force must still have been on the north bank. The
"battle" must therefore have been fought on the north bank while
a fragment of Canute's army was on the retreat, perhaps on the
point of fording the stream. At any rate, we seem hardly justi-
fied in calling the engagement at Brentford a "pitched battle."
See Oman, *England before the Norman Conquest*, 579.

[2] Oman (*ibid.*) seems to believe that Edmund retained his
forces but went into Wessex to get reinforcements. But unless
Edmund's victorious army had to a large extent melted away, it
is difficult to account for Canute's prompt return to the siege of
London.

The supply of provisions was probably running low in the Danish camp, for we next hear of a pillaging expedition into Mercia. Ordinarily that region was spared; but Eadric's defection had made it hostile territory and, furthermore, it was probably the only neighbouring section that had not been drained to the limit. Whether the entire army took part in the foray is uncertain; but the probabilities are that it was the raid mentioned by the Encomiast as undertaken by Eric with Canute's permission. Part of the host may have remained on the Isle of Sheppey in the mouth of the Medway, where a camp appears to have been established.

The fleet sailed north to the Orwell in Suffolk, and thence the host proceeded westward into Mercia, "slaying and burning whatever they came across, as is their wont."[1] As the crops had just been garnered, the raiders did not return empty-handed. Laden with plunder they began the return to the Medway, the footmen in the ships, the horsemen by land, driving the plundered flocks before them.[2]

With the forces of the enemy thus divided, Edmund's opportunity had come. With his

---

[1] *Anglo-Saxon Chronicle*, 1016. On this raid Eric seems to have met and defeated Ulfketel, who "gat ugly blows from the thingmen's weapons," as we are told by Thorrod in the *Eric's Praise. Corpus Poeticum Boreale*, ii., 105. The raid seems also to be alluded to in the Lithsmen's Song (*ibid.*, 107).

[2] Florence of Worcester, *Chronicon*, i., 176.

fourth army, collected from "all parts of England,"
he crossed the Thames at Brentford and dashed
after the Danes, who, encumbered with b oty,
were hurrying eastward through Kent.   At Otford,
in the western part of Kent, Edmund came up
with the raiders and slew a number of them; but
much fighting there could not have been, as the
Danes were apparently unwilling to make a stand
and hurried on to Sheppey.   If Edmund had been
free to make use of the advantage that was his,
it seems that he might have destroyed a considerable part of the Danish host; but at Aylesford he
was evidently detained by a quarrel with Eadric
and the raiders escaped.[1]

Canute's position in the autumn of 1016 must
have been exceedingly difficult and serious, even
critical.   After a year of continuous warfare—
marches, battles, sieges—he seemed as far as ever
from successful conquest.   Edmund had, indeed,
won no great victories; still, he had been able to

---

[1] The account in the *Chronicle* of what occurred at Aylesford
is ambiguous and has been variously interpreted: "and the King
slew as many as he could come upon; and Eadric ealdorman
turned against [or toward?] the king at Aylesford.   Nor was there
ever worse counsel adopted than that was."   Some writers have interpreted this to mean that Eadric joined Edmund at Aylesford
and not after Sherstone, as stated by Florence.   But the Saxon
gewende ongean has a hostile rather than a favourable colour.
The probabilities are that Eadric opposed Edmund's plans at
Aylesford and thus rendered further pursuit impossible.   Such
is Florence of Worcester's version (*Chronicon*, i., 177).   For a
different view see Hodgkin (*Pol. Hist. of Eng.*, i., 397) and Oman
(*England before the Norman Conquest*, 580).

relieve London, to stay the current of Danish successes, to infuse hope and patriotic fervour into the hearts of the discouraged English. But too much must not be inferred from the fact that Canute, too, had been only moderately successful on the battle-field; he was one of those commanders, who are not attracted by great battles. In two respects he possessed a decided advantage: he had a splendid army that did not desert; he had a great fleet to which he could retire when too hotly pursued. In the autumn of 1016, Edmund had come with a strong force to the lower Thames; the enemy, however, was out of reach on the Isle of Sheppey. It was not to be expected that Canute would long lie idle; but operations in the direction of London were impossible in the presence of Edmund's army. Canute accordingly embarked his men, crossed the estuary once more, and proceeded to devastate East Anglia.

Edmund started in pursuit, and on the 18th (or 19th) of October he came upon the Danes at Ashington in Essex, as they were on their way back to their ships. There seem to have been divided counsels among the English as to the advisability of making an attack, Eadric in particular advising against it.[1] But Edmund was determined to strike, and about the middle of the afternoon the battle began. The English had the advantage of numbers; but there was a traitor in camp:

[1] *Encomium Emmæ*, ii., c. 12.

Eadric sulked and refused to order his forces of
men from Hereford into battle. The fight continued till nightfall, and did not cease entirely
even then. Darkness finally put an end to the
carnage, and the Angles fled from the field.

It is said that Canute was not eager to fight;
but the feeling in his army must have been different. The banner of the invaders was the ancient
Raven Banner, the raven being Woden's own bird.
It is said of this banner that it was made of plain
white silk and bore no image of any sort; but, when
battle began, Woden's bird appeared upon its
folds, its behaviour indicating the outcome. In
the presence of victory it showed great activity
in bill and wings and feet; when defeat was imminent, it hung its head and did not move. We are
told that it was reported in Canute's army that the
raven had appeared and showed unusual excitement.[1] Perhaps of even greater importance was
military skill and experienced generalship. The
tactics employed seem to have been such as the
Northmen frequently used: at the critical moment,
the Danes pretended to retreat; but when the lines
of the pursuing English were broken, they closed
up the ranks and cut the Saxon advance in pieces.
During the night, the Danes encamped on the
battle-field; the next day they buried their fallen
comrades and removed all articles of value from

[1] The Encomiast admits that the tale is hard to believe, but
avers that it is true (ii., c. 9). The story of the raven is old and
occurs earlier in the English sources.

ANGLO-SAXON WARRIORS
(From a manuscript in the British Museum, reproduced in *Norges Historie*, i., ii.)

THE RAVEN BANNER
(From the Bayeux Tapestry.)

Oxford as the place, which also seems unlikely, if Eadric, who apparently resided at Oxford,[1] had played the traitor's part at Ashington. It seems clear that these writers have placed Edmund's death at Oxford because they believed that Eadric was in some way the author of it.[2]

For so opportunely did the end come, that the suggestion of foul play was inevitable, and coarse tales were invented to account for the manner of death. There is, however, not the least hint in any contemporary source that Canute was in any way guilty of his rival's untimely decease. The simple-minded Encomiast again sees an illustration of Providential mercy:

But God, remembering his teaching of olden time, that a kingdom divided against itself cannot long endure, very soon afterwards led Edmund's spirit forth from the body, having compassion on the realm of the English, lest if, perchance, both should continue among the living, neither should reign securely, and the kingdom be daily annihilated by renewed contention.[3]

It is difficult to form a just estimate of Edmund Ironside, as our information is neither extensive nor varied. It is possible that he was born of a connection that the Church had not blessed;

[1] Sigeferth and Morcar were slain in Eadric's house at the Oxford gemot. (*Anglo-Saxon Chronicle*, 1015.)

[2] See Freeman (*Norman Conquest*, i., Note xx) whose argument seems conclusive.

[3] *Encomium Emmæ*, ii., c. 14.

at least such seems to have been the belief when William of Malmesbury wrote.[1] A late writer tells us that his mother was the daughter of Earl Thoretus[2]; an earl by such a name actually did flourish in the closing decade of the tenth century; he was one of the chiefs to whom Ethelred entrusted his fleet in 992. From his name we should judge that he was of Norse ancestry. There can be no doubt as to Edmund's bravery on the battle-field; perhaps he was also in possession of some talent in the way of generalship. But on the whole, his military exploits have been exaggerated: we know them chiefly from an ecclesiastic who was doubtless honest, but warmly patriotic and strongly partisan; it was natural for him to magnify skirmishes into battles. Edmund was the victor in several important engagements, but in no great battle. There was no heavy fighting at Penselwood; Sherstone was at best a drawn battle; Brentford and Otford seem to have been partly successful attacks on the rear of a retreating foe; Ashington was a decisive defeat. We cannot tell what sort of a king he might have become but the glimpses that we get of his character are not reassuring. We get sight of him first about 1006 when he sought to come into possession of

[1] *Gesta Regum*, i., 213–214. The author merely tells us that Edmund's mother was of ignoble birth; but a woman of low degree would scarcely be made queen of England.

[2] Ethelred of Rievaux. See Freeman, *Norman Conquest*, i., Note ss.

the bodies of their Saxon adversaries, the corpses being left to the wolf and the raven.

The English aristocracy suffered heavily at Ashington. The sources mention six magnates among the slain: Godwin the ealdorman of Lindsey; an ealdorman Alfric whose locality is unknown; Ulfketel, ealdorman of East Anglia; Ethelward, son of an earlier East Anglian ealdorman; also the bishop of Dorchester and the abbot of Ramsey.[1] It is a noteworthy fact that nearly all these are from Eastern England; so far as we know not one of them came from below the Thames. It may be true that all England was represented in Edmund's host at Ashington; but we are tempted to conclude that perhaps the army was chiefly composed of East Anglians summoned by the doughty Earl Ulfketel.

By far the most prominent of all the slain was this same Earl, the ruler of Saint Edmund's kingdom. Ulfketel is said to have been Edmund's brother-in-law. As his name is unmistakably Norse, it is more than likely that his ancestry was Scandinavian. In his earldom he appears to have been practically sovereign. So impressed were the Norse scalds with the power and importance of the Earl that they spoke of East Anglia as Ulfkelsland.[2] The sagas accuse him of having instigated the slaughter of the thingmen, especially

---

[1] *Anglo-Saxon Chronicle*, 1016. Florence of Worcester, *Chronicon*, i., 178.

[2] Snorre, *Saga of Saint Olaf*, c. 14.

of having destroyed Heming's corps at Slesswick.
Thurkil is naturally mentioned as his banesman.[1]

Eadric's behaviour at Ashington furnishes an
interesting but difficult problem. To the Saxon
and Norman historians it was the basest treachery,
premeditated flight at the critical moment. Still,
after the battle he appears in the councils of the
English in apparently good standing, even as a
leader. From the guarded statements of the
Encomiast, we should infer that Eadric had advised against the battle, that his counsel had been
rejected, that he therefore had remained neutral
and that he had withdrawn his forces before the
battle was joined.[2]

From Ashington Edmund fled westward to the
Severn Valley; Canute returned to the siege of
London. Once more Edmund tried to gather an
army, this time, however, with small success;
England was exhausted; her leaders lay on the
field of Ashington. Soon the Danes, too, appeared
in Gloucestershire. Some sort of a council must
.have been called to deliberate on the state of the
country, and the decision was reached to seek
peace on the basis of a divided kingdom. Eadric
seems particularly to have urged this solution.
Edmund reluctantly consented, and ambassadors
were sent to Canute's camp to offer terms of peace.

It seems at first sight rather surprising that
Canute should at this time be willing even to
negotiate; apparently he had Edmund in his

---

[1] *Jómsvíkingasaga*, c. 52.   [2] *Encomium Emmæ*, ii., c. 12.

power, and England showed no disposition to continue the war. Still, the situation in his own host was doubtless an argument for peace. After more than a year of continued warfare, his forces must have decreased appreciably in numbers. Recruiting was difficult, especially must it have been so on the eve of winter. Without a strong force he could do little in a hostile country. The campaign had been strenuous even for the vikings, and the Danes are represented as thoroughly tired of the war.[1] Canute therefore accepted the offer of the English, with the added condition that Danegeld should be levied for the support of his army in Edmund's kingdom as well as in his own.

On some little island near Deerhurst in Gloucestershire,[2] the two chiefs met and reached an agreement which put an end to the devastating war and pillage that had cursed England for more than a generation. It was agreed that Edmund should have Wessex and Canute Mercia and Northumbria; or, in a general way, that the Thames should be the dividing line between the two kingdoms. As to the disposition of East Anglia and Essex there is some doubt: Florence holds that these territories with the city of London were assigned to Edmund. So far as London is concerned, this seems to be erroneous: Canute took immediate

---

[1] *Encomium Emmæ*, ii., c. 13.

[2] Probably not the isle of Olney, but some other islet that has since disappeared. See Oman, *England before the Norman Conquest*, 581.

possession of the city and made preparations to spend the winter there, which seems a strange proceeding if the place was not to be his. The kingdom of England was thus dissolved. There is no good evidence that Canute understood his position to be that of a vassal king; he had without doubt complete sovereignty in his own domains. On the other hand, the fact that Edmund agreed to levy Danegeld in his own kingdom of Wessex looks suspiciously like the recognition of Canute as overlord of the southern kingdom.

The compact of Olney, says Florence of Worcester, was one of "peace, friendship, and brotherhood." Other writers state that the two kings agreed to become sworn brothers and that the survivor should inherit the realm of the other brother.[1] We cannot affirm that such a covenant was actually made, as the authority is not of the best. There is, however, nothing improbable in the statement; the custom was not unusual in the North. Twenty years later, Canute's son, Harthacanute, entered into a similar relationship with his rival, King Magnus of Norway, who had been making war on Denmark. In Snorre's language,

it was agreed that the kings should take the oath of brotherhood and should maintain peace as long as

[1] Henry of Huntingdon, *Historia Anglorum*, 185; *Knytlingasaga*, c. 16. The saga says distinctly that there was to be inheritance only if either died without children.

both were on earth; and that if one of them died son-
less, the survivor should inherit his realm and subjects.
Twelve men, the most eminent of each kingdom, took
the oath with the kings that this agreement should
be kept as long as any of them lived.[1]

It is possible that some such qualification in favour
of male heirs was also inserted in the Severn
covenant; still, the whole matter would have been
of slight importance had the magnates on Edmund's death been in position to insist on the
ancient principle and practice of election. Witnesses similar to those mentioned in the later
instance there seem to have been at Deerhurst;
for, after the death of Edmund, Canute summoned
those to testify before the assembly, "who had
been witnesses between him and Edmund" when
the agreement was made, as to the details of the
treaty.[2]

The reign of Edmund as king of Wessex was
destined to be brief. The covenant of Deerhurst
was probably made in the early days of November
(it could scarcely have been earlier, as the battle
of Ashington was fought on October 18) and
by the close of the month (November 30) he
was dead. Florence of Worcester tells us that he
died in London, which is improbable, as it seems
strange that he should have ventured into the
stronghold of his late enemy. Other writers give

[1] *Saga of Magnus the Good*, c. 6.
[2] Florence of Worcester, *Chronicon*, i., 179.

Oxford as the place, which also seems unlikely, if
Eadric, who apparently resided at Oxford,[1] had
played the traitor's part at Ashington.   It seems
clear that these writers have placed Edmund's
death at Oxford because they believed that
Eadric was in some way the author of it.[2]

For so opportunely did the end come, that the
suggestion of foul play was inevitable, and coarse
tales were invented to account for the manner
of death.   There is, however, not the least hint
in any contemporary source that Canute was in
any way guilty of his rival's untimely decease.
The simple-minded Encomiast again sees an
illustration of Providential mercy:

But God, remembering his teaching of olden time,
that a kingdom divided against itself cannot long
endure, very soon afterwards led Edmund's spirit
forth from the body, having compassion on the realm
of the English, lest if, perchance, both should continue among the living, neither should reign securely,
and the kingdom be daily annihilated by renewed
contention.[3]

It is difficult to form a just estimate of Edmund
Ironside, as our information is neither extensive
nor varied.   It is possible that he was born of a
connection that the Church had not blessed;

[1] Sigeferth and Morcar were slain in Eadric's house at the
Oxford gemot. (*Anglo-Saxon Chronicle,* 1015.)
[2] See Freeman (*Norman Conquest,* i., Note xx) whose argument
seems conclusive.
[3] *Encomium Emmæ,* ii., c. 14.

at least such seems to have been the belief when William of Malmesbury wrote.[1] A late writer tells us that his mother was the daughter of Earl Thoretus[2]; an earl by such a name actually did flourish in the closing decade of the tenth century; he was one of the chiefs to whom Ethelred entrusted his fleet in 992. From his name we should judge that he was of Norse ancestry. There can be no doubt as to Edmund's bravery on the battle-field; perhaps he was also in possession of some talent in the way of generalship. But on the whole, his military exploits have been exaggerated: we know them chiefly from an ecclesiastic who was doubtless honest, but warmly patriotic and strongly partisan; it was natural for him to magnify skirmishes into battles. Edmund was the victor in several important engagements, but in no great battle. There was no heavy fighting at Penselwood; Sherstone was at best a drawn battle; Brentford and Otford seem to have been partly successful attacks on the rear of a retreating foe; Ashington was a decisive defeat. We cannot tell what sort of a king he might have become but the glimpses that we get of his character are not reassuring. We get sight of him first about 1006 when he sought to come into possession of

---

[1] *Gesta Regum*, i., 213–214. The author merely tells us that Edmund's mother was of ignoble birth; but a woman of low degree would scarcely be made queen of England.

[2] Ethelred of Rievaux. See Freeman, *Norman Conquest*, i., Note ss.

an estate in Somerset: "and the monastic household dared not refuse him."[1] His rebellious
behaviour in the Danelaw, his raid into English
Mercia, give little promise of future statesmanship. Edmund Ironside was an English viking,
passionate, brave, impulsive, but unruly and
uncontrollable.

When the year closed there was no question
who should be the future ruler of England. Fate
had been kind to Canute; still, the outcome must
be ascribed chiefly to the persistent activity of
the invader. But while the name of the young
King is necessarily made prominent in the narrative, we should not forget that he was surrounded
and assisted by a group of captains who probably
had no superiors in Europe at the time. There
was the tall and stately Thurkil with the experience of more than thirty years as a viking chief;
the resourceful Eric with a brilliant record as a
successful general; the impetuous and volcanic
Ulf; doubtless also Ulf's brother, Eglaf the Jomviking. These were the men who helped most to
win the land for the Danish dynasty; they also
formed Canute's chief reliance in the critical
years following the conquest.

The gain in Britain was, however, in a measure
counterbalanced by the loss of Norway in the
same year, though in this Canute was not directly
interested at the time. After the battle of the
Nesses, King Olaf sailed north to Nidaros (Thrond-

[1] Kemble, *Codex Diplomaticus*, No. 1302.

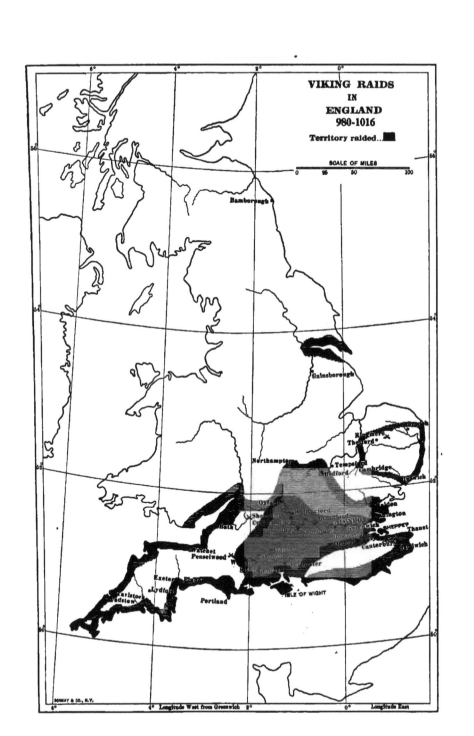

VIKING RAIDS
IN
ENGLAND
980-1016

Territory raided..

SCALE OF MILES
0   25   50   100

hjem) where he now received unquestioned allegiance. He rebuilt the city and made it the capital of his kingdom. The ruined Church of Saint Clemens, the patron saint of all seafaring men, was raised again and became in a sense the mother church of Norse Christianity. Without delay he began his great work as legislator, organiser, and missionary, a work of enduring qualities. But Canute did not forget that in this way his dynasty was robbed of one of its earliest possessions outside the Dane-lands. A clash between the great rivals was inevitable. For the present, however, Olaf's throne was safe; there was much to do before Canute could seriously think of proceeding against his virile opponent, and more than a decade passed before the young King of England could summon his chiefs and magnates into solemn imperial councils in the new capital of Nidaros.

CHAPTER V

THE RULE OF THE DANES IN ENGLAND

1017–1020

FOR eight months after the death of Ethelred there was no king of England. Neither Edmund nor Canute had an incontestable claim to the royal title, as neither had been chosen by a properly constituted national assembly. There is some evidence that Edmund was crowned, perhaps in May, 1016[1]; but even consecration could hardly remove the defect in the elective title. And after the agreement of Olney, there was, for a few weeks, no English kingdom. But, in December, it was possible once more to reunite the distracted land. In the North of England there was no vacant kingship; only Wessex and East Anglia needed a ruler. As the latter region possessed a strong Scandinavian element that might be depended upon to declare for Canute, the only doubtful factor in the situation was the

---

[1] The evidence is late and not of the best; the earliest authority to mention it is Ralph de Diceto who lived a century and a half later. But see Freeman, *Norman Conquest*, i., Note tt.

attitude of the nobility south of the Thames. Wessex, however, had more than once showed a desire to give up the struggle: the old spirit of independence was apparently crushed. London, the great rallying point of the national party, was in Canute's hands. Beyond the Thames were the camps of the dreaded host that had come from the North the year before. The Danish fleet still sailed the British seas. No trusted leader appeared to take up the fight for the house of Alfred; Ethelred's many sons seem nearly all to have perished, and only children or princes of doubtful ability remained as possible candidates for the kingship. In addition there was no doubt a feeling that England should be one realm. The accession of Canute was therefore inevitable.

The Dane evidently realised the strength of his position. There was consequently little need of hasty action; it was clearly best to observe constitutional forms and to give the representatives of the nation ample time to act. It was a Northern as well as a Saxon custom to celebrate the Yule-tide with elaborate and extended festivities; and there was every reason why Canute and his warriors in London should plan to make this year's celebration a memorable event. To these festivities, Canute evidently invited the magnates of England; for we learn that a midwinter gemot was held in London, at which the Danish pretender received universal recognition as king of all England.[1]

---

[1] Florence of Worcester, *Chronicon*, i., 179.

To say that this assembly elected a king would be incorrect; Canute gave the lords no opportunity to make an election. In a shrewd fashion he brought out the real or pretended fact that in the agreement of Deerhurst it was stipulated that the survivor should possess both crowns. Those who had witnessed the treaty were called on to state what had been said in the conference concerning Edmund's sons and brothers; whether any of them might be permitted to rule in England if Edmund should die first. They testified that they had sure knowledge that no authority was left to Edmund's brothers, and that Canute was to have the guardianship of Edmund's young sons until they were of sufficient age to claim the kingship. Florence of Worcester believes that the witnesses were bribed by Canute and perjured themselves grossly; but the probabilities are that their statement was accurate. Canute's object in submitting the problem of the succession in the South to the witan seems to have been, not exactly to secure his own election, but rather to obtain the highest possible sanction for the agreement with Edmund.

To the Northern mind the expedient adopted was both legal and proper. We know very little about the constitutional framework and principles of the Scandinavian monarchies at this period; but, so far as we can discern, the elective principle played an incidental part only; the succession was in fact hereditary. To the Anglo-Saxons the whole must have resolved itself into finding some legal form for surrender and submission. Oaths were taken and loyalty was pledged. Once more the Saxon began to enjoy real peace and security. At the same time, all the rejoicing can scarcely have been genuine; for English pride had received a wound that for some years refused to heal. It must also be said that the opening years of the new reign were not of such a character as to win the affections of unwilling subjects.

The task that the young monarch undertook in the early months of 1017 was one of peculiar difficulty. It must be remembered that his only right was that of the sword. Important, too, is the fact that at the time England was his only kingdom. As a landless prince, he had crossed the sea, landless except for possible rights in Norway; had led with him a host of adventurers most of whom were probably heathen; had wrested large areas from the native line of English Kings; and now he was in possession of the entire kingdom.

Something of a like nature occurred in 1066, when William of Normandy conquered England; but there are also notable differences. William was the lord of a vigorous duchy across the narrow Channel, in which he had a storehouse of energy that was always at his disposal. Young Canute had no such advantages. Before he was definitely recognised as king in the Danelaw, he had no territorial possessions from which to recruit and

provision his armies.   Not till 1019 did he unite
the crowns of England and Denmark.

Historians generally have appeared to believe
that in governing his English kingdom, Canute
pursued a conscious and well-defined course of
action, a line of political purposes originating
early in his reign.   He is credited with the purpose
of making England the central kingdom of an
Anglo-Scandinavian empire, of governing this
kingdom with the aid of Englishmen in preference
to that of his own countrymen, of aiming to rule
England as a king of the Saxon type.   It is true
that before the close of his reign Canute made
large use of native chiefs in the administration of
the monarchy; but such was not the case in the
earlier years.   There were no prospects of empire
in 1017 and 1018: his brother Harold still ruled in
Denmark; the Norsemen were still loyal to the
vigorous Olaf.   And at no time did the kingdoms
that he added later consider themselves as standing in a vassal relation to the English state.   In
Canute's initial years, we find no striving after
good government, no dreams of imperial power.
During these years his chief purpose was to secure
the permanence and the stability of his new title
and throne.

Nor should we expect any clear and definite
policy in the rule of a king who was still inexperi-
enced in dealing with the English constitution.
At the time of his accession, Canute is thought
to have been twenty-one or twenty-two years

old.[1] Younger he could scarcely have been, nor is it likely that he was very much older. Ottar the Swart in the *Canute's Praise* is emphatic on the point that Canute was unusually young for a successful conqueror: "Thou wast of no great age when thou didst put forth in thy ship; never younger king set out from home."[2] As Ottar's other patron, Olaf the Stout, was only twelve when he began his career as a viking, we should hardly expect the poet to call attention to Canute's youth if he had already reached manhood when he accompanied his father to England. The probabilities favour 995 as the year of his birth; if the date be correct he would be about seventeen in 1012, when the invasion was being planned, nineteen at the death of his father in 1014; and twenty-one (or twenty-two, as it was late in the year) when he became king of all England. But whatever his age, he was young in training for government. So far as we know, he could have had but little experience as a ruler before the autumn of 1016, when the battle of Ashington secured his position in England. His training had been for the career of a viking, a training that promised little for the future.

It seems, therefore, a safe assumption that in shaping his policy the King's decision would be

---

[1] Steenstrup places his age at twenty-two (*Danmarks Riges Historie*, i., 385). Munch thinks that he was several years older. (*Det norske Folks Historie*, I., ii., 126–127).

[2] *Corpus Poeticum Boreale*, ii., 155. (Vigfusson's translation.)

influenced to a large degree by the advice of
trusted counsellors. In the first year of Canute's
reign, there stood about the throne three prominent leaders, three military chiefs, to whom in
great measure the King owed his crown. There
was the sly and jealous Eadric the Mercian, a man
with varied experience in many fields, but for
obvious reasons he did not enjoy the royal confidence. Closer to the King stood Eric, for fifteen
years earl and viceroy in Norway, now the ruler
of Northumbria. Eric was a man of a nobler
character than was common among men of the
viking type; but he can have known very little
of English affairs, and for this reason, perhaps,
Canute passed his kinsman by and gave his confidence to the lordly viking, Thurkil the Tall. For
a stay of nearly ten years in England as viking
invader, as chief of Ethelred's mercenaries, and as
Canute's chief assistant in his campaign against the
English, had surely given Thurkil a wide acquaintance among the magnates of the land and considerable insight into English affairs.

Whatever the reason for the King's choice, we
seem to have evidence sufficient to allow the
conclusion that for some years Thurkil held a
position in the kingdom second only to that of the
King himself. Wherever his name appears in
Canute's charters among the earls who witness
royal grants, it holds first place. In a royal
proclamation that was issued in 1020, he seems to
act on the King's behalf in the general administra-

tion of justice, whenever royal interference should
become necessary:

Should any one prove so rash, clerk or layman,
Dane or Angle, as to violate the laws of the Church or
the rights of my kingship or any secular statute, and
refuse to do penance according to the instruction of
my bishops, or to desist from his evil, then I request
Thurkil the Earl, yea, even command him, to bend
the offender to right, if he is able to do so.[1]

In case the Earl is unable to manage the business
alone, Canute promises to assist. There is something in this procedure that reminds one of the
later Norman official, the justiciar, who was chief
of the administrative forces when the King was in
England and governed as the King's lieutenant
when the ruler was abroad. That Thurkil's
dignity was not a new creation at the time of the
proclamation is evident from the preamble, in
which Canute sends "greetings to his archbishops
and bishops and Thurkil earl and all his earls and
all his subjects." The language of the preamble
also suggests that Thurkil may have acted as the
King's deputy during Canute's absence in Denmark. It is further to be noted that of all the
magnates he alone is mentioned by name. In the
account of the dedication of the church at Ashington later in the same year, Thurkil is again given
prominent mention. In this instance general reference is made to a number of important officials,

[1] Liebermann, *Gesetze der Angelsachsen*, i., 274.

but Earl Thurkil and Archbishop Wulfstan are the only ones that the Chronicler mentions by name.[1] It is evident that the English, too, were impressed by the eminence of the tall earl.

The first and the most difficult problem that Canute and Thurkil had to solve was how to establish the throne among an unfriendly people; for the conquered Saxons cannot have regarded the Danish usurper with much affection. It is generally believed that Canute took up his residence in the old capital city of Winchester, though we do not know at what time this came to be the recognised residential town. It may be true, as is so often asserted, that Canute continued, even after other lands had been added to his dominions, to make England his home from personal choice; but it may also be true that he believed his presence necessary to hold Wessex in subjection. The revolutionary movements that came to the surface during the first few years of his reign had probably much to do with determining Canute's policies in these directions. It is a fact of great significance that during the first decade of his rule in England he was absent from the island twice only, so far as we know, and then during the winter months, when the chances of a successful uprising were most remote.[2]

---

[1] *Anglo-Saxon Chronicle*, 1020.

[2] The first recorded absence was in the winter of 1019 and 1020; Canute returned in time for the Easter festivities. The Chronicler tells of another return from Denmark in 1023; as this return

Like the later William, Canute had his chiefs and followers to reward, and the process of payment could not be long delayed. The rewards took the form of actual wages, paid from new levies of Danegeld; confiscated lands, of which we do not hear very much, though seizure of land was doubtless not unknown, as it was not a Scandinavian custom to respect the property of an enemy; also official positions, especially the earl's office and dignity, which was reserved for the chiefs who had given the most effective aid. The payment of Danegeld was an old story in English history and the end was not yet. When we consider the really vast tribute that was levied from time to time and the great value of the precious metals in the Middle Ages, it becomes clear that many of the vikings who operated in England must have become relatively wealthy men. A large number evidently served in successive hosts and expeditions. A Swedish runic monument found in Uppland (the region north of Stockholm) relates that one Ulf shared three times in the distribution of Danegeld:

But Ulf has in England thrice taken "geld," the first time Tosti paid him, then Thurkil, and then Canute paid.[1]

---

was earlier than the translation of Saint Alphege in June, the absence must have been during the winter months. See the *Chronicle* for these years.

[1] Von Friesen, *Historiska Runinskrifter* (Fornvännen, 1909), 58. Von Friesen suggests that the chief Tosti who paid the first

8

Ulf was evidently one of the vikings who composed Thurkil's invading force and finally passed with their chief into Canute's service.

The earl's office was ancient in Scandinavia and counted very desirable. It did not quite correspond to that of the English ealdorman, as it usually implied a larger administrative area, a greater independence, and a higher social rank for the official thus honoured. The office was not new in England; for more than a century it had flourished in the Danelaw. In Ethelred's time such magnates as Uhtred in Northumbria and Ulfketel in East Anglia were earls rather than ealdormen.

The first recorded act of the new sovereign was the division of the kingdom into four great earldoms. Much has been made of this act in the past; the importance of the measure has been over-rated; the purpose of the King has been misunderstood. The act has been characterised as the culmination of a certain tendency in English constitutional development; as the expression of self-distrust on the part of the monarch; and much more. It seems, however, that Canute at this time did little more than to recognise the *status quo*. England was during the later years of Ethelred's reign virtually divided into four great

---

geld may have been Skogul-Tosti, the father of Sigrid the Haughty (pp. 71-72). For other monuments alluding to the Danegeld, see *ibid.*, 58, 74-75; Montelius, *Kulturgeschichte Schwedens*, 267: the Össeby Stone.

jurisdictions, three of which, Northumbria, Mercia, and East Anglia, were governed by the King's sons-in-law, Uhtred, Eadric, and Ulfketel. How much authority was assigned to each cannot be determined; but practically the earls must have enjoyed a large measure of independence. In the fight against the Danes, Uhtred seems to have taken but small part; Ulfketel comes into prominence only when East Anglia is directly attacked.

This arrangement, which was not accidental but historic, Canute had accepted before the reputed provincial division of 1017. Eadric had long been a power in parts of Mercia; any attempt to dislodge him at so early a moment would have been exceedingly impolitic. Eric was already earl of Northumbria, having succeeded the unfortunate Uhtred, perhaps in the spring of 1016. It is only natural that Canute should reserve the rule of Wessex to himself, at least for a time. Provision naturally had to be made for Thurkil; and as the earl of East Anglia had fallen at Ashington, it was convenient to fill the vacancy and honour the old viking at the same time.[1]

It seems never to have been Canute's policy to keep England permanently divided into four great provinces; what evidence we have points to a wholly different purpose. During the first decade

---

[1] The statement of the *Chronicle* (1017) that he divided England into four parts may imply that some sort of sanction was sought from the witan; but such an act would merely recognise accomplished facts.

of the new reign, fifteen earls appear in the charters as witnesses or otherwise. Three of these may, however, have been visiting magnates from elsewhere in the King's dominions, and in one instance we may have a scribal error. There remain, then, the names of eleven lords who seem to have enjoyed the earl's dignity during this period. Of these eleven names, seven are Scandinavian and four Anglo-Saxon; but of the latter group only one appears with any decided permanence.[1]

Thurkil, while he was still in England, headed the list. Thurkil was a Dane of noble birth, the son of Harold who was earl in Scania. He was a typical viking, tall, strong, and valorous, and must have been a masterly man, one in whom warriors readily recognised the qualities of chieftainship. He had part in the ill-fated expedition that ended in the crushing defeat of Hjörunga Bay. He also fought at Swald, where he is said to have served on the ship of his former enemy, Eric the Earl.[2] In 1009 he transferred his activities to England and from that year he remained almost continuously on the island till his death about fifteen years later.

The old viking had several claims on the King's gratitude. Had he not deserted Ethelred at such an opportune moment, Canute might never have won the English crown. The statement of the sagas that Thurkil was Canute's foster-father has

[1] For the evidence see the author's paper in *American Historical Review*, xv., 725.
[2] Munch, *Det norske Folks Historie*, I., ii., 392.

been refefred to elsewhere. The foster-relationship, if the sagas are correct, would not only help to explain how Thurkil came to hold such eminent positions in Canute's English and Danish kingdoms, but may also account for the confidence that Canute reposed in Thurkil's son Harold, who may have been the King's foster-brother. The battles of Sherstone and Ashington no doubt also had a share in securing pre-eminence for the tall pirate. Sherstone, says the Encomiast, gained for Thurkil a large share of the fatherland.[1] He is prominently mentioned as one of those most eager to fight at Ashington, especially after it was reported that the raven had appeared with proper gestures on the Danish banner.[2]

In his old age Thurkil married an Englishwoman, Edith, probably one of Ethelred's daughters, the widow of Earl Eadric.[3] He ruled as English earl from 1017 to 1021. After Canute's return from Denmark in 1020, some misunderstanding seems to have arisen between him and the old war-chief; for toward the close of the next year Thurkil was exiled. The cause for this is not known; perhaps Canute feared his growing influence,

[1] *Encomium Emmæ*, ii., c. 7.

[2] *Ibid.*, ii., c. 9.

[3] Florence tells us that Thurkil's wife bore the name Edith (*Chronicon*, i., 183). The *Jómsvikingasaga* (c. 52) has Thurkil marry Ethelred's daughter Ulfhild, Ulfketel's widow. However, Ethelred had a daughter Edith who was married to Eadric. (Florence, *Chronicon*, i., 161.) For a discussion of the subject see Freeman, *Norman Conquest*, i., Notes nn and ss.

especially after his marriage to the former King's daughter. A reconciliation was brought about a year later; but for some reason the King preferred to leave him as his lieutenant in Denmark, and he was never restored to his English dignities.

Eric, Earl of Northumbria, governed this region from 1016 to 1023. He seems to have been Earl Hakon's oldest son, and is said to have been of bastard birth, the son of a low-born woman, who had attracted the Earl in his younger years. He grew up to be extremely handsome and clever, but never enjoyed his father's good-will.[1] The circumstances of Eric's promotion to the Northern earldom have been discussed in an earlier chapter. As the Scandinavian colonies north of the Humber were Norwegian rather than Danish, the appointment of a Norse ruler was doubtless a popular act.

Eadric was allowed to continue as governor of Mercia. Whether all the old Mercian region made one earldom is uncertain; most likely it did not extend to the western limits, as several smaller earldoms appear to have been located along the Welsh border. For one year only was Eadric the Grasper permitted to enjoy his dignities; at the first opportunity Canute deprived him not only of honours but of life.

Eglaf, Thurkil's old companion in arms, seems to have been given territories to rule in the lower Severn Valley.[2] Eglaf was one of the leaders in

[1] Snorre, *Saga of Earl Hakon*, c. 3.
[2] *American Historical Review*, xv., 727.

the great expedition of 1009. He was evidently
one of those who entered Ethelred's service when
peace was made; but during the closing years of
the conflict, he was doubtless fighting for Canute.
He was consequently one of the chiefs who might
claim a particular reward. He was also of high
lineage, the son of a powerful Danish chief,
Thorgils Sprakaleg, and the brother of Ulf, who
was married to Canute's sister Estrid.

In the Worcester country an Earl Hakon was
placed in control. He was evidently Eric's son
and Canute's nephew, the young Hakon whom
King Olaf drove out of Norway in the autumn of
1015. The youthful earl (he was probably not
more than twenty years old in 1017, perhaps even
younger) is described as an exceedingly handsome
man with "hair that was long and fair like silk"[1];
but warfare was evidently not to his taste. For a
decade or more he remained in Canute's service
in England. In 1026, hostilities broke out between Norway and Denmark; the result was the
final expulsion of King Olaf and the restoration of
Hakon to his Norse vice-royalty. Soon afterwards he perished in shipwreck.

Godwin is the first English earl of importance
to appear among Canute's magnates. From 1019
to the close of the reign his name appears in almost
every charter, and invariably as earl or with some
corresponding title. The fact that Godwin found
it possible to be present so frequently when grants

[1] Snorre, *Saga of Saint Olaf*, c. 30.

were to be witnessed would indicate that he could not have been located far away from the local court; perhaps he was closely attached to it. Though his ancestry is a matter of doubt, he was probably not connected with the Old English aristocracy. This defect Canute remedied by giving him a noble Danish woman of his own household for wife.[1] Godwin was consequently closely associated with the new dynasty.

Of the remaining magnates, Ethelwerd, Leofwine, Godric, Ulf, and Ranig, little is really known. Ethelwerd seems to have had some authority in the extreme Southwest. Ranig's earldom was the modern shire of Hereford. There is nothing to indicate what territories were controlled by Godric and Ulf. Leofwine probably succeeded to Eadric's position as chief ruler in Mercia. In the list we should probably include Eadulf Cudel who seems to have succeeded to some power north of the Tees after the murder of his brother Uhtred[2]; but whether he was under the lordship of Eric or held directly from Canute cannot be known.

These were the men with whom Canute shared his authority during the first ten years of his reign. It will be seen that the more important places in the local government were given to Danes and Northmen. So far as we know, only two of

---

[1] She was sister of the earls Ulf and Eglaf. Her Danish name was Gytha, which the Saxons changed to Edith.

[2] Simeon of Durham, *Opera Omnia*, ii., 197.

Ethelred's ealdormen were retained in their offices[1]; of these the one soon suffered exile, while the other appears to have played but a small part in the councils of Canute. Two appointments were made from the native population, those of Godwin and Leofwine. In the case of Godwin it is to be observed that he was bound to the new dynasty by the noble ties of marriage. As to Leofwine's ancestry we are not informed; but there are indications that some of his forefathers may have been Northmen.[2]

The more prominent of Canute's earls were drawn from three illustrious families in the North, one Norwegian and two Danish. Thurkil's descent from the Scanian earls has already been noted. Eric and his son Hakon represented the lordly race of Earl Hakon the Bad. A great Danish chief, Thorgils Sprakaleg, had two sons who bore the earl's title in England, Ulf and Eglaf, a son-in-law, Godwin, and a few years later a nephew, Siward the Strong, the lord of Northumbria. Two of these earls were married to sisters of Canute: Eric to Gytha, and Ulf to Estrid. Godwin was married to Canute's kinswoman. Hakon was the King's nephew. Thurkil was his reputed foster-father. It seems that

---

[1] Ethelwerd and Godric. Ethelwerd was exiled in 1020.

[2] Leofwine had a son named Northman, and it is possible that his father also bore that name. See Freeman, *Norman Conquest*, i., Note ccc. The occurrence of the name "Northman" in a family living in or near the Danelaw may indicate Norse ancestry.

Canute at first had in mind to establish in England a new aristocracy of Scandinavian origin, bound to the throne by the noble ties of kinship and marriage. To this aristocracy the North contributed noble and vigorous blood.

In the King's household, so far as we can learn anything about it, we find the same preference for men of Northern ancestry. Ordinarily, the thegns who witnessed royal grants may be taken to have been warriors or officials connected with the royal court. The signatures of more than half of these show names that are unmistakably Scandinavian. Usually, the Northmen sign before their Saxon fellows. The Old Norse language was probably used to a large extent at court; at least we know that the scalds who sang in praise of the "greatest king under heaven" composed their lays in Canute's native language.[1]

The year 1017, which witnessed the exaltation of the foreigners into English officialdom, also beheld a series of executions that still further weakened the English by removing their natural leaders. Most of these are associated with a Christmas gemot, when Canute was celebrating the first anniversary of his rule as king of England. Of the victims the most famous was Eadric, the Earl of Mercia. For ten years he had been a power in his region, though at no time does it

[1] For the court poetry of the scalds see Vigfusson and Powell, *Corpus Poeticum Boreale*, ii. Their verses have in part come down to us. See below, pp. 292 ff.

appear that his word of honour or his pledge of loyalty could have had any value. In all the English sources he is represented as endowed with the instincts of treason, though the Encomiast. is careful to apply no term stronger than turncoat. At the same time, it is clear that Eadric the Grasper was a man of real abilities; in spite of the fact that he held allegiance lightly, he seems to have retained his influence to the last. He was, says one writer,

a man of low origin, one whom the tongue had brought riches and rank, clever in wit, pleasant in speech, but surpassing all men of the time in envy, perfidy, crime, and cruelty. [1]

The murder of Eadric was directly in line with Canute's policy of building up a new Scandinavian aristocracy, devoted to himself, and endowed with large local authority. The new order could not be built on such men as Eadric; by his marriage to Ethelred's daughter he was too closely connected with the old order of things. Furthermore, a man who found it so easy to be disloyal could not safely be entrusted with such great territorial authority as the earlship of Mercia. There had been in this same year extensive plotting among the survivors of the Anglian nobility, and it is likely that Eadric was involved in this. It is also related that the Earl was not satisfied with

[1] Florence of Worcester, *Chronicon*, i., 160.

the King's reward,[1] which may mean that he
objected to having independent earldoms carved
out of Western Mercia. At any rate, Canute was
not reluctant to remove him. Eric appears to
have acted as executioner; and the career of the
Grasper came to a sudden end. The murder, so
far as we can see, was popular; among the men of
power Eadric can have had few friends or perhaps
none at all.

Three other lords are mentioned as having
suffered death on the same occasion: Northman,
the son of Leofwine, and two lords from the South-
west.[2] There can be little doubt that these men
were convicted of treacherous plotting and that
the punishment was regarded as merited. It is a
remarkable fact that Northman's death did not
alienate his family from the new dynasty: his
father Leofwine succeeded to Eadric's dignities
and his brother Leofric to Northman's own place
of influence; "and the king afterwards held him
very dear."[3]

Some of these executions should probably be
placed in connection with certain measures taken
against the former dynasty. Here again we have
anxious care to secure the new throne. Six sons
appear to have been born to Ethelred before his
marriage to the Norman Emma; but of these only
two or at most three seem to have survived their

[1] *Encomium Emmæ*, ii., c. 15.
[2] *Anglo-Saxon Chronicle*, 1017.
[3] Florence of Worcester, *Chronicon*, i., 182.

father. After Edmund Ironside's death, Edwy alone remained[1]; he is said to have been Edmund's full brother and a youth of promise. Evidently Canute intended to spare his life, but ordered him to go into exile. But the Etheling secretly returned to England and hid for a time in Tavistock monastery. He was evidently discovered, and Canute procured his death.[2] As Tavistock is in Devonshire, the execution of the two magnates from the Southwest may readily be explained on the supposition that they were plotting in Edwy's favour.

The London assembly seems to have assumed that certain rights were reserved to the infant sons of Edmund, but that the guardianship of the children had been given to Canute. They were scarcely a problem in 1017; still, it was necessary to make them permanently harmless. It will be remembered that Edmund married Sigeferth's widow some time in the year 1015, perhaps in early summer. It is, therefore, extremely doubtful whether the two boys, Edward and Edmund, were both the sons of the unfortunate Aldgyth; if they were they must have been twins, or the younger must have been born a posthumous child, some time in 1017, the year of their banishment.

[1] Excepting the two sons of Emma who were now in Normandy, there seems to be no record of any other surviving son. Florence of Worcester speaks of Edmund's "brothers" in narrating the discussions at the gemot of Christmas, 1016; but he may have thought of Queen Emma's children. (*Chronicon*, i., 179.)

[2] William of Malmesbury, *Gesta Regum*, i., 218.

But if Florence's account is trustworthy, the status of the two was discussed at the Christmas gemot following Edmund's death in 1016.

To slay the children of a "brother" who had committed them to his care and protection must have seemed to Canute a rude and perhaps risky procedure; it was therefore thought best to send them out of the land. Accordingly the ethelings were sent to the "king of the Slavs,"[1] who was instructed to remove them from the land of the living. This particular king was evidently Canute's maternal uncle, the mighty Boleslav, duke and later king of Poland. Boleslav took pity on the poor children and failed to dispose of them as requested. In 1025, he was succeeded by his son Mieczislav, who entered into close relations with King Stephen of Hungary.[2] It was probably some time after 1025, therefore, that the ethelings were transferred to the Hungarian court, where they grew to manhood. After forty years of exile, one of them returned to England, but died soon after he had landed.

It seems to have been Canute's purpose finally to destroy the house of Alfred to the last male descendant. The two most dangerous heirs were, however, beyond his reach: the sons of Ethelred

[1] Florence's writing *ad regem Suanorum* was probably due to an error of information or of copying; *ad regem Sclavorum*, or some such form, is probably the correct reading (i., 181).

[2] Steenstrup, *Normannerne*, iii., 303–308. Mieczislav's father was married to Stephen's sister.

and Emma were safe with their mother in Normandy. There was close friendship between the lords of Rouen and the rulers of the North; still, Duke Richard could not be expected to ignore the claims of his own kinsmen. So long as the ethelings remained in Normandy, there would always be danger of a Norman invasion combined with a Saxon revolt in the interest of the fugitive princes, Alfred and Edward.

Canute was a resourceful king: these princes, too, could be rendered comparatively harmless. If their mother Emma should be restored to her old position as reigning queen of England, her Norman relatives might find it inconvenient to support an English uprising. This seems to be the true motive for Canute's seemingly unnatural marriage. Historians have seen in it a hope and an attempt to conciliate the English people, as in this way the new King would become identified with the former dynasty. But such a theory does scant justice to the moral sense of the Anglo-Saxons. Furthermore, neither Ethelred nor Emma had ever enjoyed real popularity. There is no doubt that a princess of the blood royal could have been found for a consort, if the prime consideration had been to contract a popular marriage. It seems rather that in this matter Canute acted in defiance of English public sentiment and for the express purpose of averting a real danger from beyond the Channel. Apparently, Emma took kindly to Canute's plans, for she is said to have stipulated that if sons were born to them, they should be preferred to Canute's older children[1]; thus by inference the rights of her sons in Normandy were abandoned.

Earlier in his career, Canute had formed an irregular connection with an English or Anglo-Danish woman of noble birth, Elgiva, the daughter of Elfhelm, who at one time ruled in Deira as ealdorman. Her mother's name is given as Ulfrun, a name that is Scandinavian in both its component parts.[2] The family was evidently not strictly loyal to the Saxon line, for in 1006, just after Sweyn's return to Denmark, Elfhelm was slain and his two sons blinded by royal orders.[3] Elgiva must have had relatives at Northampton, for the Chronicler knows her as the woman from Northampton. She was a woman of great force of character, ambitious and aggressive, though not always tactful, as appears from her later career in Norway. She was never Canute's wife; but, in the eleventh century, vague ideas ruled concerning the marriage relation, even among Christians. Her acquaintance with Canute doubtless began in 1013, when he was left in charge of the camp and fleet at Gainsborough. Two sons she bore to him, Harold Harefoot and Sweyn. On Emma's re-

---

[1] *Encomium Emmæ*, ii., c. 16.

[2] Florence of Worcester, *Chronicon*, i., 190. On the subject of proper names ending in *run*, see Björkman, *Nordische Personennamen in England*, 194.

[3] Florence of Worcester, *Chronicon*, i., 158.

turn to England, Elgiva seems to have been sent
with her children to Denmark.   We find her later
taking an active part in the politics of Wendland,
Norway, and probably of England.

The Queen, who now came back from Normandy
to marry her husband's old enemy, was also a
masterful woman.   If heredity can be stated in
arithmetical terms, she was more than half Danish,
as her mother Gunnor was clearly a Danish, woman while her father had a non-Danish mother
and also inherited some non-Danish blood on
the paternal side.   She was evidently beautiful,
gifted, and attractive: her flattering Encomiast
describes her as of great beauty and wisdom.[1]
But the finer instincts that we commonly associate
with womanhood cannot have been highly developed in her case; what we seem to find is love of life,
a delight in power, and an overpowering ambition
to rule.   At the time of her second marriage she
was a mature woman; it is not likely that she was
less than thirty years old, perhaps she was nearer
forty.   At all events, she must have been several
years older than Canute.   Two children were
born to this marriage: Harthacanute, who ruled
briefly in Denmark and England after the death
of his father and of his half-brother Harold; and
Gunhild, who was married to the Emperor Henry
III.   Emma lived to a ripe old age and died in
1052, fifty years after her first marriage.

The wedding was celebrated in July, 1017, the

[1] *Encomium Emmæ,* ii., c. 16.

9

bride presumably coming from Normandy. The object sought was attained: for more than ten years there seems to have been unbroken peace between England and Normandy. When trouble finally arose after the accession of Robert the Devil, Canute was strong enough to dispense with further alliances.

One of the chief necessities was some form of a standing army, a force that the King could depend upon in case of invasion or revolt. Much reliance could obviously not be placed on the old military system; nor could the army of conquest be retained indefinitely. In 1018, or perhaps late in the preceding year, steps were taken to dismiss the Scandinavian host.[1] It has been conjectured that this was done out of consideration for the Saxon race; the presence of the conquerors was an insult to the English people. It had clearly become necessary to disband the viking forces, but for other reasons. A viking host was in its nature an army of conquest, not of occupation, except when the warriors were permitted to seize the land, which was evidently not Canute's intention. In a land of peace, as Canute intended England to be, such a host could not flourish. It should also be remembered that a large part was composed of borrowed troops furnished by the rulers of Denmark, Norway, and Sweden; these could not be kept indefinitely. Another Danegeld was levied, 82,500 pounds in all, to pay off the

[1] *Anglo-Saxon Chronicle*, 1018.

host; and most of the Northmen departed, to the evident satisfaction of all concerned.

The dismissal of one host was followed by the immediate reorganisation of another. Far more important than the departure of the fleet is the fact that the crews of forty ships remained in the royal service: this would mean a force of between three thousand and four thousand men. But the North knew no continuous body of warriors except the military households of chiefs and kings; such a household was now to be organised, but one that was far greater and more splendid than any organisation of the sort known in Scandinavia. According to Sveno's history, Canute had it proclaimed that only those would be admitted to his new guard who were provided with two-edged swords having hilts inlaid with gold.[1] Sveno also tells us that the wealthy warriors made such haste to procure properly ornamented weapons that the sound of the swordsmith's hammer was heard all through the land. In this way, the King succeeded in giving his personal guard an aristocratic stamp.

The guard of housecarles or "thingmen," as they were called in the North, was organised as a guild or military fraternity, of which the King ranked as a member, though naturally a most important one. In many respects its rules

[1] *Historiola Legum Castrensum Regis Canuti Magni,* c. 2. The *Historiola* is found in Langebek, *Scriptores Rerum Danicarum,* iii.

remind us of the regulations enforced in the Jomburg brotherhood, though its organisation was probably merely typical of the viking fraternities of the age.   The purpose of the guild laws, as reported by Sveno and Saxo, was to promote a spirit of fellowship among the members, to secure order in the guard, and to inculcate proper behaviour in the royal garth.   When the housecarles were invited to the King's tables, they were seated according to their eminence in warfare, priority of service, or nobility of birth.   To be removed to a lower place was counted a disgrace.   In addition to daily fare and entertainment, the warriors received wages which were paid monthly, we are told.   The bond of service was not permanent, but could be dissolved on New Year's Day only. All quarrels were decided in an assembly of the housecarles in the presence of the King.   Members guilty of minor offences, such as failing to care properly for the horse of a fellow guardsman, were assigned lower places at the royal tables. If any one was thrice convicted of such misdeeds, he was given the last and lowest place, where no one was to communicate with him in any way, except that the feasters might throw bones at him if they were so disposed.   Whoever should slay a comrade should lose his head or go into exile. Treason was punished by death and the confiscation of the criminal's property.[1]

These laws were put into writing several genera-

[1] Sveno, *Historiola*, cc. 5–9.   Saxo, *Gesta Danorum*, 351 ff.

tions after the guard was formed, and it is not likely that all existed from the very beginning. There is, however, nothing in the rules that might not have applied in Canute's own day. It is said that the King himself was the first who seriously violated the guard-laws, in that he slew a house-carle in a moment of anger. Repentance came swiftly; the guard was assembled; kneeling the King confessed his guilt and requested punishment. But the laws gave the King the power of judgment in such cases, and so it must be in this instance as in others. Forty marks was the customary fine, but in this case the King levied nine times that amount and added nine marks as a gift of honour. This fine of 369 marks was divided into three parts: one to go to the heirs of the deceased; one to the guard; and one to the King. But Canute gave his share to the Church and the poor.[1]

Though the housecarles are presumed to have possessed horses, the guard was in no sense a cavalry force. Horses were for use on the march, for swift passage from place to place, not for charging on the field. The housecarles were heavily armed, as we know from the description of a ship that Earl Godwin presented to Harthacanute as a peace offering a few years after Canute's

---

[1] Langebek, *Scriptores*, iii., 151 (note). The story is probably mythical; but I give it as a fitting companion to the English stories of Canute and the tide, and of his improvised verses inspired by the chants of the monks of Ely.

death. Eighty warriors, housecarles no doubt, seeing that it was a royal ship, manned the dragon,

of whom each one had on each arm a golden armring weighing sixteen ounces, a triple corselet, on the head a helmet in part overlaid with gold; each was girded with a sword that was golden-hilted and bore a Danish ax inlaid with silver and gold hanging from the left shoulder; the left hand held the shield with gilded boss and rivets; in the right hand lay the spear that the Angles call the *ætgar*.[1]

It is not to be supposed that the whole guard was always at the court—it was distributed in the strong places throughout the kingdom,[2] especially no doubt in the South. It seems likely that individual housecarles might have homes of their own; at any rate, many of them in time came into possession of English lands as we know from Domesday.[3] No doubt Anglo-Saxon warriors were enrolled in the guard, but in its earlier years, at least, the greater number must have been of Scandinavian ancestry. In the province of Uppland, Sweden, a runic monument has been found that was raised by two sons in memory of their father, who "sat out west in thinglith."[4] As thinglith was the Old Norse name for Canute's corps of housecarles, we have here contemporary

[1] Florence of Worcester, *Chronicon*, i., 195.
[2] Saxo, *Gesta Danorum*, 351.
[3] Larson, *The King's Household in England*, 163–167.
[4] The Kolstad Stone. Montelius, *Kulturgeschichte Schwedens*, 267.

mention of a Swede who served in the guard. Another stone from the same province records the fact that Ali who raised it "collected tribute for Canute in England."[1]   Housecarles were sometimes employed as tax collectors, and it seems probable that Ali, too, was a member of the great corps.   It is likely that housecarles are also alluded to in the following Scanian inscription:

Sweyn and Thurgot raised this monument in memory of Manna and Sweyn.   God help their souls well.   But they lie buried in London.[2]

The sagas are evidently correct in stating that the force of housecarles "had been chosen from many lands, though chiefly from those of the Danish [Old Norse] tongue."

So long had the wealth of England been regarded as legitimate plunder, that the Scandinavian pirates found it difficult to realise that raids in South Britain were things of the past.   They now had to reckon, not merely with a sluggish and disorganised militia, but with a strong force of professional warriors in the service and pay of a capable and determined king.   In the year 1018, says the German chronicler Thietmar of Merseburg,

the crews of thirty viking ships have been slain in England, thanks be to God, by the son of Sweyn, the king of the English; and he, who earlier with his

---

[1] The Össeby Stone.   Montelius, *ibid.*

[2] The Valleberga Stone.   Wimmer, *De danske Runemindesmærker*, iii., 165.

father brought invasion and long-continued destruction upon the land, is now its sole defender.[1]

This seems to have been the first and last attempt at piracy in England during the reign of Canute. So far as his dominions extended, viking practices were outlawed. The check that the movement received in 1018 was the beginning of a rapid decline in its strength, and before the close of Canute's reign, the profession of the sea-king was practically destroyed.

The Welsh, too, seem to have found it hard to repress their old habits of raiding the English frontier. It was probably this fact that induced Canute to establish so many earldoms in the Southwest, particularly in the Severn Valley. A few years after the signal defeat of the viking fleet, apparently in 1022, Eglaf, one of the earls on the Welsh border, harried the lands of South-western Wales.[2] As the sources nowhere intimate that Canute ever planned to conquer Wales, and as this was evidently the year of Canute's absence in the Baltic lands, the conclusion must be that this expedition was of a punitive character. The Angles and Saxons were soon to learn that the new regime meant a security for the property as well as the persons of loyal and peaceful citizens, such as they had not enjoyed for more than a generation.

[1] *Chronicon*, viii., c. 5. Thietmar's account is strictly contemporary.   [2] *Annales Cambriæ*, 23.

CHAPTER VI

1019–1025

THE first three or four years of Canute's government in England can have given but little promise of the beneficent rule that was to follow. To the conquered Saxon they must have been a season of great sorrow. On the throne of Alfred sat an alien king who had done nothing as yet to merit the affectionate regard of his subjects. In the shire courts ruled the chiefs of the dreaded Danish host, chiefs who had probably harried those same shires at an earlier date. A heavy tax had been collected to pay the forces of the enemy, but a large part of those forces still remained. The land was at peace; but the calm was the calm of exhaustion. The young King had shown vigour and decision; thus far, however, his efforts had been directed toward dynastic security rather than the welfare of his English subjects.

But with Canute's return from Denmark in 1020 begins the second period in the history of the reign. After that date, it seems that more intelligent efforts were made to reconcile the Saxons to foreign rule. For one thing, Canute must have come to appreciate the wonderful power of the Church; for an attempt was made to enlist its forces on the side of the new monarchy. Perhaps he had also come to understand that repression could not continue indefinitely.

This change in policy seems to be the outgrowth principally of the new situation created by Canute's accession to the Danish throne. Harold, his older brother, king of Denmark, appears to have died in 1018.[1] Little is known of Harold; he died young and evidently left no heirs. For a year there seems to have been no recognised king in Denmark, as Canute did not leave England before 1019. In that year he sailed to the Baltic to claim the throne in person, taking with him nine ships, fewer than one thousand men; the rest of the new force of housecarles was doubtless left in Britain as a matter of security. Thurkil, Earl of East Anglia, seems to have been left behind as English viceroy.

Various reasons may be assigned for this delay in securing the ancestral crown. Harold died in the year when Canute was reorganising the military forces of the realm; before his great corps of housecarles was complete, it would not have been safe to leave the country. Perhaps the King also felt that he must take some steps to reconcile the two racial elements of his kingdom. He may

[1] Langebek, *Scriptores*, i., 159 (note).

have concluded that with two kingdoms to govern it would be impossible to give undivided attention to English affairs and movements. To prevent rebellion in his absence, it might be well to remove, so far as possible, all forms of hostility; we read, therefore, of a great meeting of the magnates, both Danes and Angles, at Oxford in 1018, where the matter of legislation was evidently the principal subject. At this assembly, it was agreed to accept Edgar's laws as the laws for the whole land.[1] It is significant that the comparatively large body of law that was enacted in Ethelred's day was ignored or rejected. The chief reason for this may have been that Canute was not yet willing to enforce the rigid enactments against heathen practices that were such a distinctive feature of Ethelred's legislation. There can be small doubt that in the Scandinavian settlements and particularly in the alien host heathendom still lingered to some extent.

The delay was also due, perhaps, in large part to a serious trouble with Scotland. The term Northumbria is variously used; but in its widest application it embraced territories extending from the Humber to the Forth. The northern part of this kingdom, the section between the Tweed and the Forth, was known as Lothian; on this region the kings of Scotland had long cast covetous eyes. In 1006, while the vikings were distressing England, King Malcolm invaded Lothian, crossed

[1] *Anglo-Saxon Chronicle*, 1018.

the Tweed, and laid siege to Durham. The aged
Earl Waltheof made practically no attempt at
resistance; but his young son Uhtred placed himself at the head of the Northumbrian levies and
drove the invader back into Scotland.[1] Uhtred
succeeded to his father's earldom and was apparently recognised as lord throughout the entire
ancient realm. While Uhtred lived and ruled,
the neighbours to the north seem to have kept the
peace; but in 1016, as we have seen, the great
warrior was slain, probably at Canute's instigation
and his earldom was assigned to Eric. Whatever
Canute's intentions may have been, it seems likely
that the new Earl did not come into immediate
and undisputed control of the entire earldom;
for we find that in the regions north of Yorkshire,
the old kingdom of Bernicia, Uhtred's brother,
Eadulf Cudel, "a very sluggish and timid man,"
sought to maintain the hereditary rights of the
family.

Two years after Uhtred's death, Malcolm the
son of Kenneth reappeared in Lothian at the head
of a large force gathered from the western kingdom
of Strathclyde as well as from his own Scotia.
The Northumbrians had had ample warning of
troubles to come: for thirty nights a comet had
blazed in the sky; and after the passage of another
period of thirty days, the enemy appeared. An

[1] Simeon of Durham, *Opera Omnia*, i., 216. The account of
the siege of Durham is not by Simeon but by some writer whose
identity is unknown.

army gathered mainly from the Durham country met the Scotch forces at Carham on the Tweed, near Coldstream, but was almost completely destroyed.[1] There is no record of any further resistance; and when Malcolm returned to the Highlands he was lord of Lothian, Eadulf having surrendered his rights to all of Northumbria beyond the Tweed.

Canute apparently acquiesced in this settlement. So far as we know, he made no effort to assist his subjects in the North, or to redeem the lost territory. We cannot be sure of the reason for this inactivity; but the general situation on the island appears to offer a satisfactory explanation. It will be remembered that 1018 was the year when Canute disbanded his Scandinavian army. As we are told that the bishop of Durham, who died in 1019, took leave of earth a few days after he had heard the news of the great defeat,[2] it seems likely that the battle of Carham was fought late in the year 1018, and after the host had departed for Denmark. Canute, therefore, probably had no available army that he could trust; to call out his new subjects would have been a hazardous experiment. There is also the additional fact that the sluggish Eadulf was in all probability regarded as a rebel, whom Canute was not anxious to assist.

As to the terms of the surrender of Lothian, nothing definite is known. Our only authority in the matter puts the entire blame on Eadulf,

[1] Simeon of Durham, *Opera Omnia*, i., 84.   [2] *Ibid.*

and apparently would have us believe that Malcolm merely stepped into the earl's position as vassal of Eric or Canute. If such were the case, Canute could hardly have been left in ignorance about the cession, and he may have cherished certain pretensions to overlordship, which Macolm evidently did not regard very seriously. In one way the cession of Lothian was a great loss to England; on the other hand, it added an Anglian element to the Caledonian kingdom, which in time became the controlling factor, and prepared the northern state for the union of the kingdoms that came centuries afterwards.

The following year, Canute was finally in position to make the deferred journey to Denmark. The Danish situation must have had its difficulties. In a proclamation issued on his return, the King alludes to these, though in somewhat ambiguous terms:

> Then I was informed that there threatened us a danger that was greater than was well pleasing to us; and then I myself with the men who went with me departed for Denmark, whence came to you the greatest danger; and that I have with God's help forestalled, so that henceforth no unpeace shall come to you from that country, so long as you stand by me as the law commands, and my life lasts. [1]

Most probably, the difficulty alluded to was some trouble about the succession. There may have

---

[1] Liebermann, *Gesetze der Angelsachsen*, i., 273 (sec. 5).

been a party in Denmark to whom the thought of calling a king from England was not pleasant; or it may be that a conservative faction was hoping for a ruler of the old faith. Any form of invasion from Denmark at this time, when the nation was even kingless, is almost beyond the possible. But no doubt there had been a likelihood that Canute would have to call on his English subjects for military and financial support in the effort to secure his hereditary rights in the North.

Canute chose to spend the winter in Denmark, as during the winter season there was least likelihood of successful plots and uprisings. As early as possible in the spring of 1020, he returned to England. Evidently certain rebellious movements had made some headway during his absence, for Canute immediately summoned the lords to meet in formal assembly at the Easter festival. The plotting was apparently localised in the south-western shires, as we infer from the fact that the gemot sat in an unusual place, Cirencester in the Severn country. Its chief act seems to have been the banishment of Ethelwerd, earl in the Devon country, and of a mysterious pretender whom the Chronicler calls Edwy, king of churls.[1] It seems natural to associate the destinies of these two men and to conclude that some sort of conspiracy in the pretender's favour had been hatching, but we have no definite information.

[1] *Anglo-Saxon Chronicle*, 1020.

It was probably at this gathering that Canute issued his proclamation to the English nation; at least there seems to be no doubt that it was given in 1020. It is a remarkable document, a message to a restless people, an apology for the absence in Denmark, and a promise of future good government. It hints darkly at what may have been the disturbances in the Southwest and the measures taken at Cirencester in the following terms:

Now I did not spare my treasures while unpeace was threatening to come upon you; with the help of God I have warded this off by the use of my treasures.[1]

In a measure the Proclamation of 1020 contains the announcement of a new governmental policy in England, one that recognises the English subjects as citizens who may be trusted with some share in the administration of the realm, and not merely as conquered provincials whose rebellious instincts can be kept down by a continuous policy of coercion only. There was, it is true, little need of coercion after 1020; the natural leaders of the native population were gone. But the importance of the union with Denmark with respect to politics in England must not be overlooked: it removed what fear had remained as to the stability of Canute's conquered throne. At the first indication of an uprising, it would be possible to throw a Danish force on the British coast, which, com-

[1] Sec. 4.

bined with the King's loyal partisans in England, could probably stifle the rebellion in a brief campaign.

The purpose to make larger use of the native energies is indirectly shown in the command to the local functionaries that they heed and follow the advice of the bishops in the administration of justice:

And I make known to you that I will be a kind lord and loyal to the rights of the Church and to right secular law.

And also my ealdormen I command that they help the bishops to the rights of the Church and to the rights of my kingship and to the behoof of all the people.

And I also command my reeves, by my friendship and by all that they own, and by their own lives, that they everywhere govern my people justly and give right judgments by the witness of the shire bishop, and do such mercy therein as the shire bishop thinks right and the community can allow.[1]

The significance of this appears when we remember that the local prelates were probably English to a man.

There is, however, no evidence for the belief so frequently expressed, that Canute by this time, or even earlier, had concluded to dispense with his Scandinavian officials, and to rule England with the help of Englishmen only. In the Proc-

---

[1] Secs. 2, 8, and 11. For a translation of the entire document see Appendix i.

10

lamation the King speaks of Danes and Angles, not of Angles and Danes. Among the thegns who witnessed his charters, Danes and Saxons continue to appear in but slightly changed ratio till the close of the reign. The alien guard was not dismissed. Local government continued in the hands of Norse and Danish earls. Time came when these disappeared from their respective earldoms, but for reasons that show no conscious purpose of removal because of nationality or race. As the field of his operations widened, as the vision of empire began to take on the forms of reality, Canute found it necessary to use his trusted chiefs in other places and in other capacities. Consequently the employment of native Englishmen in official positions became more common as the years passed.

The following year about Martinsmas (November 11, 1021), came the first real break in Canute's political system: Thurkil the Tall, who stood second to the King only in all England, was outlawed. Florence of Worcester adds that his wife was exiled with him.[1] The reason for this act is not clear; but we may perhaps associate it with a lingering dislike for the old dynasty. If Edith was actually Ethelred's daughter, Thurkil's marriage may have been a source of irritation or even supposed danger to Canute and possibly also to the lady's stepmother, the callous Queen Emma.

[1] *Chronicon*, i., 183.

It is also possible that the King in this case simply yielded to pressure from the native element, particularly from the Church. Thurkil's prominence in the kingdom can hardly have been a source of pleasure to the men who recalled the part that he had played in the kingdom at various times. In the Proclamation he is entrusted with the task of enforcing the laws against heathen and heretical practices. But to assign such a duty to the man who was in such a great measure responsible for the martyrdom of Saint Alphege must have seemed a travesty upon justice to the good churchmen of the time. The conjecture that the banishment of the Earl was not wholly the result of royal disfavour receives some support from the fact that, a few months later, Canute and Thurkil were reconciled, and the old Earl was given a position in Denmark analogous to the one that he had held in England.[1] Canute still found him useful, but not in the western kingdom. At the same time, the shrewd King seems not to have felt absolutely sure of the Earl's loyalty, for we read that he brought Thurkil's son with him to England, evidently as a hostage.

In 1023 another great name disappears from the documents: Earl Eric is mentioned no more.

[1] *Anglo-Saxon Chronicle*, 1023. The story given by later writers that Thurkil was slain by a Danish mob soon after his exile cannot be credited. It doubtless originated in a desire that the persecutor of Saint Alphege should suffer retribution. See especially the life of this saint in Langebek, *Scriptores*, ii., 453.

Later stories that he, too, suffered exile are not to
be believed. Eric seems to have died in possession
of all his Northumbrian dignities and of the King's
favour at a comparatively advanced age; for the
warrior who showed such signal bravery at Hjörunga Bay nearly forty years before could not
have been young. In all probability he had passed
the sixtieth milestone of life, which was almost
unusual among the viking chiefs of the period. We
are told that in his last year he contemplated a
visit to Rome which was probably never made.
Most reliable is the story that he died from the
effects of primitive surgery. Just as he was about
to set out on the Roman journey, it was found
necessary for him to have his uvula treated. The
surgeon cut too deep and a hemorrhage resulted
from which the Earl died.[1] That the story is old
is clear, for some of the accounts have the additional information that the leech acted on the
suggestion of one who can be none other than
Canute. This part of the story is probably
mythical.

The spirit of chivalry was not strong in the

[1] One of the sagas (*Fagrskinna*, c. 24) tells us that Eric actually
made the pilgrimage and died soon after the return. That such
a journey was at least planned seems probable; Eric's brother-in-
law, Einar, is said to have made a pilgrimage during the earlier
years of the decade; they may have planned to make the journey
together. The earliest English writers who account for Eric's
disappearance on the theory of exile are William of Malmesbury
(*Gesta Regum*, i., 219), and Henry of Huntingdon (*Historia
Anglorum*, 186).

viking; but, so far as it existed, it found its best
representative in Eric, the son of Hakon the Bad.
He was great as a warrior, great as a leader in the
onslaught. He possessed in full measure the
courage that made the viking such a marvellous
fighter; the joy of the conflict he seems to have
shared with the rest. But when the fight was
over and the foeman was vanquished, nobler
qualities ruled the man; he could then be merciful
and large of soul. As a statesman, on the other
hand, he seems to have been less successful; in
Norway he permitted the aristocracy to exercise
local authority to a greater extent than the welfare of Norse society could allow. As to his rule
in Northumbria we know nothing.

The next year we have the closing record of
still another Scandinavian earl in England:
Eglaf signs a grant for the last time in 1024.[1]
Doubtless some trouble had arisen between him
and the King, for two years later he appears to be
acting the part of a rebel. Still later, he is said
to have joined the Varangian guard of Scandinavian warriors at Byzantium, where he closed his
restless career in the service of the Greek Emperor.[2]

There still remained Norse and Danish earls in
England, such as Ranig and Hakon; but the men
who were most intimately associated in the English
mind with conquest and cruel subjection were
apparently out of the land before the third decade

[1] Kemble, *Codex Diplomaticus*, No. 741.
[2] *Jómsvikingasaga*, c. 52.

of the century had finished half its course. It is probable that Hakon succeeded his father in the Northumbrian earldom, as Leofwine of Mercia seems to be in possession of Hakon's earldom in Worcestershire in 1023,[1] the year when Hakon's father presumably died.

After the banishment of Thurkil, we should expect to find Eric, while he still lived, as the ranking earl in the kingdom and the chief adviser to the King. But Eric's earldom was in the extreme north; his subjects were largely Norwegian immigrants and their descendants, as yet, perhaps, but imperfectly Anglicised; he was himself an alien and his circle of ideas scarcely touched the field of Saxon politics. He could, therefore, be of small assistance in governing the kingdom as a whole. Furthermore, it is doubtful whether Canute really felt the need of a grand vizier at this time. An excellent assistant, however, he seems to have found in the Saxon Godwin. It has been thought that Godwin's exalted position of first subject in the realm belongs to a date as early as 1020.[2] But this is mere conjecture. It is evident that his influence with Canute grew with the passage of time; still, it is likely that historians have projected his greatness too far back into his career.

[1] In an agreement of that year involving lands in Worcester and Gloucester, Leofwine ealdorman signs as a witness. Kemble, *Codex Diplomaticus*, No. 738.

[2] Freeman, *Norman Conquest*, i., 285.

A position analogous to that of the tall earl he could not have held before the closing years of the reign. If Canute left any one in charge of the kingdom during his absences after 1020, it could not have been Godwin. When the fleet sailed against the Slavs on the south Baltic shores in 1022, Godwin appears to have accompanied the host. Tradition tells us that he fought valiantly in the Swedish campaign of 1026. A Norse runic monument records his presence in some expedition to Norway, presumably that of 1028.[1] Canute did not employ English forces to a large extent in any of his foreign wars, possibly because he was distrustful of them: only fifty English ships made part of that vast armada that overawed the Norwegians in 1028. Canute's probable reluctance about arming the Saxons after the battle of Carham and the consequent loss of Lothian has already been referred to. The presence of Godwin as a chief in Canute's host may, therefore, be taken as a mark of peculiar confidence on the King's part.

Godwin was never without his rival. In the Midlands Leofwine and after him his son Leofric were developing a power that was some day to prove a dangerous barrier to the ambitions of the southern Earl and his many sons. The family of Leofwine had certain advantages in the race for power that made for stability and assured possession of power once gained: it was older as a member of the aristocracy; it seems to have had Anglo-

[1] *Afhandlinger viede Sophus Bugge's Minde,* 8.

Danish connections, presumably Danish ancestry; it was apparently controlled by a spirit of prudence that urged the acceptance of de-facto rule. But in the matter of aggressive abilities and statesmanlike ideas the Mercians were far inferior to their Saxon rivals; the son and grandsons of Leofwine never attained the height of influence and power that was reached by Godwin and his son Harold.

While these changes were going on in England, an important advance had been made in the direction of empire. In his message from Rome to the English people (1027) Canute claims the kingship of England, Denmark, Norway, and parts of Sweden. The copies of the document that have come down to us are, however, not contemporary, and it is not likely that the sweeping claim of the salutation was found in the original. For at no time was Canute lord of any Swedish territory as the term was understood and the frontier drawn in the eleventh century. It has been pointed out that in this case we probably have a scribal error of Swedes for Slavs.[1] As King of Denmark, Canute inherited pretensions to considerable stretches of the south Baltic shore lands, and consequently could claim to rule a part of the Slavic lands. Early in his reign he made an expedition to these regions, of which we have faint echoes in both English and Scandinavian sources.

[1] Steenstrup, *Normannerne*, iii., 326–328.

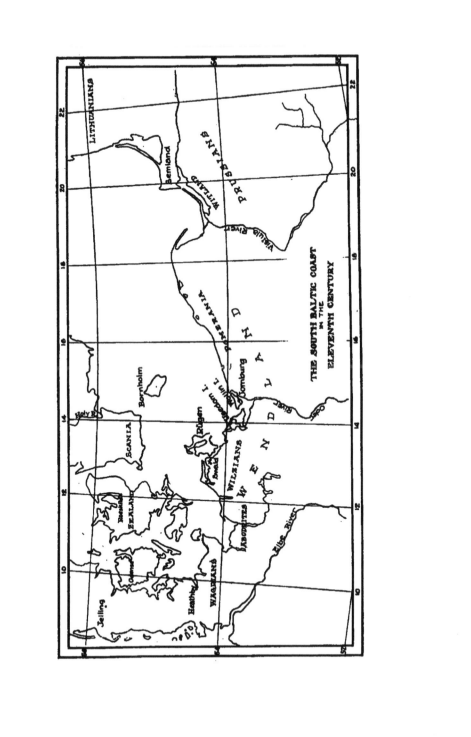

THE SOUTH BALTIC COAST
IN THE
ELEVENTH CENTURY

1

From the Elbe eastward along the Baltic shores, at least as far as the Vistula, where the Lithuanian settlements appear to have begun,[1] Slavic tribes were evidently in full possession all through the viking age. There was, however, no consolidated Slavic power, no organised Slavic state. The dominions of Bohemia and Poland were developing but neither had full control of the coast lands, The non-Slavic peoples who were interested in this region were the Danes and the Germans. The eastward expansion of Germany across and beyond the Elbe had begun; but in Canute's day Teutonic control of Wendish territories was very slight.

We find the Danes in Wendland as early as the age of Charlemagne, when they were in possession of a strong and important city called Reric, the exact location of which is not known.[2] The Danish interest appears to have been wholly a commercial one: horses, cattle, game, fish, mead, timber products, spices, and hemp are mentioned as important articles of the southern trade.[3] There was also, we may infer, something of a market for Danish products. At all times, the intercourse seems to have been peaceful; Danes and Wends appear to have lived side by side on the best of terms. The Germans, on the other hand, were not regarded with much favour by their Slavic neighbours. The feeling of hostility and

[1] Steenstrup, *Venderne og de Danske*, 3.
[2] *Ibid.*, 24–25.
[3] *Danmarks Riges Historie*, i., 322–323.

hatred that the Wend cherished was reciprocated on the German side; the German mind scarcely thought of the Slav as within the pale of humanity.

The most famous of all Danish settlements in these regions was Jom, a stronghold near the mouth of the Oder, sometimes called Jumne, Jumneta, or Julin. In the eleventh century Jom was a great city as cities went in those days, though it was probably not equal to its reputation. The good Master Adam, who has helped us to so much information regarding Northern lands and conditions in his century, speaks of the city in the following terms:

It is verily the greatest city in Europe. It is inhabited by Slavs and other peoples, Greeks and barbarians. For even the Saxons who have settled there are permitted to live with the rest in the enjoyment of the same rights; though, indeed, only so long as they refrain from public profession of their Christian faith. For all the inhabitants are still chained to the errors of heathen idolatry. In other respects, especially as to manners and hospitality, a more obliging and honourable people cannot be found.[1]

The city was located on the east side of the island of Wollin, where the village of Wollin has since been built. For its time it enjoyed a very favourable location. Built on an island, it was fairly safe from land attacks, while its position some distance from the sea secured it from the

[1] *Gesta*, ii., c. 19.

common forms of piracy.[1] Back into the land ran the great river highway, the Oder, while a few miles to the north lay the Baltic with its long coast line to the east, the west, and the north.

To secure Danish influence in the city, Harold Bluetooth built the famous fortress of Jomburg and garrisoned it with a carefully chosen band of warriors, later known as the Jomvikings. According to saga, Palna Toki, the viking who is reputed to have slain King Harold, was the founder and chief of the brotherhood; but the castle probably existed before Toki became prominent in the garrison, if he ever was a member. The fortress was located north of Jom near the modern village of Wollin, where abundant archæological evidence has definitely identified the site.[2] The harbour or bay that served as such has since filled with the rubbish of time; but in the tenth century it is reported to have had a capacity of three hundred dragons.

The existence of a military guild at Jomburg seems well attested. Only men of undoubted bravery between the ages of eighteen and fifty years were admitted to membership; and, in the admission, neither kinship nor friendship nor considerations of exalted birth should be taken into account. As members of the brotherhood, all the Jomvikings assumed the duties of mutual

[1] Steenstrup, *Venderne og de Danske*, 33-34.
[2] *Danmarks Riges Historie*, i., 325-326. Steenstrup, *Venderne og de Danske*, 49.

support and the revenge of a fallen comrade. Strict discipline was enjoined in the fortress; absence for more than three days at a time was forbidden; no women were to be admitted to the castle. There was to be no toleration of quarrelsome behaviour; plunder, the fruitful source of contention, was to be distributed by lot. In all disputes the chief was the judge.[1]

It seems evident that the chief of these vikings was something more than the captain of a garrison; he bore the earl's title and as such must have had territorial authority in and about the city. Supported by the Jomvikings he soon began to assert an independence far beyond what the Danish kings had intended that he should possess. However, till the death of Harold Bluetooth, the brotherhood appears to have been fairly loyal to their suzerain; it was to Jomburg that the aged King fled when his son rebelled against him; it was there that he died after the traitor's arrow had given him the fatal wound. The rebel Sweyn was not immediately recognised by the Earl at Jom; the vikings are said to have defied him, to have captured him and carried him off. Only on the promises of marriage to Gunhild, the sister of Earl Sigvaldi's wife, and of the payment of a huge ransom, was he permitted to return to his throne. The saga story has probably a great measure of truth in it. Sweyn seems to have been determined on the destruction of the fraternity, and most

[1] *Jómsvíkingasaga*, c. 24.

THE VALLEBERGA STONE

likely had some success; for toward the close of his reign, we find the Jomvikings no longer terrorising the Baltic shores, but plundering the western isles.

In 1021, toward the close of the year, we read of the exile of Thurkil the Tall, who will be remembered as an old Jomviking, the brother of Earl Sigvaldi, and the leader in the descent of these vikings upon England in 1009. We do not know where the exile sought a new home, but one is tempted to conjecture that he probably returned to the old haunts at the mouth of the Oder. It is an interesting fact that a few months later Canute found it advisable to make a journey to that same region.

In the entry for 1022, the Chronicler writes that "in this year King Canute fared out with his ships to Wiht," or, as one manuscript has it, to "Wihtland." Apparently, the movement, whatever it was, did not interest the scribe; far more important in his eyes was the news that Archbishop Ethelnoth, when in Rome to receive the pallium, was invited to say mass in the papal presence, and was afterwards permitted to converse with the Holy Father. Historians have thought with the monk that the journey with the fleet can have had but little importance, that it was merely a mobilisation of the navy at the Isle of Wight, perhaps for the purpose of display.

It was the Danish historian Steenstrup who first suggested that Wiht or Wihtland probably did not mean Wight in this case, but the old Witland

that we read of in the writings of Alfred: Wulfstan
the wide-farer informed the royal student that
"the Vistula is a mighty stream and separates
Witland from Wendland and Witland belongs to
the Esthonians."[1] Evidently the Angles understood Witland to be the regions of modern Prussia
east of the Vistula. That Canute's expedition
actually went eastward seems extremely probable
for we read that the next year he returned from
Denmark and had become reconciled with Earl
Thurkil.[2]

There were Danish colonies at the mouths of
the Oder, the Vistula, and the Düna[3]; all these,
no doubt, submitted to the conqueror from England. The expedition probably first went to
Jom in Wendland; thence eastward to the Prussian
regions of Witland and the still more distant
Semland, a region near the Kurisches Haff that is
reported to have been conquered by one of Harold
Bluetooth's sons.[4] Canute's possessions thus extended along the Baltic shores from Jutland almost to the eastern limits of modern Germany;
he may also have had possessions farther up the
eastern coast of the sea. It is not likely that these
possessions were anything more than a series of

[1] *Normannerne*, iii., 322–325.
[2] *Anglo-Saxon Chronicle*, 1023.
[3] Steenstrup, *Normannerne*, i., 195–199; iii., 322–325.
[4] Saxo, *Gesta Danorum*, 328. The Sembrians are described by
Adamus in his history (iv., c. 18) as a very barbarous but humane
race.

stations and settlements; but these would serve
as centres of influence from which Danish power
would penetrate into the interior to the protection
of Danish trade and commerce.

Later English writers have a story to tell of this
expedition, especially of the valorous part that was
played by the Earl Godwin. In the expedition
against the Vandals, Godwin, without first inform-
ing the King, made a night attack on the enemy
and put them to rout. When Canute prepared to
make an attack early in the morning, he missed
the English and feared that they had fled or
deserted. But when he came upon the enemy's
camp and found nothing there but bloody corpses
and plunder, light dawned on the King, and
he ever afterward held the English in high
esteem.[1]

Jomburg apparently retained its old pre-eminence as the centre of Danish control on the southern shore. The King's brother-in-law, Ulf, seems
to have been left in control, probably with the
title of earl. But after the death of Thurkil, who
had been left as viceroy of Denmark, Ulf was apparently transferred to that country and Canute's
son Sweyn, under the guidance of his mother
Elgiva, was appointed the King's lieutenant in
Wendland.[2]

[1] Henry of Huntingdon, *Historia Anglorum*, 187. The author
dates this expedition in 1019, which is probably incorrect. An
expedition to Wendland earlier than 1022 is quite unlikely.

[2] Steenstrup, *Venderne og de Danske*, 66.

The extension of Danish influence among the Wends brought Denmark into closer contact and relations with the Empire. Two years after Canute's expedition to the Slavic lands, Henry the Saint passed to his reward, and Conrad the Salic succeeded to the imperial dignities. On the death of Henry II. the great Polish Duke Boleslav hastened to assume the regal title, and evidently planned to renounce the imperial suzerainty. This policy of hostility to the Empire was continued by his son and successor, Mieczislav, who also may have hoped to interest his cousin King Canute in the welfare of the new kingdom.

Conrad also felt the need of a close alliance with the Danish conqueror, and called upon Archbishop Unwan of Hamburg-Bremen for assistance as a mediator. Unwan was Canute's friend and succeeded in bringing about the desired understanding. Possibly the price of the alliance may have appealed to Canute as much as the Archbishop's arguments; for Conrad bought the friendship of his Northern neighbour with the Mark of Sleswick to the Eider River.[1]

The exact date of this alliance is a matter of doubt, but the probabilities appear to favour 1025, when the Emperor Conrad was in Saxony. Some historians believe that the mark was not ceded at this time but ten years later, when Canute's daughter Gunhild was betrothed to Conrad's son Henry, as Adam of Bremen seems to

[1] Adamus, *Gesta*, ii., c. 54

associate these two events.[1] But Adam's chronology is confused on these matters. Canute's friendship was surely more difficult to purchase in 1025 when his star was rapidly ascending than in 1035 when his empire had begun to collapse. While we cannot be sure, it seems extremely likely that the boundary of Denmark was extended to the Eider in 1025.

[1] See Manitius, *Deutsche Geschichte unter den sächsischen und salischen Kaisern*, 370.

DANISH COINS FROM THE REIGN OF
CANUTE, MINTED AT LUND,
ROESKILDE, RINGSTED

CHAPTER VII

1017–1026

THE English Church enjoyed Canute's favour
from the very beginning: the King was a
Christian; furthermore, he no doubt saw in the
Church a mighty force that should not be antagon-
ised. At the same time, there is no evidence of any
close union between church and monarchy before
1020; and even then it was more like an *entente
cordiale* than an open aggressive alliance, as it
later came to be. Canute was a Christian, but
he was also a shrewd statesman and a consummate
politician. The religious situation among his
Danish supporters in England as well as the general
religious and political conditions in the North
probably made it inexpedient, perhaps impossible,
to accede to the full demands of the Church without danger to his ambitions and probable ruin to
his imperialistic plans.

When the eleventh century opened, the North
was still largely heathen. Missionaries had been
at work for nearly two centuries—ever since

AN ENGLISH BISHOP OF THE ELEVENTH
CENTURY

(From the Bayeux Tapestry.)

POPPO'S ORDEAL

(Altar decoration from about 1100. Danish National Museum.)

Saint Ansgar entered the Scandinavian mission field in the days of Louis the Pious—and the faith had found considerable foothold in Denmark, especially on the Jutish peninsula. Canute's father Sweyn had been baptised; but other indications of his Christian faith are difficult to find. His queen, Sigrid the Haughty, was almost violent in her devotion to the old gods. Sweden remained overwhelmingly heathen for some years yet, while the progress of the Church in Norway depended on royal mandates supported by the sword and the firebrand. Only five years before the death of Canute, Norse heathendom won its last notable victory, when Saint Olaf fell before the onslaught of the yeomanry at Stiklestead (1030).

The army that conquered England for Canute was no doubt also largely heathen. It seems, therefore, safe to assume that during the early years of the new reign, the worship of the Anse-gods was carried on in various places on English soil; surely in the Danish camps, perhaps also in some of the Danish settlements. This situation compelled the Christian King to be at least tolerant. Soon there began to appear at the English court prominent exiles from Norway, hot-headed chiefs, whose sense of independence had been outraged by the zealous missionary activities of Olaf the Stout.[1] Canute had not been lord of England more than six or seven years before the Norwegian

[1] Snorre, *Saga of Saint Olaf*, cc. 130, 131, 139.

problem began to take on unusual interest. Before long the missionary King found his throne completely undermined by streams of British gold. The exiles who sought refuge at Winchester and the men who bore the bribe-money back to Norway were scarcely enthusiastic for the faith that frowned on piracy; consequently it continued to be necessary for Canute to play the rôle of the tolerant, broad-minded monarch, who, while holding firmly to his own faith, was unwilling to interfere with the religious rites of others. In his later ecclesiastical legislation, Canute gave the Church all the enactments that it might wish for; but it is a significant fact that these laws did not come before the Northern question had been settled according to Canute's desires and his viceroy was ruling in Norway. Edgar's laws, which were re-enacted in 1018, at the Oxford assembly, deal with the matter of Christianity in general terms only. The more explicit and extensive Church legislation of Ethelred's day was set aside and apparently remained a dead letter until it was in large measure re-enacted as a part of Canute's great church law late in the reign.

The early surroundings of the King had not been such as to develop in him the uncompromising zeal that characterised the typical Christian monarch in mediæval times. We do not know when he was baptised; it may have been in childhood, and it must have been before the conquest of England, as the Christian name Lambert, which was added in baptism to the heathen name by which we know him, would suggest that the rite was administered by a German ecclesiastic.[1] It is believed that he was confirmed by Ethelnoth the Good, the English churchman who later became Archbishop of Canterbury.[2] We do not know when the rite of confirmation was administered, but the probabilities point to the winter months of 1015–1016; for during these months Canute was several times in South-western England where Ethelnoth lived at the time

The subjection of England to an alien, half-heathen aristocracy must have caused many difficulties to the English Church. How the problems were met we do not know. The Mediæval Church, however, was usually to be found on the side of power: the Church loved order and believed in supporting good and efficient government

[1] Adamus, *Gesta*, ii., c. 50: schol. 38. It seems to have been customary to add a Christian name in baptism.

There is an allusion to Canute's conversion in the Chronicle of Adémar de Chabannes (ii., c. 55), who seems to believe that Canute became a Christian after the conquest of England. But the authority of the Aquitanian chronicler, though contemporary, cannot be so weighty as that of the records of the church of Bremen which the Scholiast seems to have used in the entry cited above. For Adémar's statement see Waitz, *Scriptores* (*M. G. H.*), iv., 140.

[2] Langebek, *Scriptores*, ii., 454: Osbern's tract concerning the translation of Saint Alphege. Osbern tells us that Ethelnoth was dear to Canute because he had anointed him with the sacred chrism. This cannot refer to his coronation, nor is it likely to have reference to his baptism, as Ethelnoth, would scarcely have given Canute a German name. It seems, therefore, that it must allude to his confirmation.

whenever circumstances would permit it. Soon
after the meeting at Oxford, apparently in 1019,
Archbishop Lifing made a journey to Rome; we
may conjecture that he went to seek counsel and
to obtain instructions as to what attitude the
English clergy should assume toward the new
powers, but we do not know. It is clear, however,
that the subject was seriously discussed at the
papal court, for the archbishop brought back a
letter to Canute exhorting him to practise the
virtues of Christian kingship. It must have
flattered the young Dane to receive this, for he
refers to it in his Proclamation:

I have taken to heart the written words and verbal
messages that Archbishop Lifing brought me from the
pope from Rome, that I should everywhere extol
the praise of God, put away injustice, and promote
full security and peace, so far as God should give me
strength.[1]

That same year the venerable Primate died, and
Ethelnoth the Good was appointed to succeed
him as Archbishop of Canterbury.[2] The choice
was evidently the King's own and the two men
seem to have laboured together in singular
harmony. But though Ethelnoth was primate,
the dominant influence at court seems to have
been that of an abbot in Devonshire. When
Abbot Lifing was yet only a monk at Winchester,

---

[1] Liebermann, *Geschichte der Angelsachsen*, i., 273.
[2] Florence of Worcester, *Chronicon*, i., 183.

he seems to have attracted the King's attention; at any rate, we are told by the historian of Malmesbury that he became an intimate friend of Canute and exerted great influence with him.[1] It may have been this friendship that secured to Lifing the abbacy of Tavistock, perhaps in 1024, in which year he witnessed charters for the first time as abbot.

Lifing's advance to power was rapid. Two years after his first appearance in the documents as abbot, we find that he had been elevated to the episcopal office, having probably been advanced to the see of Crediton.[2] The Devonshire country had been the centre of a persistent anti-Danish movement, it appears, and it was surely a prudent move to place a strong partisan of the new order in control of the Church in the southwestern shires. In the same year, the King further honoured him with landed estates in Hampshire. This must have been just prior to the Holy River campaign in Sweden, on which expedition the bishop probably accompanied his royal master (William of Malmesbury tells us that he frequently went to Denmark with Canute); at all events, when Canute without first returning to England made his journey to Rome, in the early months of 1027, the

---

[1] *Gesta Pontificum,* 200.

[2] Kemble, *Codex Diplomaticus,* No. 743. Florence of Worcester, *Chronicon,* i., 185. To this he afterwards added the see of Worcester, to which he was appointed by Harold in 1038. *Ibid.,* 193.

bishop of Crediton was an important member of the King's retinue. It was Bishop Lifing who was sent back to England with Canute's famous message to the English Church and people, the King himself going on to Denmark. William of Malmesbury describes him as a violent, wilful, and ambitious prelate; when he died (in 1046) the earth took proper notice and trembled throughout all England.[1]

The year 1020 was one of great significance for English history in the reign of Canute. In that year he returned to England as Danish king; in that same year he issued his Proclamation to his Anglian subjects and announced his new governmental policy; the same year saw the appointment of a new and friendly primate of the Anglican Church; in that year, too, began a series of benefactions and other semi-religious acts that made Canute's name dear to the English churchmen and secured him the favour of monastic chroniclers. These took various forms: new foundations were established and many of the older ones received increased endowments; monasteries that had been defiled or destroyed in the Danish raids were repaired or rebuilt; the fields where the Lord of Hosts had given the victory to Canute's armies were adorned with churches where masses were said for the souls of the slain; saints were honoured; pilgrimages were made; heathen practices were outlawed.

[1] *Gesta Pontificum*, 200–201.

The series properly begins with the consecration of the church on Ashington field in 1020. The church itself was apparently a modest structure, but the dedication ceremonies were elaborate. As the primacy was evidently vacant at the time, Archbishop Lifing having died about mid-year (June 12),[1] the venerable Wulfstan of the northern province was called on to officiate. With him were numerous ecclesiastics, bishops, abbots, and monks. King Canute and Earl Thurkil also graced the occasion with their presence.[2] It is interesting to note that the office of chapel priest at Ashington was given to a clerk of Danish blood, the later prelate Stigand, one of the few Danes who have held ecclesiastical offices in England. Stigand for a time sat on the episcopal throne in the cathedrals of Winchester and Canterbury. Doubtless a Dane could perform the offices on this particular field with a blither spirit than a native Englishman. If the intention was to impress the English Church, Canute clearly succeeded. Though details are wanting, it is understood that similar foundations soon graced the other fields where Canute had fought and won.

In that same year, apparently, monks were substituted for secular clerks as guardians of Saint Edmund's shrine. Grievously had the Danes sinned against the holy East Anglian King. Five generations earlier he had suffered ignomini-

[1] Stubbs, *Registrum Sacrum Anglicanum*, 31.
[2] *Anglo-Saxon Chronicle*, 1020.

ous martyrdom at the hands of the vikings. The saint had again suffered outrage in the closing months of King Sweyn's life by what seemed to be petty persecution of the priests who served at his sacred shrine. As we have already seen, the King's sudden death while the matter of tribute was still unsettled gave rise to the legend that Saint Edmund struck down the Dane "in like manner as the holy Mercurius slew the nithing Julian."

It was charged that the priests of the holy place led disorderly lives, and on the advice of the neighbouring bishop, Elfwine of Elmham, it was determined to eject them. Earl Thurkil's consent was asked and received. Monks to the number of twenty were brought from Saint Benet Hulme and Ely.[1] The same year a new church was begun, that the relics of the martyr might have a more suitable home. The monks naturally organised themselves into a monastic community, which seems to have enjoyed full immunity from the very beginning: a trench was run around Saint Edmund's chapel on the edge of which all tax-gathering was to stop. In addition it is said that the Lady Emma pledged an annual gift of four thousand eels from Lakenheath, though this was probably a later contribution. The brethren of the monastery also claimed that Canute granted them extensive jurisdiction over the manors that belonged to the new foundation.[2] It is evident

[1] *Memorials of Saint Edmund's Abbey*, I., xxvii, 47, 126.
[2] *Ibid.*, i., 343.

that large endowments were given and Canute in
this way became in a sense the founder of one of the
most important sanctuaries of mediæval England.

William of Malmesbury tells us that Canute disliked the English saints, but the evidence indicates
the contrary. The only instance of ill-will recorded is in the case of Saint Edith, King Edgar's
holy daughter. Saint Edith rested at Wilton,
where there was a religious house for women that
had enjoyed her patronage. Canute expressed a
doubt as to the sanctity of a daughter of the im-
moral Edgar and ordered the shrine to be opened.
The offended princess arose, we are told, and struck
the impious King in the face.[1] Canute acknowledged his error and did penance. There may be
some truth in the story so far as it relates to the
King's hostility or incredulity, for Saint Edith was
the sister of Canute's old enemy, King Ethelred.

It may have been the vigorous argument of
Saint Edith, or genuine piety, or political considerations that wrought the change, but it is clear that
Canute soon developed a profound respect for
the saints that rested in England. He caused the
relics of Saint Wistan to be translated from
Repingdon to a more suitable home in the honoured
abbey of Evesham.[2] The remains of Saint Felix
were brought back to Ramsey in the face of strong
opposition from the jealous monks of Ely.[3] On

[1] William of Malmesbury, *Gesta Pontificum*, 190.
[2] *Chronicon Abbatiæ de Evesham*, 325-326.
[3] *Historia Rameseiensis*, 127-128.

one of his northern journeys the King turned
aside to Durham to adore the bones of the mighty
Saint Cuthbert. Five miles did the King walk
with bare feet to the Durham sepulchre, and after
showing proper respect and veneration, he concluded his visit with a royal gift of lands, two
manors, we are told, with all their belongings.[1]
Toward the close of his reign, by legislative act,
he gave the strenuous Dunstan a place on the
calendar of English saints.[2]

By far the most famous act of homage of this
sort was the translation of Saint Alphege from
London to Canterbury in 1023, famous not because of its peculiar importance, but because
certain literary monks saw fit to write long accounts of it. This, too, was an act of expiation:
so far as the sins of Canute's people were concerned
the case of Bishop Alphege was much like that of
the martyred King Edmund. Alphege was from
Western England and became a monk at Deerhurst
in Gloucestershire. He was for a time abbot of
Bath and later bishop of Winchester. It was
he who confirmed Olaf Trygvesson and thus
indirectly began the work that resulted in the
conversion of Norway. As Archbishop of Canterbury he seems to have taken a pastoral interest in
the Danish besiegers, for which he was rewarded
with indignities and death. His bones had been
laid at rest at Saint Paul's in London; but Canter-

[1] Simeon of Durham, *Opera Omnia*, i., 90.
[2] Liebermann, *Gesetze der Angelsachsen*, i., 298.

bury was naturally anxious to have her first martyred bishop in her own house, while London, on the other hand, is said to have watched over the sacred remains with a jealous care that bore the marks of avarice rather than of veneration.

We are told that Canute earlier had formed the purpose of translating the relics and that certain calamities had recalled the intention to his mind. He suggested the project to Archbishop Ethelnoth, who doubted the feasibility of the venture. According to the highly-coloured report of the monk Osbern who claims to have his information from an eye-witness, the King and the Archbishop secretly removed the body from its resting-place and gave it to a monk who bore it to the Thames where the King's ship lay ready to receive it. The attention of the Londoners was diverted to other parts of the city by feigned excitement at the farther gates, for which the King's housecarles were responsible. Meanwhile, the royal ship, with Canute himself at the rudder, was conveying the remains to Southwark, where they were given into the keeping of the Archbishop and his companions, who bore them joyfully on to Rochester. Here the party was joined by Queen Emma and the five-year-old princeling Harthacanute accompanied by a strong force of housecarles. The translation was effected in June and occupied seven days.[1]

[1] Most of these details are from Osbern's tract on the life and translation of Saint Alphege. See Langebek, *Scriptores*, ii.,

The Dane's interest in the Church also expressed itself in frequent and important endowments. While it is not always possible to verify these grants, there can be little doubt that the monastic records are usually correct on the points of possession and donors, though the extant charters are frequently forgeries produced at a time when titles were called into question. In some of these gifts, too, we see clearly a desire to atone for past wrongs. Canterbury, which had suffered heavy losses at the hands of Thurkil and his wild comrades, was assured of its liberties and immunities early in the reign.[1] Another act of expiation was the visit and gift to Glastonbury, the famous monastery that had received the bones of Edmund Ironside. A century after Canute's time Edmund's grave was covered with a "pall of rich materials, embroidered with figures of peacocks." Legend ascribes the gift to Canute, and may in this case be trustworthy. With the King at Edmund's grave stood Archbishop Ethelnoth, who was at one time a monk at Glastonbury.[2] The visit seems to have been made in 1026, perhaps on the eve of Canute's expedition against the Norwegians and Swedes.

Perhaps Canute's most famous gift was the

---

or Wharton's *Anglia Sacra*, ii. The account in the *Chronicle* is briefer but more reliable.

[1] Kemble, *Codex Diplomaticus*, Nos. 727 and 731; of these the former is scarcely genuine.

[2] William of Malmesbury, *Gesta Regum*, i., 224.

golden cross at Winchester. Some time in the early years of his reign, apparently in 1019, probably just before his visit to Denmark, he gave to the New Minster a "magnificent golden cross, richly ornamented with precious stones"; in addition to this, "two large images of gold and silver, and sundry relics of the saints."[1] It seems to have been a gorgeous present, one that was keenly appreciated by the recipients, and the history of which was long recounted. The gift was apparently accompanied by a donation of valuable lands.[2]

Canute also showed an interest in the monastery of Saint Benet Hulme, to which three manors were given.[3] It is claimed that he granted certain immunities to the church of Saint Mary Devon in Exeter, but the evidence is not trustworthy.[4] The great abbey of Evesham was not forgotten: the blessed Wistan was given a black chasuble and other ornaments, probably at the time of his translation.[5] It may be that in making this gift the King wished to show his appreciation of the abbot as well as to honour the saint: Abbot Elfward is said to have been Canute's cousin; if such was the case he must have been the son of the ill-starred Pallig.

Gifts there also were of a more personal character, gifts to various ecclesiastics, monks, and priests whom the King wished to honour; especially may

---

[1] *Liber de Hyda*, xxxvi.   [2] *Ibid.*, 324.
[3] Kemble, *Codex Diplomaticus*, No. 740.
[4] *Ibid.*, No. 729.   [5] *Chronicon Abbatiæ de Evesham*, 83.

we mention the grants to Bishop Burhwold and to Bishop Lifing.[1] But such donations were not numerous; Canute seems to have preferred to honour foundations, probably because in mediæval times the institution was of greater consequence than the individual.

The gifts enumerated were made during the first half of the reign. Grants were made in the second period as well: Abingdon claims to have enjoyed his favour[2]; the Old Minster at Winchester was endowed with lands and adorned with specimens of the goldsmith's art[3]; a considerable gift of lands was made to York cathedral[4]; but these seem to reveal a different spirit and purpose in the giver. Before his career closed the great Dane became an ardent Christian; but in his earlier years, the politician left little room to the churchman: the Church was a factor merely, though a great factor, in the political situation. Other kings have gloried in new foundations as monuments to religious zeal; Canute selected the long-established, the widely-influential shrines and houses and gave his favour chiefly to them. In return he doubtless expected the favour of Saints Cuthbert, Alphege, Edmund, Felix, and Dunstan, and the support of Canterbury, Evesham, Winchester, and the other great institutions that he

---

[1] Kemble, *Codex Diplomaticus*, Nos. 728, 743.
[2] *Chronicon Monasterii de Abingdon*, i., 434 ff.
[3] *Annales Monastici*, ii., 16.
[4] Kemble, *Codex Diplomaticus*, No. 749.

endowed. It is to be noted that nearly all the institutions that shared the royal bounty were located in the Anglo-Saxon South where Canute especially needed to build up a personal following. The exceptions were York, Durham, and Coventry where the faithful rejoiced in an arm of Saint Augustine, a relic of peculiar value that Canute is said to have bestowed on the city.[1]

Whatever his motives were, it is clear that Canute showed an interest in matters ecclesiastical far beyond what the Church might reasonably expect from a king whose training had scarcely been positively Christian, and who still kept in close touch with the non-Christian influences that dominated so much of the North. Still, one desire remained unsatisfied: thus far the King had done nothing to make the Christian faith compulsory in England. The Proclamation of 1020 looks in that direction; but it contains no decree of the desired sort. It is a peculiar document, remarkable more for what it omits than for what it actually contains. God's laws, by which the rules of the Church are doubtless meant, are not to be violated; but the important task of bringing the violators to justice is committed to the old pirate, Thurkil the Tall, whose appreciation of Christian virtues and divine commandments cannot have been of the keenest.[2] Certain charac-

[1] Gervase of Canterbury, *Historical Works*, ii., 56. The arm was brought to England from Rome by Archbishop Ethelnoth. William of Malmesbury, *Gesta Regum*, i., 224.   [2] Sec. 9.

12

teristically heathen sins are to be avoided: among
the things forbidden is to consort with witches
and sorceresses.[1] But the only crime of this
nature for which the document prescribes a specific
penalty is that of marrying a nun or any other
woman who has taken sacred vows:

And if any one has done so, let him be an outlaw
before God and excommunicated from all Christendom, and let him forfeit all his possessions to the king,
unless he quickly desist from sin and do deep penance
before God.[2]

It is evident, however, that Canute believed
that the process of education in the church from
Sunday to Sunday would eventually solve the
problem of heathenism in England; for he closes
his Proclamation with an exhortation to all his
subjects to attend faithfully the divine services:

And further still we admonish all men to keep the
Sunday festival with all their might and observe it
from Saturday's noon to Monday's dawning; and let
no man be so bold as to buy or sell or to seek any court
on that holy day.
And let all men, poor and rich, seek their church
and ask forgiveness for their sins and earnestly keep
every ordained fast and gladly honour the saints, as
the mass priest shall bid us,

[1] Sec. 15. As the term used for sorceress seems to be Norse,
this prohibition was evidently aimed at practices in the Danelaw.
[2] Sec. 17.

that we may all be able and permitted, through the mercy of the everlasting God and the intercession of His saints, to share the joys of the heavenly kingdom and dwell with Him who liveth and reigneth forever without end. Amen.[1]

[1] Secs. 18-20.

CHAPTER VIII

THE TWILIGHT OF THE GODS

THE question what attitude to assume toward the organised English Church may have caused Canute some embarrassment; but the English problem was simple compared with the religious complications that the young King had to face in the North. England was Christian, at least officially, while Scandinavia was still largely heathen; though every day saw the camps of Christendom pitched a little farther toward the Arctic. In all the Northern kingdoms missionaries were at work planting the seeds of the new faith. By the close of the millennium Christianity had made great progress in the Danish kingdom; it was firmly rooted in Jutland and had found a foothold on the islands and in Scania. Amo g the Norwegians the new worship had also made some progress; but in Sweden the darkness of heathendom still hung heavy and low.

Norse Christianity doubtless filtered in with the viking raids: with the plunder of the Catholic South and West, the sea-kings also appropriated many of the forms and ideas of Western civilisation,

HAMMERS OF THOR
(From the closing years of heathendom.)

and it is not to be supposed that the fields of religious thought were neglected or overlooked. King Hakon the Good became a Christian at the court of his foster-father, Ethelstan, the grandson of Alfred.[1] The sons of Eric Bloodax were also baptised in England, where their father had found an exile's refuge.[2] Olaf Trygvesson found his faith and his mission while fighting as viking in England. Olaf the Saint received baptism in Rouen on his return from a raid as viking mercenary. Thus Norway had been in close touch with the new faith for nearly a century; and yet, Christianity had made but little actual progress. During the reign of Canute the Danish Church reached the stage of effective organisation, while in Norway the religious activities were still of the missionary type.

The forces of the Anse-gods were in retreat all along the religious frontier; but it is not to be supposed that they were panic-stricken. To their zeal for the ancestral worship was added a love for the conflict which inspired the faithful to contest every inch of the Christian advance. The challenge of Thor has a sort of historic reality in it:

[1] Snorre, *Saga of Harold Fairhair*, c. 41. Hakon's dates according to saga are 935–961. The earlier date should probably be corrected to 945 or a later year, perhaps 947. See *Norges Historie*, I., ii., 139.

[2] Snorre, *Saga of Hakon the Good*, c. 3. Eric Bloodax was Hakon's half-brother. For a time he ruled Northumbria as vassal of the English King. *Anglo-Saxon Chronicle*, 952. The vassal relationship is asserted in the sagas.

in a sense the issue of religion was settled in the
North by wager of battle.   In his admiration for
strength and force, many a Northman seemed
willing to follow the lead of the stronger cult.

The Anse-faith of the viking age seems to have
been a development of an ancient form of heaven
worship or possibly of sun worship, traces of which
have been found in the North from the days of the
stone age.[1] In time the deity came to be viewed
from various angles, and each particular aspect was
individualised and made the object of separate
worship.   Thus, apparently, arose the three great
divinities, Thor, Woden, and Frey.   Thor is the
god of strength, the mighty defender of gods and
men.   His name (O. Eng. *Thunor*), his flaming
beard, the crash of his hammer-stroke show that
the Thor-conception was closely associated with
early notions of thunder and lightning.   Similarly,
the name of Woden[2] associates his divinity with
the untamed forces of nature, the fury of the
tempest, the wrath of the storm.   He is, therefore,
the god of the battle rush, the divine force that
inspires the athletic frenzy of the berserk.   Thor is
armed with a hammer, Woden with a spear.   Thor
rides in a cart drawn by rams; Woden's mount is

[1] Montelius, *Kulturgeschichte Schwedens*, 312.   Two symbols
of sun worship, the wheel and the axe (the symbol of lightning
which later developed into Thor's hammer), can be traced back to
the close of the stone age.   *Ibid.*, 55.   The worship of the bright
sky may have preceded that of the sun.

[2] German *Wotan*.   Cf. Mod. Ger. *Wuth*.

a swift eight-footed horse. But Woden is more than a mere god of conflict; he is wise and cunning and knows the mysteries of the world. Frey is the god of fruitfulness, the sun-god as giver of life and growth. He should be worshipped by tillers of the soil.

In the course of time, new deities were admitted to the Scandinavian pantheon; some of these were no doubt developed from older conceptions; others were evidently introduced from neighbouring cults. Gradually the old, rude beliefs came to be overlaid with myths, a series of strange tales, bold, strong, and weird. Recent scholars have held that many of these were borrowed from the bulging storehouse of Christian faith and legend— the result of intellectual contact between the old races and the Norse immigrant on the Western Islands.[1] But even where this borrowing can be clearly traced, the modifying touches of the Norse imagination are clearly in evidence.

The Northern peoples also developed a system of ethics of which we have a remarkable statement in the Eddic poem, the "Song of the High One." While of a lower character than that associated with Christianity, it was, when we consider the soil from which it sprang, a remarkable growth. Candour, honesty, courage, strength, fidelity, and hospitality were enjoined and emphasised. The Northman was impressed

[1] Particularly the late Sophus Bugge in *The Home of the Eddic Poems* and elsewhere.

with the fact that all things seem perishable; but
he hoped that the fame of a good life would continue after death.

> Cattle die, kinsmen die,
> Finally dies one-self;
> But never shall perish the fame of him
> Who has won a good renown.

> Cattle die, kinsmen die,
> Finally dies one-self;
> But one thing I know that always remains,
> Judgment passed on the dead.[1]

But the duties toward the hostile and the weak,
that Christianity strove to inculcate, the Northman did not appreciate: slavery was common;
weak and unwelcome children were often exposed
at birth; revenge was a sacred duty.

It is not the intention to enter upon a full discussion of Old Northern faith and morals: in the
conversion of a people that had reached the particular stage of culture that the Norsemen occupied
in the eleventh century, neither is of prime import-
tance. It is doubtful whether the vikings were
much interested in the intricacies of dogma, be it
heathen or Christian. It also seems unlikely that
Christian morals as practised at the time could
have proved very attractive. In the life of Saint
Olaf, for instance, there was little that we should
regard as saintly, but much that was cruel, sinful,

[1] *Hávamál*, 39–40. (*Corpus Poeticum Boreale*, i, 8.)

and coarse. The Celtic Church, with which the Norwegians first came into close contact, seems to have put a somewhat liberal construction on the ten commandments. The forms of worship, however, were of the first importance: in the gorgeous ritual of the mediæval Church the heathen could not fail to see a tangible excellence that his own rude worship did not possess.

The Anse-faith knew no priesthood: the various local officials were charged with the duty of performing the ancient rites, though some evidently had peculiar responsibilities in this matter. In the family the father had certain sacerdotal duties. The gods were worshipped in temples, though not exclusively so; sacred groves and fountains were also used for such purposes. Frequently, also, the great hall of a chief was dedicated to the gods and used for sacrificial feasts.[1]

Most famous of all the Old Scandinavian sanctuaries was that at Upsala in Eastern Sweden, built, we are told, by the god Frey himself. It was a large wooden structure, highly ornamented with gold. Within were rude images of the three major divinities, Thor, Woden, and Frey, with Thor's image in the chief place. Near the temple there grew, according to the account in Adam's chronicle, an exceedingly large tree that always kept its verdure, in winter as well as in summer. There was also a fountain where the victims were sometimes drowned; if the corpse did not reappear,

[1] Montelius, *Kulturgeschichte Schwedens*, 321.

the favour of the gods was assured. In the sacred grove about the sanctuary, the sacrificial victims were hung—horses, dogs, and other beasts, frequently also human beings. The corpses were not removed but permitted to hang from the trees. Adam reports that an eye-witness once counted seventy-two such sacrificial victims.[1]

Every ninth year the entire Swedish nation was summoned to sacrifice at Upsala. The feast was celebrated shortly before the vernal equinox and continued nine days. At least one human being was sacrificed each day. Great multitudes were in attendance—king and people all sent their offerings to Upsala. It seems, however, that Christians were released from the duty of attendance on the payment of money.[2] It is clear that the gathering had a national as well as a religious significance. Elaborate festivities were combined with the sacrifices.

Three times in the year did the Northmen gather in this manner to feast and to invoke the gods: at Yule-tide in January, at the vernal equinox, and late in the autumn. Of these gatherings the sagas speak somewhat explicitly and seem to give reliable information.

It was the old way, when a sacrifice was to be, that all the franklins should come to the place where the temple was, and carry thither the victuals that they wished to have as long as the feast lasted. All

[1] *Gesta*, iv., c. 27 and schol. 134, 137.　　　[2] *Ibid.*

were to have a drinking together, and there were also slaughtered all kinds of cattle and also horses.

And all the blood that came thereof was then called sortilege-blood, and sortilege-bowls those wherein the blood stood, and sortilege-twigs that were made like a sprinkler. With this blood were all the altars to be sprinkled withal, and also the walls of the temple without and within, and also sprinkled on the people, but the meat was seethed for the entertainment of the people.

There had to be fires in the midst of the floor of the temple, and kettles over them, and the toasts were carried across the fire.

And he that made the feast or was chief had to make a sign over the toast and the sanctified meat.

First must come Woden's toast: that was drunk to victory and power of the king; and then Niard's toast; and Frey's toast for good seasons and peace.

It was many men's wont to drink Brage's toast after that.

Men also would drink a toast to their kinsmen that had been laid in their barrows, and that was called the memory toast.[1]

This description applies more especially to the great Yule-festivities, but its more prominent features, the gathering, the sacrificial slaughter, the blood-sprinkling, the toasts, and the feasting, were evidently common usages, though places and occasions probably developed varieties of customary worship. On the same occasions, the will

[1] Vigfusson and Powell, *Origines Islandicæ*, i., 309–310. From the *Hakonar Saga*.

of the gods was ascertained by the casting of lot or other processes of sortilege. Vows were pledged and oaths were registered.

A ring of two-ounce weight or more must lie on the altar in every head temple. This ring every *godĕ* (temple-official) must carry in his hand to any law-moot that he himself was to preside over, and he must first redden it in the blood of the sacrificial beast which he sacrificed there himself.[1]

In the myth Ragnarok the Sibyl has told of the end of all things, even of the divinities; how the twilight shall settle down upon the life of the Anses; how their strength shall wither and age steal upon them; and how at last Swart, the lord of the fire-world, shall come to the attack wrapped in flames.

> Swart from the south comes
> With flaming sword;
> Bright from his blade
> The sun is blazing.
> Stagger the stony peaks,
> Stumble the giants;
> Heroes fare Hel-ward
> And heaven yawns.[2]

It is an awful picture that the prophetess unrolls for us of all the personified forces of destruction mustering to do battle against the gods. The

[1] Vigfusson and Powell, *Origines Islandicæ*, i., 311. From the *Landnáma-bóc.*

[2] Voluspá, ll. 155–158. (*Corpus Poeticum Boreale*, i., 199.)

THE TJÄNGVIDE STONE
(Monument from the Island of Gotland. The stone shows various mythological
figures; see below, page 302.)

forces of evil win, for weakness has stolen upon the
world in the "twilight" preceding the final conflict: "an age of lust, of ax and sword, and of
crashing shields, of wind and wolf ere the world
crumbles."[1] Then comes the end of all things:

> Swart is the sun,
> Earth sinks in the ocean,
> The shining stars
> Are quenched in the sky.
> Smoke and steam
> Encircle the Ash-tree,
> Flame-tongues lick
> The lofty heaven.[2]

The prophecy of destruction as well as an expressed hope of future regeneration shows quite
clearly the result of Christian influence on thought
and imagery. The poem must consequently have
been produced after the North had come under the
spell of Western culture, some time, perhaps, in
the tenth century. Less than a century later the
"twilight of the gods" had set in.

The union of the Anglo-Saxon to the Danish
crown could not fail to affect missionary operations
in the North. It would seem at first sight as if
the work would be strengthened and hastened, for
now the Christianising energies of Britain would be
added to those of Germany. As a matter of fact
the situation became more complex and difficult:

[1] Voluspá, ll. 133-134.   [2] *Ibid.*, ll. 175-178.

the union brought out the question whether the primacy of the new church should belong to Hamburg-Bremen or to Canterbury. It seems that Canute at one time held out hopes to Archbishop Ethelnoth of rising to metropolitan authority of the Danish as well as of the English nation. Such an arrangement would seem natural and highly desirable: the empire that Canute ruled from Winchester could be more readily held together if its ecclesiastical concerns were all directed from the cathedral at Canterbury.

These new plans with respect to the young Danish Church apparently date from the years immediately following Canute's return to England as Danish king (1020). His new interest in English ecclesiastical matters has been discussed elsewhere. In 1022, Ethelnoth consecrated three bishops for Danish sees: Gerbrand for Zealand (Roeskild); Reginbert for Funen (Odense); and Bernhard for the Scanian lands.[1] The sources also state that many other English bishops were sent to Denmark from England, but no names are given. It is to be noted that the names given above are not Anglo-Saxon but German. It has therefore been thought that these bishops were from Flanders or Lorraine, in which regions there was an ecclesiastical movement of some importance in the days of Canute.[2]

Of these three the most important was doubt-

[1] Stubbs, *Registrum Sacrum Anglicanum*, 33.
[2] Steenstrup, *Normannerne*, iii., 383.

less Gerbrand, whose cathedral was located at Roeskild, the royal residential city. At this time Unwan was archbishop of Hamburg-Bremen. Unwan was an aggressive and ambitious prelate; it was not with pleasure that he learned of the new bishops from the West; without the North as its mission-field, Bremen would be a sorry province. Bishop Gerbrand on his journey to his new parish, —he was probably sailing along the German coast according to custom,—was captured and brought before Archbishop Unwan who forced him to do proper homage. Apparently the German Prelate made a favourable impression on Bishop Gerbrand for through his influence the Archbishop induced Canute to agree that future bishops should be consecrated at Bremen.[1]

Tradition is doubtless correct in ascribing to Canute considerable activity in the endowment of churches. The statement that he established monasteries in Denmark is probably an error; if he attempted to do so, his efforts failed[2]; some time still had to pass before the viking could find contentment in the cloister. Danish monasticism dates from the closing years of the century, when twelve monks from Evesham on the Avon came on request of King Eric to found a monastery at Odense. It seems likely that the payment of Peter's pence dates from this reign. As to the amount of this tax nothing is known; but it is

[1] Adamus, *Gesta*, ii., c. 53.
[2] *Danmarks Riges Historie*, i., 403, 500–501.

probable that the sum was a very modest one, as the Danes in England seem to have been specially favoured in this matter, the tax in the Danelaw being half as large as in the rest of England.[1]

Across the Sound in Scania, the introduction of Christianity was a slower process. We learn that in Sweyn's time an Englishman, Godebald, was appointed bishop there, and that he occasionally preached in the neighbouring sections of Sweden and Norway.[2] The results were evidently meagre, but it is significant that the preacher came from England.

The Norwegian Church is in a peculiar sense a daughter of the English Church. The first serious attempt at mission work in Norway was made about the middle of the tenth century, when King Hakon built a few churches and sent for English priests to officiate in them. One of these apparently bore the episcopal title, Sigfrid, a monk of Glastonbury.[3] The yeomanry gathered and slew the missionaries and the work came to nought.

When Olaf Trygvesson seized the kingship (995), he came accompanied by English priests. Among these was Bishop Sigurd, who was probably a Northumbrian of Norse ancestry, and evidently a man of strength and discretion. After the battle of Swald he seems to have continued

---

[1] *Danmarks Riges Historie*, i., 403.

[2] Adamus, *Gesta*, ii., c. 39.

[3] Taranger, *Den angelsaksiske Kirkes Indflydelse paa den norske*, 143.

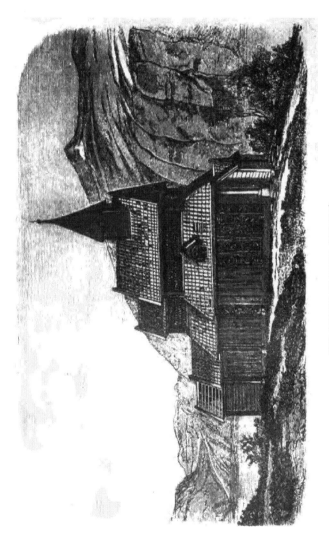

THE CHURCH AT URNES (NORWAY)

(From about 1100.)

his labours in Sweden. English missionaries also came with Olaf the Stout.

He was accompanied by a number of priests and bishops from England through whose doctrine and instruction he prepared his heart for God, and to whose guidance he entrusted the people who were subject to him. Among these were men who were famous for learning and virtue, namely Sigfrid, Grimkell, Rudolf, and Bernhard.[1]

It is to be observed once more that none of these bears an Anglo-Saxon name: Sigfrid and Grimkell were doubtless natives of the Danelaw, of Norse blood, but English in culture and faith; Bernhard may have been a German from the country of the lower Rhine; Rudolf is said to have been a kinsman of Edward the Confessor; as his name is Norman, we shall have to conclude that he was a relative of Queen Emma, Edward's mother. Late in life he received from the Confessor an important appointment as abbot of Abingdon (1050).[2] So long as King Olaf lived Grimkell seems to have held the office of chief bishop.

These were the men who laid the foundation of the Norwegian Church; later missionaries from Britain continued the work along the earlier lines. The result was that the new Church came largely to be organised according to English models. Its ceremonial came to reflect Old English practices.

[1] Adamus, *Gesta*, ii., c. 55.
[2] *Anglo-Saxon Chronicle*, 1050. *Anglia Sacra*, i., 167.

13

Its terminology was formed according to Anglo-Saxon analogies.[1]   Characteristic of both the English and the Norse Church was an extensive use of the vernacular. And many remarkable parallels have been found in the church legislation of King Ethelred and the ecclesiastical laws attributed to Saint Olaf.[2]

It would seem most fitting that a church so intimately connected with English Christianity should pass under the metropolitan jurisdiction of the see at Canterbury, and such may have been Saint Olaf's original intention. But the establishment of Danish power at Winchester, the appointment of Canute's friend Ethelnoth to the primacy, and Canute's designs on the Norwegian throne made such an arrangement impractical. There was consequently nothing to do but to enter into relations with the see of Bremen. Adam tells us that Olaf sent an embassy[3] headed by Bishop Grimkell

with gifts to our archbishop and bearing the request that he receive these [English] bishops favourably

[1] An illustration of this appears on a runic monument at Odderness in Southern Norway raised in memory of a godson of Saint Olaf: "Oivind, Saint Olaf's godson [*kosunr* or *gosunr*] raised this church on his allodial land."

[2] For the account of the Anglo-Saxon missionaries I am indebted to Taranger's work on the influence of the Anglo-Saxon on the Norwegian Church: *Den Angelsaksiske Kirkes Indflydelse paa den norske.*

[3] *Gesta,* ii., c. 55; iv., c. 33. The embassy was probably sent some time during the years 1020–1023, and perhaps shortly before Canute accepted the supremacy of Hamburg-Bremen in Denmark.

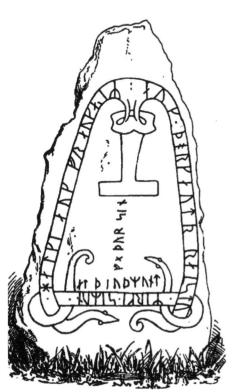

RUNIC MONUMENT SHOWS HAMMER OF THOR

THE ODDERNESS STONE

and send others of his own consecration that the rude Norwegian people might be strengthened in the Christian faith.

It is difficult to appreciate the tremendous social changes that the introduction of Christianity worked among the Northmen of the eleventh century. There was so much that was new in Christian practice that the adjustment was a difficult matter. The rigid observance of the seventh day; the numerous holidays; the frequent fasts and the long abstentions of Lent; the duties of confession and penance; the support of a new social class, the priests; all these things the unwilling convert found exceedingly irksome. In addition to this, there were certain prohibitions that also worked hardships: marriage within certain degrees of kinship; the exposure of children (except such as were born with deformities, who might be exposed after baptism); the eating of horseflesh, and other honoured Northern customs. Much that was heathen could not be rooted out. The churches were frequently built near the old sanctuaries and the new worship unavoidably came to be associated in many minds with much that was heathen.[1]

While Canute was organising the Church in Denmark, Olaf was striving to reshape Norwegian society and uproot the old faith. With force and

[1] This paragraph is summarised from Professor Bugge's discussion in *Norges Historie*, I., ii., 379–381.

fair words he won many for the new order, but
many more refused to receive baptism. Ten years
passed with growing discontent; so long as the nation was still heathen in morals and view of life,
resistance was inevitable. Finally the partisans
of the old rites and practices turned to Canute,
the great Christian King. And he who should
have been a defender of the faith heard their complaints with unfeigned joy.

CHAPTER IX

CANUTE AND THE NORWEGIAN CONSPIRACY

1023–1026

THE sons of Earl Hakon, Eric and Sweyn, who ruled Norway for fifteen years after the fall of Olaf Trygvesson, were not aggressive rulers. They were not of the blood royal, they were vassals of alien kings, both seem by nature to have been of an easy-going disposition; hence they were not able to command obedience to the extent that a strong monarchy demanded. As a result, the Norwegian aristocracy arrogated to itself a great measure of independence. The peasantry resumed their old habits and practices; in many places the old worship was wholly restored, including the sacrificial festivals. The Earls were Christians, but did not interfere.

Of a different type was King Olaf Haroldsson. He was determined and forceful, equipped with a vigorous intellect and a will that could brook no opposition. Though his policies extended far beyond the religious field, his chief anxiety was to make Norway a Christian kingdom. His zeal

was that of the convert, the passion of the devotee;
but it was more than that: it was the purpose of the
far-seeing statesman. In his viking adventures
he had become acquainted with the advantages
of the European political system. He wished to
introduce this into his own kingdom, to Euro-
peanise Norway. This was the great king-thought
for which Saint Olaf lived and fell. But at the
basis of the European system lay Christianity.
In his proselyting endeavours, he met opposition
from the very beginning; but for a time he was
able to overcome all resistance. However, the
spirit of rebellion was silenced only; after five years
of missionary effort, King Olaf found that Christian progress was apparent rather than real. He
also found that the devotees of the old worship
were still determined and that a group of chiefs
were organising an opposition that might overturn
his throne.

The opposition was of two sorts: on the one hand
the Christian was opposed by the partisan of the
old gods; on the other hand Olaf's strong kingship
was disliked by the chiefs who recalled the freedom that they had enjoyed in the days of the two
earls. Distances were great in Norway; travel
was difficult; the ocean was the best highway.
But with sail and oar it took time to reach the
settlements on the long coast line, and the King
soon learned that promises to renounce the Anses
were easily forgotten or broken. Then followed
crop failures in the far North: it was clear that

Frey was angry and wished to punish the apostacy of his people.[1]

In the aristocratic opposition five chieftains bear special prominence. At Soli on the wide plains of Jæderen in South-western Norway, not far from the modern city of Stavanger, lived Erling, the son of Skjalg. Erling had sailed with King Olaf to Wendland, but had had no part in the fight at Swald. Later the Earls found it advisable to make peace with the Soli family and gave Erling Skjalgsson a magnificent fief in the South-west. From the Naze to the Sogn Firth his was the ruling influence. Of all the Norwegian magnates Erling was unquestionably the most powerful; and though both Earl Eric and King Olaf had looked askance at his power, he maintained his position for a quarter of a century. Five active sons and a spirited daughter grew up in Erling's house. The lord of Soli never was an ideal subject; but after his nephew Asbjörn slew one of King Olaf's servants in the royal presence during the Easter festivities, a quarrel broke out that had fatal consequences.[2]

The island of Giski some distance north of Cape Stadt was the ancestral seat of the famous Arnung family, which for several generations held a prominent place in the councils of Norway. According to tradition the family was founded by one Finnvid who was found in an eagle's nest, and hence was known as Finnvid Found. The family

[1] Snorre, *Saga of Saint Olaf*, c. 106.
[2] *Ibid.*, cc. 22, 23, 116 ff.

took its name from Arne, a prominent chief in Saint Olaf's day and a good friend of the King. Seven sons and a daughter were born to Arne and his good wife Thora. The oldest of the sons married the only daughter of the mighty Erling. Arne's daughter became the wife of another prominent lord and enemy of Olaf, Harek of Tjotta. For a time all the sons of Arne supported the King and Kalf alone finally joined his enemies. Olvi of Egg, a wealthy Thronder, was found to have continued the old sacrificial practices in secret, and on the King's orders was slain. Kalf Arnesson married his widow, and from that day his loyalty was shaken.[1]

Far to the north lived two chiefs who were also counted among the King's opponents: Harek of Tjotta and Thor the Dog. Thor was the ill-fated Asbjörn's uncle and the brother-in-law of the slain Olvi. He lived on the Bark-isle beyond the Arctic Circle and was easily the most powerful man in those regions.[2] Harek lived on the isle of Tjotta, a little to the south of the Polar Circle. He seems to have had something of a monopoly of the Finnish trade and from this and other sources amassed great wealth. In the Norse nobility few stood higher than Harek: he counted among his kinsmen the reigning King as well as his predecessors the Earls.[3] In the rebellion that finally

---

[1] Snorre, *Saga of Saint Olaf*, cc. 106–110.
[2] *Ibid.*, c. 106.   [3] *Ibid.*, c. 104.

cost King Olaf his life, Thor and Harek were prominent leaders.

In the Throndelaw, some distance south of Nidaros, dwelt Einar Thongshaker. Einar, the strongest and most athletic Norseman of his day, the archer who could pierce a damp ox-hide with a blunt shaft, was also a man of great personal influence. Married to Earl Eric's sister, he was naturally in sympathy with the dynastic claims of the Earl's family. For some years after the defeat at the Nesses, he had lived in exile in Sweden; but finally he was reconciled to King Olaf and was permitted to return.[1]

It does not appear that any of these leaders had any enthusiasm for the old faith; Erling Skjalgsson and Einar Thongshaker seem to have been zealous Christians. But among their kinsmen were many who clung to the worship of Woden and Thor. Wherever the King found heathen rites celebrated in open or secret, harsh measures were employed—loss of property, of limb, and even of life. Thus the chiefs saw many a kinsman dishonoured or dead, and to their disinclination to obey the royal mandate was joined the motive of private revenge. Soon dissatisfaction was rife everywhere, and over the North Sea fled yearly a band of exiles who had resisted the royal will.

Among those who went west was Einar Thong-

[1] On the subject of the Norse chiefs in King Olaf's day, see Munch, *Det norske Folks Historie*, I., ii., 659–670; *Norges Historie*, I., ii., 340–348.

skaker, though he went ostensibly as a pilgrim, not as a plotter. Soon after his return from Sweden he found it advisable to seek expiation at Rome for earlier sins, and in 1022 or 1023 he left for the Eternal City. It seems probable that his brother-in-law Eric joined him in this expedition or planned to do so, for the sagas persist in connecting Eric's death, which must have occurred about 1023, with a pilgrimage to Rome, at least projected and perhaps carried out. In England Einar is said to have visited young Earl Hakon, possibly in his earldom in the Severn Valley; he also had an interview with Canute "and was given great gifts."[1] Einar's visit was probably just after Canute's return from his expedition to the Slavic lands. Whether the pilgrimage was more than a mere pretext we do not know, though it probably was made in good faith. After his return to Norway he was not active in King Olaf's service, though he showed no open hostility.

Many magnates or sons of prominent franklins had fared to Canute on various errands; but all who came to King Canute were given their hands full of wealth. There one could see greater splendour than elsewhere, both as to the multitude of people in daily attendance and in the other arrangements on the manors that he possessed and occupied. Canute the Mighty gathered tribute from the lands that were

[1] Snorre, *Saga of Saint Olaf*, c. 121. According to Snorre's reckoning, he left in the summer of 1023 and returned the following summer.

the richest in the North; but in the same measure as
he had more to receive than other kings, he also gave
much more than any other king. . . .

But many of those who came from Norway lamented
the loss of their liberties and hinted to Earl Hakon
and some to the King himself, that the men of Norway
were now surely ready to renew their allegiance to
King Canute and the Earl, and to receive their old
liberties from them.   These speeches suited the Earl's
mind, and he suggested to Canute that Olaf be called
on to surrender the kingdom to them, or to agree to
divide it.[1]

Snorre attributes Canute's delay in claiming the
Norse kingship to a difference between himself and
his cousin, Earl Hakon, as to who should possess
and rule the country.   It is evident, however,
that before 1023 Canute was hardly in a position
to press a claim of such a doubtful character.
But in that year the situation was more favourable:
he was in uncontested possession of the English
and Danish crowns; he had successfully fought
and subdued the Slavs to the south of Denmark;
his prestige was consequently greater than ever
before.   That year, the subject of Norse conquest
must have been discussed quite seriously at
Winchester, for as soon as the winter was past, an
embassy was on its way to King Olaf's court to
demand the kingdom of Norway for Canute.

Among the various regions that composed the
Norwegian realm, two enjoyed a peculiar promin-

[1] Snorre, *Saga of Saint Olaf*, c. 130.

ence: the Wick and the Throndelaw. The Throndelaw was a group of "folks" or shires about the Throndhjem Firth, a region that had developed considerable solidarity and in one sense was reckoned as the heart of the kingdom. Here was for some time the capital of the nation, as it has remained in ecclesiastical matters to this day, at least nominally. The Wick was the country that bordered on the great "Bay" in the extreme south. It was this region that first came into contact with European civilisation and where culture and Christianity had perhaps taken firmest root. In a sense the Wick was disputed territory: it had earlier been under Danish overlordship, and a part of it had also for a brief period been subject to Sweden; national feeling was therefore not strong on these shores. For this reason, perhaps, King Olaf had established a royal residence at Tunsberg near the mouth of the Firth on the western shore. Here the King held his court in the winter of 1024–1025; it was here that he received the English embassy.

It was a splendid company that Canute sent to Norway, but Olaf was not pleased with their errand. For several days he kept them waiting before he was willing to grant them an audience.

But when they were permitted to speak with him they brought into his presence Canute's writ and recited their message, that Canute claims all of Norway as his possession and asserts that his ancestors

have possessed the realm before him; but whereas
King Canute offers peace to all lands, he will not fare
to Norway with war shields if another choice is
possible. But if King Olaf Haroldsson wishes to rule
Norway, let him fare to King Canute and receive the
land from him as a fief and become his man and pay
such tribute as the earls had earlier paid.[1]

Such a proposal was an insult to the Norse
nation, and it is not likely that Canute expected
a favourable reply. But in its apparent modera-
tion, in its appeal to historic rights, the demand
served well the intended purpose: to extort a
challenge that would make hostilities unavoidable
and make Olaf appear as the aggressor. King
Olaf's anger did not permit a diplomatic reply:

I have heard tell in olden story that Gorm the Dane-
king was an excellent ruler, but he ruled Denmark
only; but the Dane-kings who have come since his
day do not seem to have been satisfied with that.
It has come to this now that Canute rules Denmark
and England and in addition has subjected a large
part of Scotland. Now he challenges my inheritance.
He should, however, learn to be moderate in his
avarice,—or does he plan to govern all the Northlands
alone? Or does he intend to eat alone all the cabbage
in England? He will be able to accomplish that before
I shall pay him tribute or do him any sort of homage.
Now you shall tell him these my words, that I will
defend Norway with point and edge as long as life

[1] Snorre, *Saga of Saint Olaf*, c. 131.

days are granted me; but never shall I pay tribute for my kingdom to any man.[1]

Such is Snorre's account. The speeches are doubtless the historian's own; but they reveal a keen insight into the shrewd diplomacy of Canute and the impetuous methods of Olaf. The ambassadors soon prepared to retire, little pleased with the outcome. It is reported that in conversation with Sighvat the Scald they expressed their surprise at the Norse King's rashness. The lord of England was gentle and forgiving.

Only recently two kings came from north in Scotland, from Fife, and he laid aside his wrath and let them keep all the lands that they had earlier possessed and gave them great gifts of friendship in addition.

The poet later put his reply into verse:

> Able kings have carried
> Their heads to Canute, coming
> From Fife in the far north
> (Fair was the purchase of peace).
> Olaf has never sold
> (Oft has the stout one conquered)
> Here in the whole world
> His head to any man.[2]

There could be no question about unpeace after Olaf's defiance had been repeated to Canute. It is said that Norsemen looked on cabbage eaters

[1] Snorre, *Saga of Saint Olaf*, c. 131.
[2] *Corpus Poeticum Boreale*, ii., 133-134.

as naturally stupid; hence the taunt, if given, had a sharp point. The great King is said to have remarked that Olaf should find something besides cabbage within his ribs. That summer two of Erling's sons, Aslak and Skjalg, appeared at the English court. "And King Canute gave the brothers large revenues."[1]

During the succeeding summer (1025) King Olaf remained in the South. Rumour had it that Canute was coming from England with a powerful host, and the Norwegian King made preparations to meet him. The chiefs were summoned to the Wick and seem to have appeared with their retainers in large numbers. Olaf's spies were everywhere on the lookout for the English fleet. Merchant ships were eagerly sought for news. But Canute was not yet ready to fight and did not appear before autumn. He spent the winter in Denmark but mainly for precautionary purposes; hostile activities were evidently to be postponed to a more favourable time.[2]

That same autumn Olaf approached the King of Sweden on the subject of an alliance against the ambitious King of Denmark. The young Anund Jacob, King Olaf's brother-in-law and admirer, was now on the Swedish throne. It was easy to convince the youthful King that his realm would not long be left in peace should Canute succeed in adding Norway to his dominions. An alliance was accordingly concluded: the king who should

[1] Snorre, *Saga of Saint Olaf*, c. 131.   [2] *Ibid.*

first need assistance should have the other's help.
A conference was also arranged for, as more
definite plans would have to be agreed upon. That
year King Olaf prepared to winter at Sarpsborg,
just across the firth from Tunsberg. King Anund
made a winter journey into Gautland toward the
Norse frontier, and tarried there for some months.
During his stay there, envoys appeared from
Canute with gifts and fair words. Anund was
assured of peace and security if he would renounce
his alliance with the Norsemen. But this embassy also had to return with unsatisfactory reports: Anund intended to be faithful to his pledge;
no friendship for Denmark was to be looked for in
Sweden.[1]

Spring came (1026) and developments were
looked for; but the unexpected happened: Canute
returned to England, leaving his young son Harthacanute, a boy of eight or nine years, as regent in
Denmark under the guardianship of Ulf, Canute's
brother-in-law, who seems to have succeeded
Thurkil the Tall as viceroy in Denmark. The
allied kings now proceeded to hold their projected
conference at Kingscrag, near the south-east corner
of Olaf's kingdom. In this conference a new
agreement seems to have been reached; the
defensive alliance was apparently changed to an

[1] Snorre, *Saga of Saint Olaf*, c. 132. The legendary *Olafs-saga*
tells us that the gifts were two golden candlesticks, a golden dish
highly jewelled for the table service, and two gold rings. Anund
is said to have remarked that he did not wish to sell Olaf for a dish.

ORNAMENTS (CHIEFLY BUCKLES) FROM THE VIKING AGE

ORNAMENTS (CHIEFLY BUCKLES) FROM THE VIKING AGE

offensive one and an attack on Canute's Danish possessions was planned.[1]

Why Canute failed to attack Norway in the autumn of 1025, or in the following spring, is not known. It seems, however, a fairly safe conjecture that he felt unprepared to meet the allied forces. He evidently preferred to wait until the spirit of disaffection and rebellion had spread more widely in Norway; for thus far only the great house of Soli had openly espoused the pretender's cause; most of the dissatisfied lords were in King Olaf's host. Doubtless he also hoped that by diplomatic means or otherwise dissension might be sown between the confederated kings, and their alliance dissolved.

Gold was the power that Canute depended upon to prepare rebellion in Norway. That the Danish King employed bribery in these years to a large extent is a well-attested fact. Florence of Worcester who wrote three generations later recounts how gold was distributed among the Norwegian chiefs in the hope that they would permit Canute to rule over them, though Florence is clearly misinformed when he tells us that the Norsemen had renounced their allegiance to King Olaf because of his simplicity and gentleness.[2] Olaf was a saint when the scribe at Worcester wrote his history; but he was not a saint of the ideal sort, and hence Florence is led into error.

[1] Snorre, *Saga of Saint Olaf*, c. 134.
[2] Florence of Worcester, *Chronicon*, i., 184.

14

Richard of Cirencester, too, has heard of these proceedings and the "great supply of gold and silver that was sent to the magnates of that country."[1] Both writers represent the Norsemen as eager for the bribes. The sagas, of course, give fuller details. The result was that King Olaf's forces to some extent were made up of men whose loyalty had been undermined, who were in the pay of the enemy. The following year (1027), the year when the most Christian monarch made his pilgrimage to the tomb of Peter, seems to have seen the greatest activity in this direction; but the probabilities are that large sums of Danegeld had found their way to Norway also in the earlier two or three years.

[1] *Speculum Historiale*, ii., 178.

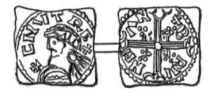

CHAPTER X

THE BATTLE OF HOLY RIVER AND THE PILGRIMAGE
TO ROME

1026–1027

ONE of the notable results of the expedition
to the South Baltic in 1022 was that a
reconciliation was effected with Thurkil the Tall.
"And he gave Denmark into the keeping of Thurkil and his son; and the King brought Thurkil's
son with him to England."[1] The son who was
thus made regent was probably Sweyn; it was
scarcely Harthacanute, as this Prince was present
at the translation of Saint Alphege from London
to Canterbury that same year (1023); of Canute's
other son, Harold Harefoot, we hear nothing until
after the King's death. The hostage that Canute
took with him to England may have been Harold
who played an important part in Northern history
two decades later. Thurkil cannot have lived
long after his promotion to the vice-royalty, for
three years later (1026), we find Harthacanute
representing royal authority in Denmark with

[1] *Anglo-Saxon Chronicle*, 1023.

Earl Ulf as guardian and actual wielder of power. This change in the regency we may, perhaps, ascribe to the activities of Queen Emma, one of whose chief purposes in life was to disinherit her husband's illegitimate offspring.

The next few months seem to have witnessed a revolution in Denmark: Earl Ulf appears to have summoned a national assembly at Viborg, an old sanctuary in the north central part of Jutland, where he announced that it was Canute's desire to have his young eight-year-old son chosen and proclaimed King of Denmark. With evident success he argued that the ancient kingdom, which always had had a ruler within its borders, was poorly served by the present arrangement of subjection to an absentee-king. He also called attention to the threatened invasion from the allied kingdoms of Norway and Sweden. The sagas assert that Queen Emma had plotted with Earl Ulf to secure the royal name for her son and that she had even forged a document to support the move. The assembly assented and Hartha-canute was proclaimed King.[1]

There are suggestions that Ulf at this time was in communication with the allied monarchs and that he had even encouraged them to invade the Danish territories. Evidence is wanting, but it is clear that Ulf's activities in 1026 were not of the proper sort.[2] The Earl was an ambitious and

[1] Snorre, *Saga of Saint Olaf*, c. 148.
[2] Steenstrup, *Normannerne*, iii., 349.

turbulent man, closely connected with both the Danish and the Swedish dynasties. He was a man of the type that finds service difficult; it is clear that Canute suspected him of treason.

After Canute's departure for England the Northern kings had their conference at Kingscrag where a closer alliance was formed and offensive operations were probably determined upon. Soon afterwards King Olaf was on his way to his northern capital to raise the host for a grand effort. It seems that the chiefs quite generally obeyed the summons; of the leaders in the northern shires Einar Thongshaker alone remained at home on his estates. A considerable fleet gathered at the rendezvous at the mouth of Throndhjem Firth; as it sailed southward there were constant additions, till it finally counted 480 ships. The royal flagship was the *Bison*, a longship that had been built the winter before, the prow of which bore the head of a bison adorned with gold.

On the journey southward, King Olaf learned that Canute was still in England, but that he was making preparations for a grand attack. He also learned that Erling Skjalgsson was now with his sons in the enemy's service. But no one knew when the English host might be expected; time passed and the Norsemen began to tire of inaction. Accordingly King Olaf dismissed the least effective part of his forces and with the remainder, sixty large and well-manned ships, sailed for the coast of Zealand, expecting later to join the Swedish armament that had gathered on the Scanian coast.[1]

Meanwhile, Canute had hastened his preparations. One of his Scanian subjects, Hakon of Stangeby, had, when the plans of the enemy had become evident, hastened to England to warn his King. It is said that Canute rewarded him with an estate in Scania for his loyalty and promptness.[2] It was a mighty fleet that sailed from southern England that summer; Canute led the expedition in person with Earl Hakon apparently as second in command. Snorre reports that Canute's ship had one hundred and twenty oars, while that of the Earl had eighty. Both ships were provided with golden figureheads; but their sails were counted particularly splendid with their stripes of blue and red and green.

Earl Ulf had by this time come to realise that Denmark could not afford to ignore the Lord of England. There was evidently much dissatisfaction with the Earl's régime, for we find that the Danes in large numbers accepted the invaders. Ulf and Harthacanute soon retreated to Jutland, and left the islands and Scania to the enemy.

The situation that Canute found when he sailed into the Lime Firth was perhaps not wholly a surprise; he must have known something about what his deputy had been plotting and doing.

[1] Snorre, *Saga of Saint Olaf*, c. 144.
[2] Saxo, *Gesta Danorum*, 347–348. There seems to be no reason to doubt that Saxo here reports a reliable tradition.

That he was angry is evident; that his wrath was
feared is also clear. Harthacanute was advised
to submit; he knelt before his father and obtained
forgiveness, as the King realised that no responsi-
bility could lodge with a witless boy. Ulf also
tried to make terms with the offended monarch,
but was merely told to collect his forces and join
in the defence of the kingdom; later he might
propose terms.

Such is Snorre's account[1]; it may be inaccurate
in details, but the main fact that Earl Ulf was
faithless to his trust seems to be correctly stated.
Elsewhere, too, Ulf is accused of opposition to his
King: Saxo charges him with treason[2]; and an
entry in the *Anglo-Saxon Chronicle* tells us that
Canute went east to fight Ulf and Eglaf.[3]   There
has been some dispute as to the identity of these
chiefs, but unless evidence to the contrary is
forthcoming, we shall have to conclude that they
were the two brothers who were earls in England
in the early days of Canute as English king.
Shortly before this (1024), Eglaf's name disappears
from the English sources. The Chronicler was
evidently not informed as to the situation in the
North; but he knew that the two brothers were
among the opponents of the King and recorded
what he knew.

Meanwhile, Olaf was on the shores of Zealand
with his longships. Saxo relates that one day

---

[1] *Saga of Saint Olaf*, c. 148.   [2] *Gesta Danorum*, 347 ff.
[3] Entry for the year 1025; this should be corrected to 1026.

while he was addressing the Danes at a public assembly with a view to winning them to his own allegiance, spies rushed up and reported that they had seen several ships approaching. An aged Dane assured the King that the ships were merchantmen only; but when sails in growing numbers began to cross the horizon, he added that they were merchantmen who had come to buy Denmark with iron.[1]

From the Lime Firth, Canute must have sailed his fleet southeastward to the upper entrance of the Sound; at any rate, King Olaf soon discovered that the homeward route had been effectually blocked. There was now nothing to do but to continue the journey eastward and to form a junction with King Anund's fleet which was harrying the Scanian coast. Canute must have followed in hot pursuit, for before the enemies could form a junction he seems to have found and defeated a part of the Swedish fleet at Stangeberg.[2] A little later, he came up with the combined strength of the allied Kings near the mouth of Holy River.

Holy River is a short stream in the eastern part of Scania that serves as the outlet of a group of lakes not far inland. Between these lakes and the sea the forest was heavy enough to conceal any activities inland. When the Kings learned that the Danish fleet was approaching, they took counsel and decided to draw up their ships in battle order

[1] *Gesta Danorum*, 348. [2] *Ibid.*

east of the river mouth, but to act on the defensive. King Anund was to remain in charge of the fleet while King Olaf, who is reputed to have been something of a military engineer, went inland to prepare a trap for the enemy. Where the river left the lakes he is said to have built a temporary dam of trees and turf, and he also improved the outlets of some of the smaller lakes, so as to increase the water masses behind the dam. Many days the work continued under Olaf's direction. Then came the message that Canute had arrived and the Norsemen hastened to their ships.

It was late in the afternoon when Anund's spies finally caught sight of the great armament approaching from the west. Swift-footed couriers at once left for the lakes to inform Olaf, who immediately prepared to break the dam, at the same time filling the course with large trees. Canute saw the enemy drawn up in line and ready for the fight; but it was then too late to proceed to the attack; moreover, the enemy had the advantage of a carefully chosen position. The Dane therefore refused battle that day. Finding the harbour at the river mouth empty, he sailed into it with as many ships as could be accommodated; the remainder were left just outside.

At dawn the next morning, a large part of Canute's forces was found to have landed; some were conversing, others seeking amusement. Then without the least warning the waters came down in torrents,

dashing the floating trees against the ships.   The ships
were injured and the waters overflowed the river
banks, drowning the men who had gone on land and
also many who were still on the ships.   Those who
were able to do so cut the ropes and allowed their
ships to drift, each in its own direction.   The great
dragon that Canute himself commanded was among
these; it was not easily managed by the oars alone
and drifted out toward the hostile fleet.   But when
the allies recognised the ship, they immediately
surrounded it; but it was not easily attacked, for the
ship was high like a castle and had a number of men
on board, who were carefully chosen, thoroughly
armed, and very reliable.   It was not long before
Earl Ulf came up alongside with his ships and men
and the battle was now joined in earnest.   Canute's
forces now came up from all sides.   Then the Kings
Olaf and Anund realised that they had now won as
much as fate had allowed them for this time; so they
ordered a retreat, withdrew from Canute's fleet, and
separated from the fight.[1]

In its disorganised condition Canute's host
could make no effective pursuit.   The Danes and
English had suffered heavy losses, while those of
the Swedes and Norsemen were slight; still their
combined forces were yet inferior to those of
Canute.   It was, therefore, agreed to avoid
further battle.   Eastward the course continued,
the intention being to stop for the night in the
harbour of Barwick on the coast of Bleking.

[1] Snorre, *Saga of Saint Olaf*, c. 150.

However, a large part of the Swedish fleet did not enter the harbour, but continued the journey eastward and northward; nor were the sails lowered before the chiefs had reached their respective homes.

Early the following morning, King Anund ordered the signal to be sounded for a council of the remaining chiefs. The entire army landed and the assembly proceeded to discuss the situation. King Anund announced that of 420 ships that had joined him in the preceding summer only 120 were now in the harbour. These with the sixty Norwegian ships did not make a force sufficient for successful operations against Canute. The Swedish King therefore proposed to Olaf that he should spend the winter in Sweden, and in the spring, perhaps, they might be able to renew hostilities. Olaf demurred: the former viking could not surrender his purposes so readily; it would still be possible, he argued, to defeat Canute as his large fleet would soon be compelled to scatter in search of provisions, his eastern coasts having been too recently harried to afford much in the way of supplies. But the outcome was that Olaf left his ships in Sweden and returned to Norway overland.

Canute kept informed as to the situation in the enemies' fleet and army but did not attempt pursuit. It would seem that a great opportunity was thus permitted to slip past; but the King probably did not so regard it. To fight the Swedes was not a part of his present plan; his hope was to detach King Anund from his more vigorous ally. When he learned that the hostile fleet was about to dissolve, he returned to Zealand and blocked the Sound, hoping, no doubt, to intercept the Norwegian King on his return northward. As we have seen, however, Olaf appreciated the danger and refused to risk an ambush. That same season saw him on the march through south-western Sweden to his manors on the shores of the great Firth. On his arrival in his own land, he dismissed the larger part of his host; only a small body of trusted men including several prominent magnates remained with him at Sarpsborg, where he prepared to spend the winter.[1]

Of this campaign we have, broadly speaking, but one detailed account,—the one given in the sagas. As these are far from contemporary, doubts have been cast upon the story, but in the main it seems reliable. That there was a battle at Holy River we know from the *Anglo-Saxon Chronicle*, which states that Canute was defeated at that place by Ulf and Eglaf supported by a large force of Swedes. As to the strategic device of King Olaf, we cannot be so sure; but the account in the sagas reveals a topographical knowledge so specific as to argue strongly for the belief that the authors must have had access to reliable sources. There is also a question as to the date of the battle: Snorre seems to place it in 1027; the *Old English*

[1] Snorre, *Saga of Saint Olaf*, cc. 154-159.

Chronicle has it in 1025.   The battle seems to have
been fought some time in September, 1026.   It
evidently occurred before Canute made his pilgrimage to Rome, where we find him at Easter,
1027.

Though Canute suffered a defeat at Holy River,
the outcome gave no advantage to his enemies.
The Swedes were discouraged and tired of a conflict which, after all, did not seem to concern them.
King Olaf was discredited: a King who had abandoned his ships was not in position to claim a
victory.   From that day he found disloyalty
everywhere.   The pretender had only to appear
on the Norwegian coasts with ships and men to
secure the enthusiastic allegiance of the rebellious
Norsemen.

Canute was not prepared, however, to move
against Olaf at this time.   Autumn was coming on,
a season that was far too short for naval operations.   And soon a tragedy was enacted at the
Danish court, the consequences of which probably
caused a complete rearrangement of Canute's
immediate plans.   The day before Michaelmas
the King proceeded to Roeskild, where Earl Ulf
had prepared an elaborate entertainment for him
and his train.   According to the sagas Ulf was
aggressive, vigorous, and brave; but he was also
tactless and careless in speech, and possessed a
temper that was not easily controlled.   The festivities did not seem to please the King—he was
moody and silent.   In the evening Ulf suggested

a game of chess, hoping, no doubt, that the play would help to restore the royal good humour.

But as they were playing at chess, King Canute and Earl Ulf, the King made a wrong move and the Earl took one of his knights. The King moved his opponent's chessman back and told him to make another play; this angered the Earl; he overturned the chessboard, rose, and left the table. Then said the King, "Are you running away now, timid Wolf!" The Earl turned in the doorway and replied, "Farther you would have run at Holy River, if you had been able. You did not then call Ulf timid, when I rushed up to help you, when the Swedes were threshing you and your men like dogs." With that the Earl left the room and went to sleep.[1]

It is not likely, however, that the Earl's rest was wholly undisturbed that night, for in the morning he was found to have sought sanctuary in Holy Trinity Church. Nor did sleep appease the King's anger; while he was dressing the next morning, he ordered his shoe-swain to go at once and slay Ulf. But the servant dared not strike him within the sacred precincts. Then the King called Ivar White, one of his guardsmen, a Norseman who is said to have been Earl Eric's nephew,[2] and sent him with similar orders. Ivar soon returned to the King with a bloody sword as evidence that his sister's husband was no more.

[1] Snorre, *Saga of Saint Olaf*, c. 153.
[2] Munch, *Det Norske Folks Historie*, I., ii., 737.

Lines from the oldest fragment of Snorre's History (written about 1260). The fragment tells the story of the battle of Holy River and the murder of Ulf.

A LONGSHIP
(Model of the Gokstad ship on the waves.)

Tales of chess games that have resulted seriously for at least one of the players appear elsewhere in mediæval literature; hence it would not be safe to accept this account without question. Still, there is nothing improbable about the tale; the insult that Ulf offered was evidently seized upon by the King as a pretext for ridding himself of a man whom he believed to be a traitor. An independent English tradition credits Canute with a passion for the game: the historian of Ramsey tells us that Bishop Ethelric once found him "relieving the wearisomeness of the long night with games of dice and chess."[1] Nor is there any reason to doubt that Ulf was actually assassinated at the time; his name disappears from the sources.

A life had been taken in God's own house; blood had been shed before the very altar; even though the King had ordered it, the Church could not overlook the crime. The priests immediately closed the church; but on the King's command, it was again opened and mass was said as before. It is recorded that large possessions were added to the church when services were resumed. To his sister the widowed Estrid, the King also owed satisfaction; we are told that she, too, received large landed estates. But her young son Sweyn, who was at this time scarcely more than eight years old, she prudently seems to have removed from her brother's kingdom; for twelve years the

[1] *Historia Rameseiensis*, 137.

future King of Denmark was a guest at the Swedish court.[1]

It seems that the scene of his recent guilt had small attraction for Canute after that fateful Michaelmas season.   He is said to have left the city and to have taken up his abode on his longship. But not many months later we find him on a pilgrimage to the capital of Christendom.   The journey must have been planned during the autumn of 1026; it was actually undertaken during the early months of the following year; apparently the pilgrims arrived in Rome toward the end of March.

We cannot be sure what induced King Canute to make this journey at this particular time.   In his message to the English people he says that he went to seek forgiveness for his sins; but this pious phrase is almost a rhetorical necessity in mediæval documents and must not be regarded too seriously. Nor can we trust the statement that the King had earlier vowed to make such a pilgrimage, but had hitherto been prevented by business of state; for the year 1027 had surely but little to offer in the way of leisure and peace.   The motive must be sought in the political situation that had developed in the North in the year of the Holy River campaign, and in the strained relations that must have arisen between the King and the Church.

No doubt the eyes of the Christian world looked approvingly on the persistent efforts that Olaf

[1] Adamus, *Gesta*, ii., c. 71.

of Norway, who was canonised four years later,
was making to extirpate heathendom in the North.
Especially must the English priesthood have
looked with pride and pleasure on the vigorous
growth of the Norse daughter Church.   But here
comes the Christian King of England with hostile
forces to interfere in behalf of King Olaf's enemies.
Canute probably protested that he would carry
on the work; but it is clear that an absent monarch
with wide imperial interests could scarcely hope
to carry out successfully a policy that implied
revolution both socially and religiously.   His
hand had also been raised against the Christian
ruler of Sweden, which was yet a heathen land,
against a prince in whom the Church doubtless
reposed confidence and hope.   Perhaps worst of
all, Canute's hand was red with the blood of his
sister's husband, his support at Holy River, whose
life had been taken in violation of the right
of sanctuary and sacred peace.   The mediæval
Church was a sensitive organism and offences of
this sort were not easily atoned for.   It was time
to pray at Saint Peter's tomb.   It is also likely
that Canute hoped to gain certain political advantages from the journey: in a strife with the Northern powers it would be well to have the Emperor a
passive if not an active ally; and this was the year
of the imperial coronation.

Norse tradition remembers Canute's pilgrimage
as that of a penitent: "he took staff and scrip,
as did all the men who travelled with him, and

15

journeyed southward to Rome; and the Emperor himself came out to meet him and he accompanied him all the way to the Roman city."[1] Sighvat the Scald, who was both Canute's and Olaf's friend, also mentions the pilgrim's staff in his reference to the royal pilgrimage.[2] Still, it is not to be thought that gold was overlooked in preparing for the journey: the saga adds that "King Canute had many horses with him laden with gold and silver," and that alms were distributed with a free hand.

The Encomiast, who saw the King in the monastery of Saint Bertin in the Flemish city of Saint-Omer, also gives us a picture, though one that is clearly exaggerated, of a penitent who is seeking forgiveness and reconciliation. With humble mien the royal pilgrim entered the holy precincts; his eyes cast down and streaming with tears, he implored the suffrages of the saints; beating his breast and heaving sighs, he passed from altar to altar, kissed the sacred stones, and left large gifts upon each, even upon the smallest. In addition alms were distributed among the needy.[3]

The route followed was the old one from Denmark south-westward along the German coast to Flanders, whence the journey went southward through Lorraine and the Rhone country. It

---

[1] *Fagrskinna*, c. 33.

[2] *Corpus Poeticum Boreale*, ii., 136. The statement in *Fagrskinna* is probably based on Sighvat's verses.

[3] *Encomium Emmæ*, ii., c. 20.

seems to have been Canute's intention to visit King Rudolf of Burgundy on the way; but he was found to have departed on a similar journey to the Eternal City. The progress was one that was doubtless long remembered in the monasteries along the route. Important institutions at some distance from the chosen route seem also to have been remembered in a substantial way; it may have been on this occasion that a gift was sent to the monastic foundation at Chartres, of which we have grateful acknowledgment in the Epistles of Bishop Fulbert[1]; and another to the church at Cologne, a costly psalter and sacramentary which some time later found their way back to England.[2]

On Easter Day (March 26), King Canute assisted at the imperial coronation ceremony; on that day King Conrad and Queen Gisela received the imperial crowns in the Church of the Holy Apostles.[3] The assembly was large and splendid and the visiting sovereigns held places of conspicuous honour. When the Emperor at the close of the ceremony left the Church, Canute and Rudolf walked beside him. It was a day of great re-

---

[1] Migne, *Patrologia Latina*, cxli, col. 231. As to its date the letter furnishes no clue. Bishop Fulbert died, according to Migne's calculations, in April, 1029, two years after Canute's journey.

[2] Wharton, *Anglia Sacra*, ii., 249; William of Malmesbury's *Vita Wulstani*. The manuscripts were illuminated by Erven, scholasticus of Peterborough.

[3] Giesebrecht, *Geschichte der deutschen Kaiserzeit*, ii., 241–243. For a collection of the relevant texts, see Bresslau's *Jahrbücher des deutschen Reichs unter Konrad II.*, i., 139.

joicing among Conrad's German followers, ending, as was customary, with a fight between them and their Roman hosts.

On the 6th of April, a great synod met at the Lateran to consider various weighty matters and to settle certain important controversies. It may have been at this meeting, though preliminary negotiations must have prepared the matter to some extent, that King Canute or his spokesman stated the complaints of the English Church. For one thing he urged that the price extorted from the English archbishops for the pallium was too high. The Pope promised to reduce the charges on condition that Peter's pence be regularly paid. Apparently the curia urged reform in church dues generally, for a little later Canute sent his English subjects a sharp reminder on this point. The Pope also agreed to exempt the English school at Rome from the customary tribute. On the whole it seems, however, that the more substantial results of the negotiations remained with the Roman curia.

The English King had another set of grievances which seem to have been discussed in the same synod, but which particularly interested the ruler of Burgundy. English and Danish pilgrims, he asserted, were not given fair and considerate treatment on their journeys to Rome: they were afflicted with unjust tolls and with overcharges at the inns; evidently Canute also felt that the highways should be made safer and justice more

accessible to those who travelled on holy errands.
In the matter of undue charges, the Burgundians
appear to have been especially guilty. The rea-
sonableness of Canute's request was apparent to
the synod, and it was decreed that the treatment of
pilgrims should be liberal and just:

and all the princes have engaged by their edict, that
my men, whether merchants or other travellers for
objects of devotion, should go and return in security
and peace, without any constraint of barriers or tolls.[1]

From Rome, Canute hurried back to Denmark,
following the same route, it seems, as on the
journey south. Soon after his return he sent a
message to the English clergy and people, advising
them as to his absence and doings in Italy.[2] From
the use of the phrase, "here in the East" in speaking
of the Scandinavian difficulties, it seems likely that
the message was composed in Denmark or some-
where on the route not far from that kingdom.
It was carried to England by Bishop Lifing of
Crediton. In this document Canute also recounts
the honours bestowed upon him in Italy; especially
does he recall the presents of Emperor Conrad:
"divers costly gifts, as well in golden and silver

---

[1] See Appendix ii.: Canute's Charter of 1027.

[2] The Anglo-Saxon original of Canute's Charter has been lost.
Our oldest version is a Latin translation inserted into the Chronicle
of Florence of Worcester (see Liebermann, *Gesetze der Angelsachsen*, i., 276, 277). Most of our information as to Canute's
pilgrimage comes from this document.

vessels as in mantles and vestments exceedingly
precious."

The document also asks that the lawful church-
dues be regularly paid,—Peter's pence, plough alms,
church scot, and tithes of the increase of animals
and of farm products.   This admonition was later
enacted into law.   At the same time he forbids
his sheriffs and other officials to do injustice to
any one, rich or poor, either in the hope of winning
the royal favour or to gain wealth for the King.
He has no need of wealth that has been unjustly
acquired.   But this lofty assertion of principle
looks somewhat strange in the light of the fact
that the King was in those very days engaged in
bribing a nation.

There can be no doubt that the visit to the
Eternal City was of considerable importance
for the future career of the Anglo-Danish King.
Doubtless Rome began to realise what a power
was this young monarch who up to this time had
probably been regarded as little better than a
barbarian, one of those dreaded pirates who had
so long and so often terrorised the Italian shores.
Here he was next to the Emperor the most redoubt-
able Christian ruler in Europe.   Probably Canute
returned to the North with the Pope's approval
of his plans for empire in Scandinavia,—tacit if
not expressed.   John XIX. was a Pope whose
ideal of a church was one that was efficiently
administered and he may have seen in Canute a
ruler of his own spirit.

CHAPTER XI

THE CONQUEST OF NORWAY

1028–1030

CANUTE was still in the Eternal City on the 6th of April, but it is not likely that he remained in the South much later than that date. With the opening of spring, hostilities might be renewed in Scandinavia at any moment. That Canute expected a renewal of the war is clear from the language of his message to Britain:

> I therefore wish it to be made known to you that, returning by the same way that I departed, I am going to Denmark, for the purpose of settling, with the counsel of all the Danes, firm and lasting peace with those nations, which, had it been in their power, would have deprived us of our life and kingdom. . . .

After affairs had been thus composed, he expected to return to England.

His plans, however, must have suffered a change. So far as we know, warlike operations were not resumed that year; and yet, if any overtures for peace were made, they can scarcely have been

successful. Some time later in the year Canute
set sail for England; but with his great purpose
unfulfilled: for he had promised in his "Charter"
to return to Britain when he had "made peace
with the nations around us, and regulated and
tranquillised all our kingdom here in the East."
Not till next year did he return to the attack on
King Olaf Haroldsson. Hostile movements across
the Scottish border seem to have been responsible for the postponement of the projected conquest. It is told in the *Anglo-Saxon Chronicle*
that as soon as Canute had returned from Rome
he departed for Scotland; "and the King of Scots
submitted to him and also two other kings, Mælbeathe and Jehmarc."

Malcolm, the son of Kenneth, was at this time
ruler of Scotia, a kingdom composed chiefly of
the region between the Forth and the river Spey,
with various outlying dependencies. We do not
know what called forth hostilities between Malcolm and Canute at this time; but it is possible
that the inciting force may have been the Norwegian King, as difficulties in Britain might lead
Canute to abandon his Norse pretensions. As
overlord of the Orkneys and probably also of the
neighbouring Scotch coast lands, King Olaf naturally would be drawn into diplomatic relations
with the kings of Scone. The *Chronicle* gives the
year of the expedition to Scotland as 1031; but it
also places it in the year of Canute's pilgrimage,
which we know to have been made in 1027.

Malcolm rendered some sort of homage in 1027, but for what territories we do not know. That he became Canute's vassal for all his possessions is unlikely; he had already for a decade been the man of the English King for Lothian; and the probabilities are that the homage of 1027 was merely the renewal of the agreements entered into after the battle of Carham in 1018. With the Northern war still unfinished, Canute cannot have been in position to exact severe terms. Furthermore, the acquisition of the Norwegian crown would bring to Canute important possessions to the north and north-west of Malcolm's kingdom and place him in a more favourable position for conquest at some future time. Whether Malcolm realised it or not, further victories for Canute in Scandinavia would mean serious dangers for the Scottish realms.

The identity of the other two kings, Mælbeathe and Jehmarc, is a matter of conjecture. Mælbeathe was probably Macbeth, who as earl ruled the country about Moray Firth, the Macbeth whom we know from Shakespeare's tragedy. Skene believes that Jehmarc, too, must have ruled in the extreme north or north-west, the region that was under Norse influence. But the language of the *Chronicle* need not mean that these kings were both from Scotland; Munch's conjecture that Jehmarc was Eagmargach, the Celtic King of Dublin after the Irish victory at Clontarf,[1] is at

[1] *Det norske Folks Historie*, I., ii., 673.

least plausible. That Canute counted Irishmen among his subjects appears from a stanza by Ottar the Swart:

> Let us so greet the King of the Danes,
> Of Irish, English, and Island-dwellers,
> That his praise as far as the pillared heaven
> May travel widely through all the earth.[1]

If Munch's identification is correct, it reveals a purpose of combining all the Scandinavian West with the older kingdoms, a policy that must have seemed both rational and practical. The homage of Malcolm and Macbeth seems to be mentioned by Sighvat though here again the chronology is defective, the submission of the kings "from far north in Fife" being dated before 1026.

In the meantime Norway was not forgotten. During the year 1027, while Canute was absent in Rome or busied with North British affairs, his emissaries were at work in Norway still further undermining the tottering loyalty of the Norwegian chiefs. No attempt was made at secrecy—it was bribery open and unblushing. Says Sighvat the Scald:

> Jealous foes of King Olaf
> Tempt us with open purses;
> Gold for the life of the lordly
> Ruler is loudly offered.

[1] *Corpus Poeticum Boreale*, ii., 157 (Vigfusson's translation with slight changes).

The poet was a Christian and seems to have taken
grim satisfaction in the teachings of the new faith
regarding future punishment:

> Men who sell for molten
> Metal the gentle ruler
> In swart Hell (they deserve it)
> Shall suffer the keenest torture.[1]

The activities of the Danish envoys appear to
have extended to all parts of the country, though
it seems likely that their success was greatest in the
West and South-west where they enjoyed the
protection and assistance of the mighty nobleman
Erling Skjalgsson, who thus added dishonour to
stubborn and unpatriotic wilfulness. After Holy
River Canute apparently dismissed his fleet for
the winter, in part at least, and Erling returned
to his estates at Soli.

With Erling Canute's envoys came north and
brought much wealth with them. They fared widely
during the winter, paying out the money that Canute
had promised for support in the autumn before;
but they also gave money to others and thus bought
their friendship for Canute; and Erling supported
them in all this.[2]

Evidence of this activity appears in a remarkable
find of English coins to the number of 1500 near
Eikunda-sound, not far from Soli. The treasure

[1] *Corpus Poeticum Boreale*, ii., 134.
[2] Snorre, *Saga of Saint Olaf*, c. 161.

was brought to light in 1836; most of the coins bear the effigies of Ethelred and Canute; all are from Canute's reign or earlier.[1] The next year (1028) Canute sailed his fleet into Eikunda-sound and remained there for some time; but there seems no reason why English money should be secreted on that occasion. More probably the treasure was part of the bribe money; the fact that it was hidden would indicate that Canute's agents found the business somewhat dangerous after all.

Gold alone does not account for Saint Olaf's downfall. There were other reasons for the defection of the aristocracy, but these have been discussed in an earlier chapter: there was dissatisfaction with the new faith; there was dissatisfaction with a régime that enjoined a firm peace everywhere, that aimed at equal justice for all without respect to birth or station, and that enforced severe and unusual punishments; there was also the memory of the days of the earls, when the hand of government was light and the old ways were respected.

In 1028, Canute was ready to strike. Soon the news spread that a vast armament was approaching Norway. "With fifty ships of English thegns,"[2] the King sailed along the Low German shores to the western mouth of the Lime Firth. Among the chiefs who accompanied him from England were the two earls, Hakon and Godwin. One of

[1] Munch, *Det norske Folks Historie*, I., ii., 741.
[2] *Anglo-Saxon Chronicle*, 1028.

Godwin's men found his death in Norway, as we learn from a runic monument raised by one Arnstein over the grave of his son Bjor, "who found his death in Godwin's host in the days when Canute sailed [back] to England."[1]

The ships that the King brought from England were doubtless large and well-manned: Canute's housecarles may have made up a considerable part of the crews. At the Lime Firth an immense Danish fleet was waiting: according to the sagas 1440 ships made up the fleet that sailed up to the Norwegian capital Nidaros. Twelve great hundreds is evidently merely a round number used to indicate unusual size; but that the armament was immense is evident from the ease with which it accomplished its work. So far as we know, the awe-stricken Norsemen made no resistance. In addition to the English and Danish ships, there were evidently not a few that were manned by the housecarles of disaffected Norwegian chiefs.

Olaf was informed of Canute's intentions and did what he could to meet the invasion. Men were dispatched to Sweden to bring home the ships that had been abandoned there nearly two years before. This was a difficult undertaking, for the Danes kept close guard over the passages leading out of the Baltic. Part of the fleet the Norsemen burned; with the rest they were able to steal through the Sound after Canute had begun his advance toward

[1] *Afhandlinger viede Sophus Bugges Minde*, 8.

Norway. King Olaf also summoned the host, but there came

> Few folk and little dragons.
> What a disgrace that landsmen
> Leave our lord royal
> Unsupported. (For money
> Men desert their duties.)

What forces the Norwegians were able to collect sailed up into Oslo Firth, where King Olaf prudently remained till Canute had again departed from the land.[1]

The northward progress of Canute's armament is told in a poem by Thorarin Praise-tongue, who had composed an earlier lay to the King's honour.[2] "The lord of the ocean" sailed from the Lime Firth with a vast fleet. Canute seems to have cut across the strait to the southwestern part of Norway, where the "war-trained men of Agdir saw in terror the advance of the hero," for Canute's dragon gleamed with steel and gold. "The swart ships glide past Lister" and soon fill Eikunda-sound. And so the journey goes on past the Hornel-mount and the promontory of Stadt, till the "sea-falcons glide into the Nid River."

At important points Canute landed and summoned the franklins to formal assemblies. The summons were generally obeyed: the franklins swore allegiance to the new King and gave the required hostages. Wherever there was occasion

[1] Snorre, *Saga of Saint Olaf*, c. 168.   [2] *Ibid.*, c. 172.

to do so, the King appointed new local officials from the elements whose loyalty he believed he could trust. He spent some time in Eikunda-sound where Erling Skjalgsson joined him with a large force. The old alliance was renewed and Erling received promise of all the region between the great headlands of Stadt and the Naze, with a little additional territory to the east of the latter point. This was more than the lord of Soli had ever controlled before. The terms have not been recorded, but Canute was always liberal in his promises.[1]

When Nidaros was reached, the eight shires of the Throndelaw were summoned to meet in a grand assembly, the Ere-thing, which met on the river sands at the mouth of the Nid. As Thrond-hjem was counted the most important region of the kingdom, the Ere-thing throughout the middle ages enjoyed a prominence of its own as the assembly that accepted and proclaimed the Nor-wegian kings. Here then, Canute was formally proclaimed the true King of Norway, and the customary homage was rendered.[2]

There was no need of going beyond Nidaros. Thor the Dog, Harek of Tjotta, and other great lords from the farther North were present at the Ere-thing and took the oaths of allegiance. Thor came in Canute's fleet; Harek joined the King at Nidaros. On these two chiefs the King de-pended for support in the Arctic regions. In re-

[1] Snorre, *Saga of Saint Olaf*, c. 170.　　　[2] *Ibid.*

turn for their allegiance they received enlarged franchises and privileges, among other things the monopoly of the trade with the Finnish tribes. [1]

The conclusions of the Ere-thing concerned Norway alone. A little later a larger assembly was called, a joint meeting of the chiefs of Norway and of the invading army—magnates from England, Denmark, and Norway; possibly the warriors, too, had some voice in this assembly. Here then, in the far North on the sands of Nidaros, was held the first and only imperial assembly, so far as our information goes, that Canute ever summoned. It was called to discuss and decide matters of interest common to all the three realms—especially was it to hear the imperial will, the new imperial policy.

Canute was yet a young man—he had not advanced far into the thirties—but prudence, perhaps also wisdom, had developed with the years. He realised that his own person was really the only bond that held his realms together; but he also understood that direct rule was impracticable. The Norse movement was essentially a revolt from Olaf, not a popular demand for union with Denmark. Among the Danes, too, there was opposition to what smacked of alien rule, as is shown by the readiness with which the magnates had received the revolutionary plans of Earl Ulf. No doubt it was with reluctance that Canute announced a system of vassal earls and kings;

[1] Snorre, *Saga of Saint Olaf*, c. 170.

however, no other solution can have seemed possible.

To his nephew Hakon he gave the vice-royalty of Norway with the earl's title and dignity. Whether the entire kingdom was to be included in Hakon's realm may be doubted; Southern Norway, the Wick, which was as yet unconquered, was an old possession of the dynasty of Gorm and may have been excepted. "Next he led his son Harthacanute to his own high-seat and gave him the kings-name with the government of the Danish realms."[1] As Harthacanute was still but a child a guardian must be found, and for this position Canute seems to have chosen Harold, the son of Thurkil the Tall,[2] his own foster-brother, if tradition can be trusted. Harold at this time was apparently in charge at Jomburg, where he had probably stood in a similar relation to Canute's older son Sweyn who was located there. It is significant that the only one who is awarded the royal title is Harthacanute, the youngest of the King's three sons; but he was also the only one who was of legitimate birth. There can be little doubt that Canute intended to make Harthacanute the heir to all his realms. Of these arrangements Thorarin Praise-tongue sings in his lay:

> Then gave the wise
> Wielder of Jutland
> Norway to Hakon
> His sister's son.

[1] Snorre, *Saga of Saint Olaf*, c. 171.   [2] *Ibid.*, c. 183.

16

And to his own son
(I say it) the old dark
Halls of the ocean,
Hoary Denmark.[1]

Among the Norwegian chiefs who thus far had remained neutral was Einar Thongshaker, the archer of Swald. But now that the Ere-thing had acted and had renounced its allegiance to Olaf, Einar promptly appeared and took the required oaths. King Canute felt the need of binding the proud magnate closely to the new order of things, and along with gifts and increased feudal income went the flattering phrases that next to those who bore princely titles Einar should be the chiefest in the kingdom, and that he or his son Eindrid seemed, after all, most suited to bear the rule in Norway, "were it not for Earl Hakon."[2]

There remained the formality of taking hostages, sons, brothers, or near kinsmen of the chiefs, "or the men who seemed dearest to them and best fitted." The fleet then returned to the South. It was a leisurely sail, we are told, with frequent landings and conferences with the yeomanry, especially, no doubt, in the shires where no assemblies had been summoned on the northward journey. When King Olaf heard of Canute's return, he moved farther up the Oslo Firth and into one of its arms, the Drammen Firth. Here

[1] *Corpus Poeticum Boreale*, ii., 159.
[2] Snorre, *Saga of Saint Olaf*, c. 171.

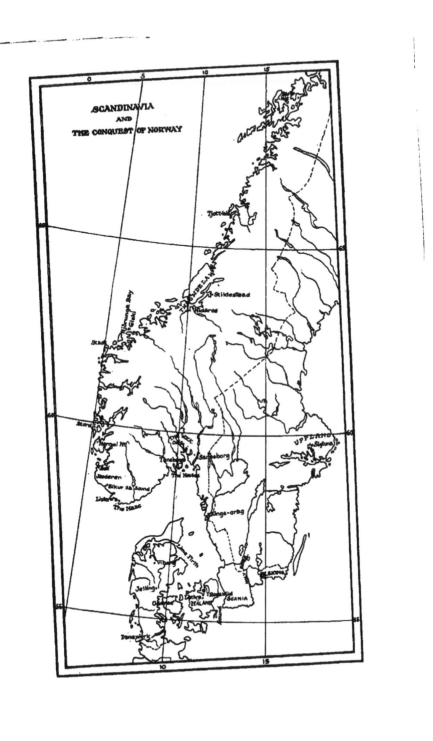

SCANDINAVIA
AND
THE CONQUEST OF NORWAY

he apparently left his ships while he and his men withdrew some distance into the interior. King Canute did not pursue him. He sailed along the south shores to the Oslo Firth and up to Sarpsborg, where an assembly of the freemen accepted him as King. From Sarpsborg he returned to Denmark, where he seems to have spent the winter. Not till the following year did he care to risk a return to England; but at that time his Norse rival was treading the path of exile across the Baltic (1029).

While Canute was being hailed as King at Sarpsborg, Olaf was in hiding two or three days' march distant, probably in the Ring-realm. When he learned of the enemy's departure, he promptly returned to Tunsberg and tried to resume his sway. The situation was desperate, but he wished to make a last appeal to the Norsemen's feeling of loyalty to Harold's dynasty. And now another fleet sailed up the western shores, this time the King's own. Only thirteen ships steered out of Tunsberg harbour and few joined later. The season was the beginning of winter, a most unfavourable time for aggressive operations. When King Olaf had rounded the Naze, he learned that his old enemy, Erling Skjalgsson, had been levying forces in considerable numbers. Olaf managed, however, to intercept Erling's ship and overpowered the old chief after a furious struggle. "Face to face shall eagles fight; will you give quarter?" Erling is reported to have said when Olaf remarked on his bravery. The King was disposed to reconciliation; but during the parley one of his men stepped up and clove the rebel's head. "Unhappy man," cried the King, "there you struck Norway out of my hand!" But the overzealous housecarle was forgiven.[1]

The news of Erling's death fired the whole coast. The magnates realised at once that retreat was now impossible: they must maintain the cause of Canute. Nowhere could King Olaf land, everywhere the yeomanry called for revenge. From the south came the sons of the murdered man in vigorous pursuit; in the north Earl Hakon was mustering the Thronder-folk. Finally King Olaf was forced into one of the long inlets that cut into the western coast. Here he was trapped; flight alone was possible; but before him lay wild mountain regions, one of the wildest routes in Norway. It was midwinter, but the crossing was successful, though the sufferings and difficulties must have been great. Exile was now the only choice; the journey continued to the Swedish border and thence across that kingdom and the Baltic Sea to Russia.[2]

When Canute returned to England, Norway was apparently loyal, peaceful, and obedient. So far as we know, he never again visited the North.

The rule of Earl Hakon was brief: a year and a half at most. Of the character of his government

[1] Snorre, *Saga of Saint Olaf*, cc. 174-176.
[2] *Ibid.*, cc. 177 ff.

we have no information; but the good-natured, easy-going son of Earl Eric was not a man to antagonise the Norwegian aristocracy. His lack of aggressive energies was thoroughly appreciated at Winchester: it is difficult to determine whether Canute's attitude toward his nephew is to be ascribed to bad faith or lack of faith; at all events, the King seems anxiously to have sought a pretext to remove him.

Among the noble families of Thronde-land, perhaps none ranked higher than the house of the Arnungs. Arne Armodsson was a mighty chief and, while he lived, a good friend of King Olaf. Of his five surviving sons four were faithful to the King till he fell at Stiklestead. As we have noted elsewhere, the family also had connections with Olaf's enemies: Arne's daughter was the wife of Harek; his son Kalf was married to the widow of Olvi who had been executed at the King's orders for practising heathen rites; somewhat later Olvi's son Thorir was slain for treason (1027?). When Olaf left Norway, Kalf deserted him and not long afterwards made peace with Earl Hakon and became his man. The sagas attribute this step to the influence of his wife Sigrid and her brother, Thor the Dog. Sigrid is represented as a woman of the legendary type, possessed of a demon of revenge. She had lost much: a husband for his fidelity to the old gods; a son for suspected treason; another in an effort to take vengeance for his brother. To this motive was added that of ambition, which was, perhaps, that which chiefly determined Kalf's actions. Canute seems to have been anxious to secure the active support of this influential noble and probably had expressed a desire for an interview; for in the spring following the conquest (1029), Kalf prepared his ship and sailed to England.[1]

It must have been clear to Canute that continued peace in the North was not to be hoped for. That King Olaf Haroldsson, who had begun his career as a viking while he was yet a mere boy and who was still young, strong, and virile, would be content with permanent exile was unthinkable. Canute must further have realised that his power in Norway had no secure foundation: bribery could not be employed forever; heathendom was a broken reed. His representative was weak, or, as Canute is said to have put it, too "conscientious"; in a crisis he was not to be trusted. Einar Thongshaker was of doubtful loyalty and furthermore had nearly passed the limits of active life. But here was Kalf, young and influential, wealthy and strong.

Canute therefore proposed to Kalf that if Olaf should reappear in Norway he was to raise the militia and lead the host against him. He thus became, in a way, Canute's personal, though unofficial, representative in the kingdom, with a higher title in prospect:

I will then give you the earl's dignity and let you govern Norway; but my kinsman Hakon shall fare

[1] Snorre, *Saga of Saint Olaf*, c. 183.

back to me; and for that he is best suited, as he is so conscientious that I scarcely believe he would do as much as hurl a single shaft against King Olaf, if they were to meet.[1]

Kalf listened joyfully; Canute's speech appealed to him; "and now he began to yearn for the earlship." An agreement was made, and soon Kalf's ship, laden with gifts, was again sailing eastward over the North Sea. Bjarne the Poet recalls these gifts and promises in a praise-lay of which we have fragments:

> The lord of London made promise
> Of lands ere you left the westlands
> (Since there has come postponement);
> Slight was not your distinction.[2]

A few months later the vice-royalty was vacant. Soon after Kalf's return to Norway, Hakon sailed to England; Canute had apparently sent for him. The sources are neither clear nor wholly agreed on this matter; but practically all place the journey in some relation to Hakon's betrothal to Gunhild, Canute's niece, the daughter of his sister Gunhild and a Slavic prince, Witigern. It was late in the year before Hakon was ready to return —sometime after Martinsmas (November 11th), says Florence of Worcester.[3] His ship never

[1] Snorre, *Saga of Saint Olaf*, c. 183.
[2] *Corpus Poeticum Boreale*, ii., 163.
[3] *Chronicon*, i., 184–185.

reached Norway; it went down in a tempest in the Pentland Firth, probably in January, 1030.

The English sources have it that Canute in fact exiled Hakon, though formally he sent him on a personal mission; but the chroniclers are evidently in error in this matter. When these writers speak of outlawry, they mean exile from England; and Hakon was no longer an English resident. Still, it is extremely probable that Hakon had been deprived of his ancestral dignities, that he had been transferred to a new field. Two possibilities appear to fit into the situation: the Earl may have been transferred to the north-western islands or to Jomburg. The Norwegian dependencies along the Scottish shores, the Orkneys and other possessions, passed to Canute when he assumed the Norwegian crown. The fact that Hakon's ship went under on the shores of the Orkneys may indicate that he had an errand in those waters, that Canute had created a new jurisdiction for his easy-going nephew.

Still more is to be said for the alternative possibility. Canute had clearly decided to supersede Hakon in Norway. He had already, it seems, selected his illegitimate son Sweyn for the Norse governorship. The promotion of Sweyn would create a vacancy in Jomburg; perhaps Hakon was intended as Sweyn's successor at that post. At any rate, the King was planning a marriage between the Earl and a kinswoman of his own who was of the Slavic aristocracy, a marriage that would secure for the Earl a certain support among the Wendish nobility. The prospective bride was probably in Wendland with her kinsmen at the time; at any rate she was not on the ship that went down in the Swelchie of Pentland Firth; for a few years later we find Gunhild the widow of one whose history is closely associated with Jomburg, Harold, the son of Thurkil the Tall, the Harold who in 1030 was administering Danish affairs in the name of Harthacanute. Florence tells us that in 1044, Gunhild was exiled from England with her two sons, Thurkil and Heming.[1] Two fierce brothers, it will be recalled, led the Jomvikings into England in 1009,—Thurkil and Heming. No doubt the exiled boys were Harold's sons, named in honour of their stately grandfather and his valiant brother.

Once more Norway was without a ruler. The news of Hakon's death was not long in reaching the Throndelaw, and the leaders of the various factions seem to have taken prompt measures to provide a satisfactory régime. Einar Thongshaker, mindful of Canute's earlier promises, got out his ship and repaired to England. As usual the diplomatic King was prodigal with promises and professions of friendship: Einar should have the highest place in the Norse aristocracy, a larger income, and whatever honours the King could give except the earl's authority,—that had been assigned to Sweyn, and messengers had already

[1] *Chronicon*, i., 199.

been dispatched to Jomburg with instructions to the young prince to assume control at Nidaros.[1]

The old warrior cannot have been pleased. It is likely that his loyalty received a violent shock. Knowing that an attempt would be made to restore Olaf to the throne, he apparently decided to assume his customary neutral attitude; at any rate, he would not fight under Kalf Arnesson's banner. So he lingered in England till the trouble was over and Sweyn was in charge of the kingdom.

Kalf did not go to England; he was busy carrying out his promises to Canute. For hardly had the merchant ships brought rumours of Earl Hakon's death, before Olaf's partisans took measures to restore their legitimate King. Some of the chiefs set out for Russia; and when midsummer came, King Olaf's banner was advancing toward the Norwegian capital. Kalf was prepared to meet him. As it was not known what route Olaf might choose to take or in what region he would set up his standard, the forces of the yeomanry were divided, the southern magnates under the leadership of the sons of Erling undertaking to meet the King if he should appear in the south-east, while the northern host under Kalf, Harek, and Thor the Dog was preparing to hold the Throndelaw.

The host that gathered to oppose the returned exile was wholly Norse: no Dane or Englishman seems to have fought for Canute at Stiklestead. The only alien who is prominently mentioned in

[1] Snorre, *Saga of Saint Olaf*, c. 194.

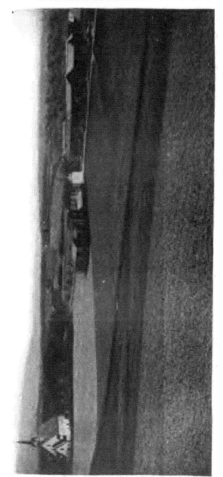

STIKLESTEAD
(From a photograph.)

this connection is Bishop Sigurd, a Danish eccle-siastic who had served as Hakon's court bishop and was a violent partisan of Canute. All the western coast as far as to the Arctic seems to have been represented in the army of the franklins, which is said to have numbered 14,400, four times the number that fought for the returned King.

Still, the disparity of forces was not so great after all. Most of the kingsmen were superb warriors, and all were animated with enthusiasm for Olaf's cause. It was otherwise in the host of the yeomanry; many had small·desire to fight for King Canute, and among the chiefs there was an evident reluctance to lead. Kalf had, therefore, no difficulty in securing authority to command— it was almost thrust upon him.

The battle was joined at Stiklestead farm, about forty miles north-east of the modern Throndhjem. The summer night is short in the Northlands and the long morning gave opportunity for careful preparation. At noon the armies met and the battle began. For more than two hours it raged, King Olaf fighting heroically among his men. Leading an attack on the hostile standard, he came into a hand-to-hand conflict with the chiefs of the yeomanry and fell wounded in three places.[1]

Saint Olaf's day is celebrated on July 29th, and it is generally held that the battle was fought on that date. Some historians have thought that it

---

[1] For details of the battle see Snorre, *Saga of Saint Olaf*, cc. 215–229.

was really fought a month later on the last day
of August. Sighvat was that year on a pilgrimage
to Rome, and was consequently not an eye-witness;
but his lines composed after his return are, nevertheless, one of the chief sources used by the saga-
men. The poet alludes to an eclipse of the sun
on the day of the battle:

> They call it a great wonder
> That the sun would not,
> Though the sky was cloudless,
> Shine warm upon the men. [1]

Such an eclipse, total in that very region at the
hour assigned to the climax of the fight, actually
occurred on August 31st. It is generally held,
however, that the eclipse came to be associated
with the battle later when the search for miracles
had begun.

The reaction was successfully met, but without
any assistance from Canute. Sweyn had prepared
a large force of Danes, commanded it seems by
Earl Harold, and had hastened northward; but
had only reached the Wick when the battle of
Stiklestead was fought. It seems strange at first
thought that no English fleet was sent to assist
Kalf and his associates. It is not likely that
Canute depended much on the fidelity of the
Northmen—he understood human nature better
than most rulers of his time; nor had he any means
of knowing how widely the revolt would spread

---

[1] *Corpus Poeticum Boreale*, ii., 142.

when the former King should issue his appeal. The key to his seeming inactivity must be sought in the international situation of the time: England was just then threatened with an invasion from the south, a danger that demanded a concentration of military resources on the shores of the Channel.

The accounts that have come down to us of the relations of England and Normandy during the latter half of Canute's reign are confused and contradictory; but a few facts are tolerably clear. Some time after the murder of Ulf (1026), Canute gave the widowed Estrid in marriage to Robert the Duke of Normandy (1027–1035).[1] It may be that on his return from Rome in the spring of 1027 Canute had a conference with Robert, who had succeeded to the ducal throne in the previous February. But whether such a meeting occurred or not, Robert had serious trouble before him in Normandy and no doubt was eager for an alliance with the great King of the North. The marriage must have taken place in 1027 or 1028; a later date seems improbable. The father of William Bastard is not famous for conjugal fidelity and may not have been strongly attracted by the Danish widow; at any rate, he soon repudiated her, perhaps to Estrid's great relief, as Duke Robert the Devil seems not to have borne his nickname in vain. The characteristics of the Duke that most im-

---

[1] The evidence for this marriage is discussed by Freeman in *Norman Conquest*, i., Note ppp.

pressed his contemporaries were a ferocious disposition and rude, untamed strength.

It is likely, however, that the break with Canute is to be ascribed not so much to domestic infelicity as to new political ambitions; at the court of Rouen were the two sons of King Ethelred, Edward and Alfred, who had grown to manhood in Normandy. It apparently became Robert's ambition to place these princes on English thrones, which he could not hope to accomplish without war. An embassy was sent to Canute (perhaps in 1029), somewhat similar to the one that Canute had sent to Norway a few years before, bearing a similar errand and equipped with similar arguments. Evidently the Norman ambassadors did not receive kind treatment at the English court. Their report stirred the Duke to great wrath; he ordered a fleet to be prepared for an invasion of England.[1] Most likely that was the time, too, of the Duchess Estrid's disgrace.

The expedition sailed, but a storm sent, as William of Jumièges believes, by an overruling Providence, "who had determined that Edward should some day gain the crown without the shedding of blood," drove the fleet in a westerly direction past the peninsula of Cotentin to the shores of Jersey. Robert was disappointed, but the fleet was not prepared in vain: instead of attacking England, the Duke proceeded against Brittany and forced his enemy Duke Alain to seek

[1] William of Jumièges, *Historia Normannorum*, vi., c. 10.

peace through the mediation of the Church at Rouen.[1]

These events must have occurred after Canute's return from the North,—in the years 1029 and 1030. No other period seems possible; it is not likely that the threatened hostilities could have been later than 1030, for in 1031 a new King, Henry I., ascended the French throne and Robert the Devil became involved in the resulting civil war.[2]

If our chronology is correct, the summer of 1030 saw the Northern Empire threatened from two directions; in Norway it took the form of revolt; in Normandy that of threatened invasion. In both instances legitimate claimants aimed to dislodge a usurper. The danger from the South was by far the greater; Olaf's harsh rule had not yet been forgotten by the Norsemen, nor had they yet experienced the rigours of alien rule. England was quiet and apparently contented; but what effect the pretensions of the Ethelings would have on the populace no one could know. We may be sure that Canute was ready for the invader; but so long as the Norwegian troubles were still unsettled, he wisely limited himself to defensive operations.

It is also related, though not by any contemporary writer, that Canute was dangerously ill at the

[1] William of Jumièges, *Historia Normannorum*, vi., cc. 10, 11.
[2] This was followed by a famine in the duchy (1033) which probably induced the Duke to make his pilgrimage to the Holy Sepulchre on the return from which he died (1035).

time of the Norman trouble, and that he at one time expressed a willingness to divide the English kingdom with the Ethelings.[1]   Whether he was ill or not, such an offer does not necessitate the inference either of despair or of fear for the outcome. The offer if made was doubtless a diplomatic one, on par with the promises to the Norwegian rebels, made for the purpose of gaining time, perhaps, until Norway was once more pacified.

But fortune had not deserted the great Dane. When autumn came in 1030, the war clouds had passed and the northern skies were clear and cheerful. Canute's Norwegian rival had gone to his reward; his Norman rival was absorbed in other interests. Without question Canute was now Emperor of the North.

[1] William of Jumièges, *Historia Normannorum*, vi., c. 12.

CHAPTER XII

THE EMPIRE OF THE NORTH

WHEN the eleventh century began its fourth decade, Canute was, with the single exception of the Emperor, the most imposing ruler in Latin Christendom. Less than twenty years earlier he had been a landless pirate striving to dislodge an ancient and honoured dynasty; now he was the lord of four important realms and the overlord of other kingdoms. Though technically Canute was counted among the kings, his position among his fellow-monarchs was truly imperial. Apparently he held in his hands the destinies of two great regions; the British Isles and the Scandinavian peninsulas. His fleet all but controlled two important seas, the North and the Baltic. He had built an empire.

It was a weak structure, founded too largely on the military and diplomatic achievements of a single man; but the King was young—in the ordinary course of nature he should have lived to rule at least thirty years longer—and with careful diplomatic effort, of which he was a master, he might be expected to accomplish great things in the way of consolidating his dominions. But instead

of thirty years, the fates had counted out less than
half a dozen. In this period he was able to do
almost nothing to strengthen the bonds of empire.
Canute's power did not long remain at its zenith—
the decline began almost immediately. In this
there is nothing strange; the marvel is in the fact
that such an empire was actually built.

Of Canute's many dominions, the kingdoms
of Denmark, England, and Norway had fairly
distinct boundaries. Lothian might be in question between England and Scotland; the Norwegian kings had claimed certain territories across
the Scandinavian watershed, Jemteland, a Norse
colony in Swedish possession; but otherwise the
limits were tolerably definite. The fourth division, the Slavic lands on the southern rim of the
Baltic, was a more indefinite area. Its limits are
unknown; perhaps it should be called a sphere of
influence rather than a province. There were,
however, certain evident nuclei; the regions about
the lower course of the Oder with Jomburg as the
chief city were doubtless the more important part;
in addition there was Semland in the extreme east
of modern Prussia, Witland a trifle farther west
where the Vistula empties into the sea; and doubtless some of the intervening territories. There
are indications that Danish settlements had also
been planted in the region of the modern city of
Riga[1]; but as to their probable relation to Canute's
empire the sources are silent.

[1] Steenstrup, *Normannerne*, i., 195–199.

In addition to England, Canute possessed important territories elsewhere in the British archipelago. The King of Scotland was his vassal, at least for a part of his dominions; and we have seen that at least one other Scottish king, probably from the extreme north of the island, had done homage to Canute. It has also been shown that the Norse-Irish kingdom of Dublin should, perhaps, be counted among his vassal states. As King of Norway, Canute was lord of the Shetlands and the Orkneys, perhaps also the Hebrides, and other Norse colonies on the west shores of Scotland. The Faroes were not wholly subject and the Icelandic republic still maintained its independence; but the straggling settlements in far-off Greenland seem to have acknowledged their dependence on the Norwegian crown.[1]

Any definite imperial policy Canute seems never to have developed. In his own day the various units were nominally ruled by earls or sub-kings, usually chosen from the King's own immediate family; but the real power was often in the hands of some trusted chief whom the King associated with the lord who bore the title. If time had been granted, some form of feudalism might have developed out of this arrangement; but it had few feudal characteristics in Canute's own day. It was evidently Canute's intention to continue the scheme of one king for the entire group of dominions, for at the imperial assembly at Nidaros, he

[1] Munch, *Det norske Folks Historie*, I., ii., 704, 705.

placed Harthacanute in the high-seat and gave him the administration of Denmark, which was, after all, the central kingdom. The Encomiast bears further testimony as to Canute's intention when he tells us that all England had taken an oath to accept Harthacanute as king.[1] It seems that Canute, to secure the succession to his legitimate son, had adopted the Capetian expedient of associating the heir with himself in the kingship while he was still living.

So long as obedience, especially in matters of military assistance, was duly rendered, few difficulties were likely to arise between the supreme lord of Winchester and his subordinates in Nidaros, Roeskild, or Jomburg. As the union was personal, each kingdom retained its own laws and its own system of assemblies, though this must have been true to a less extent in the Slavic possessions, as these seem to have been regarded almost as a Danish dependency. When the reign closed, Harthacanute was governing Denmark; Sweyn assisted by his mother Elgiva had charge of Norway, though at that moment the Norwegian rebels were in actual control. Canute ruled England himself, not because it was regarded as the chief or central kingdom, but more likely because it

---

[1] *Encomium Emmæ*, ii., c. 19. The Encomiast is intensely partisan and much given to exaggeration; but we cannot reject the statement as to the English oath without convicting him of a worse fault for which there was scarcely a sufficient motive at the time when the *Encomium* was composed.

could not with safety be entrusted to any one
else.

So far as the Empire had any capital, that distinction appears to have belonged to the ancient
city of Winchester. Here in the heart of Wessex
was the seat of English government, the royal and
imperial residence. We naturally think of Canute's household as an English court; but it is
difficult to determine what racial influences were
in actual control. Nor do we know what was the
official language in Canute's royal garth; but the
probabilities are that both Old English and Old
Norse were in constant use. The housecarles
who guarded the royal person and interests were
in large part of Scandinavian birth or blood.
The Norse poets who sang praise-lays in the royal
hall at Winchester sang in their native dialects.
Of the King's thegns who witnessed Canute's
land grants, as a rule about one half bear Scandinavian names; there can be little doubt that most of
these were resident at court, at all events those
whose names appear in more than one document.

Other nationalities, too, were represented at
Winchester. In the enrolment of housecarles,
the King asked for strength, valour, wealth, and
aristocratic birth; not, it seems, for Danish or
English ancestry. The bishops that Canute sent
from England to Denmark appear to have been
Flemings or Lotharingians. William who in a later
reign became bishop of Roeskild is said to have
come to Denmark as Canute's private secretary

or chancellor; but William is neither a Northern
nor a Saxon but a Norman name. And thus with
Dane and Angle, Norman and Norseman, Swede
and Saxon, Celt and German thronging the royal
garth the court at Winchester must have borne
an appearance that was distinctly non-English.
As at other courts, men came and went; and the
stories of the splendours at Winchester were given
wide currency. The dissatisfied Norsemen who
sought refuge in England found at Canute's court
greater magnificence than in any other place, both
as to the number in daily attendance and as to the
furnishings and equipments of the palaces that he
owned and occupied.[1]

Sighvat the Scald, who had seen Rouen and visited
Rome, was so deeply impressed with the glories
of Canute's capital that in his praise-lay he introduced the refrain:

> Canute was under heaven
> The most glorious King.[2]

There seems also to have been a notable Slavic
element in Canute's retinue. Attention has been
called to the King's Slavic ancestry; the Slavic
strain was evidently both broader and deeper
than the Danish. One of the King's sisters bore a
Slavic name, Santslave[3]; another sister, Gunhild,

---

[1] Snorre, *Saga of Saint Olaf*, c. 130.
[2] *Corpus Poeticum Boreale*, ii., 135-136.
[3] Steenstrup, *Venderne og de Danske*, 64-65. The name occurs
in the *Liber Vibæ* of Winchester in a list of benefactors. See
above p. 57.

married a Slavic "king," Wyrtgeorn or Witigern,[1] who may have been the Wrytsleof who witnessed an English land grant in 1026[2]; possibly he was visiting his English kinsfolk at the time. Among the chiefs of the imperial guard was one Godescalc, the son of a Slavic prince, though Danish on the maternal side; he, too, married into the Danish royal family.[3]

The affairs of each separate kingdom were evidently directed from the national capitals and administered largely by native functionaries. At the same time, it seems to have been Canute's policy to locate Danish officials in all his principal dominions, at least in the higher offices. The appointment of Danes to places of importance in England has been noted in an earlier chapter. With the subjection of Norway, a number of Danes received official appointments in that kingdom. A leading cause of the Norwegian revolt in 1034–1035 was the prominence given to aliens in the councils of the regent Sweyn: "Danish men had in those days much authority in Norway, but that was liked ill by the men of the land."[4] On the other hand, no Englishman seems to have received official responsibilities in the North

---

[1] Steenstrup, *Venderne og de Danske*, 65. Florence of Worcester, *Chronicon*, i., 199.

[2] Kemble, *Codex Diplomaticus*, No. 743.

[3] After Canute's death, Godescalc returned to his native country and took up the cause of Christian mission effort among the heathen Wends. Adamus, *Gesta*, ii., cc. 64, 75.

[4] Snorre, *Saga of Saint Olaf*, c. 247.

except in the Church; and it may be doubted
whether Canute sent many Anglian prelates to his
realms in the east; the bishops that we have
record of seem to have been Normans, Flemings,
or clerks from the Danelaw. When a court
bishop was to be found for the household of Earl
Hakon, the choice fell upon Sigurd, a Dane and a
violent friend of Danish rule.

Of Canute's diplomacy the sources afford us
only an occasional glimpse; but the information
that we have indicates that he entered into diplomatic relations with almost every ruler of importance in Northern and Western Europe. The King
of Scotland became his vassal. The sagas tell
of an embassy to Sweden in the years preceding
the attack on Norway. During the same period
Canute's cousin, the King of Poland, apparently
sought his alliance against the Germans. With
the Emperor he maintained the closest relations.
The Norman dukes were bound to the Danish
dynasty by the noble ties of marriage. On his
visit to Rome the English King came into personal
contact with the King of Burgundy and His
Holiness the Pope. Even to distant Aquitaine
did the mighty monarch send his ambassadors
with messages of good-will in the form of substantial presents. In a panegyric on William the
Great, the Duke of Aquitaine, Adémar of Chabannes writes that every year embassies came to
the Duke's court with precious gifts from the kings
of Spain, France, and Navarre, "and also from

Canute, King of the Danes and the Angles";
and the chronicler adds that the messengers
brought even more costly presents away.[1] On one
occasion "the King of that country [England]
sent a manuscript written with letters of gold
along with other gifts."[2] As this statement
seems to have been written in 1028, and as the
author emphasises the fact that this beautiful
codex had arrived "recently," it seems probable
that this embassy should be associated with Canute's pilgrimage to Rome the year before. It is
not strange that Canute should wish to honour a
prince like William; and it is only natural that he
should wish to placate a people who had suffered
so much, as the Aquitanians had, from the raids
and inroads of his former associates and his allies,
the vikings and the Normans.

With respect to his immediate neighbours, Canute's policy was usually absorption or close
friendship. What he felt he could add to his
dominions, he added; where this was not possible,
he sought peace and alliance. His diplomacy
must have concerned itself especially with three
states: Normandy, Sweden, and the Empire. As
to his relations with Sweden after the encounter at
Holy River, history is silent; but war was evidently

[1] *Mon. Ger. Hist., Scriptores*, iv., 134; Adémar's *Chronicle*, ii., c.
41.

[2] Migne, *Patrologia Latina*, cxli., col. 122: sermon by Adémar. Migne considers the sermon of doubtful genuineness,
possibly because he thought its delivery should go back to 998,
when in reality 1028 seems to be the correct date.

avoided. Canute probably regarded any effort to extend his territories eastward as an unwise move, so long as the disappointed Norwegian chiefs continued to show signs of unrest and rebellion.

With Normandy he lived in continuous peace for more than a decade, until Robert the Devil took up the cause of the exiled princes. That Canute feared a move in this direction seems evident; and as Queen Emma's influence at Rouen was probably weakened by the death of Richard the Good (1027), it was no doubt in the hope of strengthening his position at the ducal court that Canute sought the title of duchess for his widowed sister. As we have seen, his success was only temporary, and for a time war seemed imminent. But the confused situation in the French kingdom at this time proved Canute's salvation. In the civil war that followed the accession of Henry I. to the French throne in 1031, Robert of Normandy took a leading part on the King's side; and it was largely due to his efforts that Henry finally overcame his enemies.[1] Meanwhile, the sons of Ethelred and Emma had to wait several years before another opportunity appeared with sufficient promise to tempt the exiles back across the Channel. For soon after the French King was safely enthroned, famine came upon Normandy, an affliction that led Robert the Devil to think of a visit to the grave of Christ. The journey was undertaken but on the return the Duke died in Asia Minor

[1] Lavisse, *Histoire de France*, II., ii., 162.

(1035). His successor was William who finally conquered England; but William was a child and Canute had no longer any fears from that direction. A few months after Robert's death the King of England also closed his earthly career. Had Robert survived Canute, it is likely that some of the results of Hastings might have come thirty years earlier than they did.

After 1019, when Canute ascended the Danish throne, the attitude and plans of the Emperor became an important factor in Northern diplomacy. The Empire was a dangerous neighbour; the Ottos had apparently been ambitious to extend their authority throughout the entire Jutish peninsula. But during Canute's reign neither power could afford to offend the other; and the Danes were therefore able to keep continued peace along the southern borders of the kingdom. At one time, when the Emperor found himself in serious difficulties, Canute was able to drive a hard bargain and exchange his friendship for a strip of imperial territory.

It is not likely that the German kings looked with much favour on Danish expansion at the mouths of the Vistula and the Oder, but they were not in position to prevent it. In 1022, when Canute made his expedition to Wendland, the Emperor Henry II. was absent in Italy, striving, as usual, to reduce disorder.[1] Two years later he died, and Conrad of Franconia was chosen King

[1] Manitius, *Deutsche Geschichte*, 322–323.

of the Germans. His election was the signal for uprisings and plots almost along the whole length of the border, in Poland, in Lorraine, and in Lombardy.[1] Boleslav, King of the Poles, died in the following year (1025), but his successor continued the policy of hostility to the Germans and seems to have sought the alliance of his cousin Canute against the Teutonic foes.[2] Conrad, too, sought Canute's friendship and was able to outbid his Polish rival. It was agreed that there should be perpetual peace between Conrad and Canute, and to cement the good understanding and secure its continuance in years to come, Canute's little daughter Gunhild, who could not yet have been more than five or six years old, was betrothed to Conrad's son Henry, who was, perhaps, three years older.[3] The covenant was kept, and Henry received his bride about ten years later (1036), after the death of Canute. The bridegroom was the mighty Emperor Henry III., though he did not attain to the imperial dignity before the death of Conrad in 1039. Gunhild was crowned Queen of Germany and as a part of the ceremony received the more honoured German name Kunigund; but she never became empress, as she died in 1038.[4]

In return for his friendship, Canute received the mark of Sleswick, a strip of land between the Schley and the Eider, that Henry the Fowler had

[1] Manitius, *Deutsche Geschichte*, 360–361, 365, 389 ff.
[2] *Ibid.*, 369–370.   [3] Adamus, *Gesta*, ii., c. 54.
[4] *Danmarks Riges Historie*, i., 409.

taken from the Danes a century before. Thus the
Eider once more became the boundary of the
Danish kingdom. But apart from territorial
acquisitions, Canute was doubtless glad to conclude the treaty, as he was just then planning
the conquest of Norway. The negotiations with
Conrad were probably concluded in the year 1025
or 1026, though more likely in the former year.[1]

Perhaps at the same time the German King
invited his ally to participate in his coronation as
Emperor; for in 1027 Canute journeyed to Rome
to witness the great event. There can be little
doubt that on this occasion the pledges were
renewed. But even in the absence of formal
treaties there was small occasion for Conrad to
make trouble for his neighbour to the north. The
years following his coronation in Rome saw four
serious revolts in Germany; not till 1033 was real
order restored in Conrad's kingdom.

There was another power that Canute could not
afford to antagonise or even ignore: no mediæval
monarch could long flourish if he overlooked the
needs of the Church. During the first years of his
English kingship, Canute does not seem to have
sought to conciliate the clergy; but after a few years
he apparently adopted a new policy and strove
to ally himself with the priesthood. It was as
king of England that he first succeeded in forming
such an alliance; in his other kingdoms, the eccle-

[1] Adamus, *Gesta*, ii., c. 54. Manitius (*Deutsche Geschichte,*
370) believes the cession was not made before 1035.

siastical problem assumed a somewhat different form.

With the head of Christendom, Canute's relations seem to have been cordial throughout his entire reign. It was the papacy that made the first move to establish such relations: in 1019 Archbishop Lifing brought a message back from Rome replete with good advice which seems to have flattered the young Dane. The pilgrimage to Rome doubtless strengthened the bond; especially must the King's later efforts to see that the proper church dues were collected have pleased the Popes of that period. For the papacy had fallen low in that age: the Pope whom Canute visited was only a layman up to the day of his election to the sacred office; his successor Benedict is said to have been a mere boy when he was elevated to the papal dignity, though authorities differ as to his age. There was, therefore, little likelihood of any conflict so long as the Peter's pence were regularly transported to Rome. A new papacy was to come; but Hildebrand had not quite reached manhood when Canute went to his rest.

Canute's ecclesiastical policy in England, at least during the closing years of his reign, seems to have aimed at greater control than had been the case earlier. The friendship and active good-will of the Church could best be secured by carefully choosing the rulers of the Church. As a Christian court, the royal household at Winchester had in its employment a regular staff of priests, nine of whom are mentioned in the documents. Canute honoured his priests; he seems to have invited them to seats in the national assembly; he called them in to witness grants of land. Finally, he honoured several of them still further by appointing them to episcopal office: at least three of Canute's clerks received such appointments before the reign closed.[1] His successor inherited his policy and several more of Canute's chapel clerks were honoured in Edward's time. The policy was not new: even in Carolingian times the royal chapel had been used as a training school for future prelates, and there are traces of a similar practice in England long before Canute's time. But so far as the Dane was concerned, the plan was probably original: we cannot suppose him to have been very well informed as to precedents more than two centuries old.

In Norway the problem was how to christianise and organise the land, and Canute had no great part in either. The Danish Church, however, was growing in strength and developing under conditions that might produce great difficulties: it was the daughter of the German Church; it was governed by an alien prelate.

The primacy of the Northern churches belonged to the see of Bremen, the church from which the earliest missionaries had gone forth into Denmark and Sweden. While this primacy was in a way

[1] Larson, *The King's Household in England*, 140–142.

recognised, in practice, the Northern kings in the early years of the eleventh century paid small regard to the claims of the archbishop. The two Olafs depended mainly on England and the neighbouring parts of the Continent for priests and prelates; and Canute, as King of England, seems to have planned to make the Danish Church, too, dependent on the see of Canterbury. At this time Unwan was Archbishop of Bremen; for sixteen years he ruled his province with a resolute hand and for the most part with strength and wisdom.

Unwan was displeased when he learned that Canute was sending bishops from England to Denmark; we have already seen how he managed to make a prisoner and even a partisan of Gerbrand, who, like Unwan himself, was doubtless a German. This must have been in 1022 or 1023, more likely in the former year. Aided by Gerbrand, who acted as mediator, Unwan was able to make Canute recognise his primacy. Adam of Bremen mentions great gifts that Unwan sent to Canute,[1] but these were probably not the determining consideration. In 1022, Canute was fighting the Slavs and adding territory that would naturally belong to the mission fields of Bremen, and it would hardly be wise to make an enemy of one whose historic rights had been admitted by earlier Danish kings. Till Unwan's death in 1029, the King and the Archbishop were fast friends. Unwan served as mediator between Canute and

[1] *Gesta*, ii., c. 53.

THE HYBY STONE

(Monument from the first half of the eleventh century; raised to a Christian
as appears from the cross.)

the Emperor when the alliance was formed in
1025 (?)[1] and otherwise served the Danish King.
It seems probable that a personal acquaintance
was formed, for Adam tells us that Unwan rebuilt
Hamburg and spent considerable time there,
"whither he also invited the very glorious King
Canute . . . to confer with him."[2]

The *entente* that was thus formed seems also to
have affected mission operations in Norway. It
is likely that Unwan demanded that King Olaf
should no longer be allowed to recruit his ecclesiastical forces in England; for soon after the date
that we have assumed as that of the new treaty,
Bishop Grimkell appeared as King Olaf's am-
bassador at Unwan's court. The Bishop, who was
evidently a Northman from the Danelaw, brought
the customary gifts and the prayer that Unwan
would accept the Anglian clerks and prelates then
in Norway as of his province and that he would
further increase the clerical forces of the kingdom.[3]
Thus in the years 1022–1023, the rights of Hamburg-Bremen were recognised everywhere.

Unwan was succeeded in the province by Libentius, the nephew of an earlier Libentius who
had held the metropolitan office in Bremen before
Unwan's day. He was of Italian blood and
therefore not likely to be burdened with German
sympathies. Before everything else, says the
good Master Adam, he entered into friendly

---

[1] *Gesta*, ii., c. 54.   [2] *Ibid.*, c. 58.
[3] *Ibid.*, c. 55; iv., c. 33.

relations with the King of the Danes.[1] But during Libentius' as well as Unwan's primacy Canute seems to have selected the bishops for his Danish as well as for his English sees.

During the closing years of his life, Canute's policy was completely identified with that of the mediæval Church as regards his attitude toward heathen and un-Christian practices. So long as the Norwegian problem was unsettled, the King dared not take a decided stand against the old faith, as he was too much dependent on heathen or semi-heathen assistance against King Olaf. But after the conquest there was no reason for further delay, and the English Church got its desired legislation. In two comparatively long enactments, one ecclesiastical and one secular, all the old and important church laws were re-enacted and various new provisions added.[2] Archbishop Dunstan was canonised and given May 13th as his mass day.[3] Added protection was given to churches and to the ministers of the altar: outlawry was to be the punishment for slaying a priest.[4] It was carefully explained that the privileges of the priesthood were due to the exalted character of the divine office; for

great is the exorcism and glorious the consecration that cast out devils and put them to flight whenever baptism is celebrated or the host is consecrated; and

[1] Adamus, *Gesta*, ii., c. 62.
[2] Liebermann, *Gesetze der Angelsachsen*, i., 278 ff.
[3] *I. Canute*, c. 17, 1.   [4] *Ibid.*, cc. 3, 4; *II. Canute*, c. 39.

holy angels are present to watch over the sacred act
and through the power of God to assist the priests so
long as they worthily serve Christ.[1]

Sundays and other church holidays were to be
properly kept; and no commercial transactions
were to be tolerated on Sundays, nor were the
public courts to hold sessions on those days except
in cases of extreme necessity.[2] Due attention
was to be given to the seasons when the Church
prescribed fasting; but it was explicitly stated
that except in the case of penitents, no fasting
was to be required between Easter and Pentecost,
or from Christmas to the close of the week following Epiphany,[3] the joyous period of the Northern
Yule-tide.

It seems clear that enactments of this sort would
be necessary only in regions where there might
still be a considerable number of recent converts
with whom the observance of Christian rites and
customs had not yet become a habit. It may be,
therefore, that these laws were particularly intended for certain parts of the Danelaw. Perhaps it was the need of improving the religious
conditions in the Danish settlements that inspired the royal demand for general instruction
in the fundamentals of the Christian faith.

And we order every Christian to learn at least so
much that he can understand clearly the teachings of

---

[1] *I. Canute*, c. 4, 2.   [2] *Ibid.*, c. 15.   [3] *Ibid.*, c. 17.

the true faith, and to learn thoroughly the Pater Noster and the Credo.[1]

Some attention is also paid to ecclesiastical finance. Fines were provided for neglect in the payment of church dues; part of these were to be paid to the bishop. The Anglo-Saxons were in the habit of making contributions for church lights at the feast of the Purification (Candlemas, February 2d), at Easter Eve, and on All Saints' day (November 1st). A fortnight after Easter plough alms were to be paid. A tithe of young beasts was due at Pentecost. Peter's pence were contributed on Saint Peter's day (August 1st). A tithe of the harvested crops was due at All Saints' day. The last tax of the year was the church scot which was paid at Martinsmas (November 11th). All these contributions are specifically mentioned and urged in Canute's laws for the English Church.[2]

The second part of Canute's legislation, the secular laws, is a document of considerable length, of which only a comparatively small part is copied from the earlier "dooms." It deals with a variety of subjects, several of which may be classed as religious rather than secular. A very important act was the definition and prohibition of heathendom and heathen practices.

Heathendon is the worship of idols, namely the worship of heathen gods, and the sun or moon, fire or flood, fountains or rocks or forest trees of any sort;

---

[1] *I. Canute*, c. 22.   [2] *Ibid.*, cc. 8–10.

also to practise witchcraft or to commit murders in any manner, whether in sacrifices or in auguries, or to busy oneself with any such delusion.[1]

As it is not customary to forbid what is never performed, we have in this enactment evidence for a persisting heathendom on English soil. In the Scandinavian colonies pagan practices were probably hard to uproot; at the same time, it is not likely that the old faith was a force that needed to be considered any longer.

The matter of Christian marriage is dealt with in both the secular and the ecclesiastical laws. It was difficult to enforce the regulations of the Church on this subject and particularly among the vikings, whose ideas as to the binding force of marriage were exceedingly vague.[2] Canute forbade clandestine marriages; to the old law that a man should have but one wife he added the important provision that "she should be his legally espoused wife."[3] He also gave the protection of the state to widows and virgins who preferred to remain unmarried.[4]

Other important enactments deal with matters of finance, especially with the King's share in the fines assessed in the courts, his income from his

---

[1] *II. Canute*, c. 5, 1.

[2] On this point the Norse sources furnish evidence everywhere. For the condition among the Scandinavians in Britain, see the account of the "Siege of Durham" published among the writings of Simeon of Durham (*Opera Omnia*, 215–220).

[3] *I. Canute*, c. 7, 3.   [4] *II. Canute*, cc. 52, 52, 1, 74.

estates, and coinage and counterfeiting; there are also important laws that look toward the security of persons and of property. The principle of equality before the law is distinctly stated: the magnates were to have no unusual privileges in the courts of justice.

Many a powerful man will, if he can and may, defend his man in whatever way it seems to him the more easy to defend him, whether as freeman or as *theow* (serf). But we will not suffer that injustice.[1]

With the legislation of Canute, the development of Old English law comes to a close. Various tracts or customals of considerable importance were composed in the eleventh century, some of which may have been put into form after the close of Canute's reign; but of these we know neither the authors nor the date. The "Laws of Edward" that the Norman kings swore to maintain were in reality the laws of Canute; for when the Anglo-Norman lawyers of the early twelfth century began to investigate the subject of Old English law, they found its most satisfactory statement in the legislation of the mighty Dane. In the *Quadripartitus* these laws occupy the most prominent place; while the compilations that Liebermann has called the *Instituta Cnuti* and the *Consiliatio Cnuti* are scarcely more than translations of Canute's legislation for church and state.[2]

[1] *II. Canute*, c. 20, 1.

[2] For the text of these compilations (including the forged forest law) see Liebermann, *Gesetze der Angelsachsen*, i., 529–546, 612–

So great was the Danish King's reputation as a
lawmaker in the twelfth century that he was even
credited with enactments and institutional experi-
ments with which he never had any connection.
Toward the close of that century an official of the
royal forest, as it seems, drew up an elaborate law
for the King's hunting preserves which he tried
to give currency and authority by ascribing it to
Canute.[1] The Dane was not indifferent to the
chase, but he did not find it necessary to make it
the subject of extensive legislation. In his secular
laws the subject is disposed of in a single sentence:
"And let every man forego my hunting, wherever I wish to have it free from trespass, under
penalty of the full fine."[2]

In the so-called "Laws of Edward the Confessor" it is stated that the *murdrum* fine originated
in the reign of Canute. It is well-known that
William the Conqueror found it necessary to take
special measures for the protection of his Normans
from assassination at the hands of Englishmen who
were seeking vengeance; he decreed, therefore,
that the hundred where the murder of a Norman
was committed should see that the criminal was
given proper punishment or pay a heavy fine in
case of default. The twelfth-century lawyer who

---

626. The documents have been made the subject of a series of
studies by F. Liebermann, the results of which are summed up in
Pollock and Maitland, *History of English Law*, i., 100–101.

[1] Liebermann, *Gesetze der Angelsachsen*, i., 620.

[2] *II. Canute*, c. 80, 1.

With the Northmen came a new conception of personal honour and a new term for criminality of the most dishonourable type, the *nithing* name. Norse rules were introduced into court procedure. Administrative areas came to bear Norse appellations, as the wapentake in the Danelaw generally and the riding in Yorkshire.[1] These facts, however, belong in large measure to the earlier development, though it doubtless continued through the reign of Canute and longer.

But though Scandinavian ideas of law had long flourished on English soil, it was not till Canute's day that they were formally accepted as a part of the Anglo-Saxon legal system. In penal legislation a new spirit appeared: there was less mercy and punishments became more severe—exile, mutilation, and forfeiture of life more common. If the ordeal should convict a man of a second offence, the penalty might be the loss of the hands or the feet, or of both. Still further mutilation was decreed if the criminal should continue to commit grave offences; "but let the soul be spared."[2] The same penalties were not always provided for both sexes: a faithless husband might have to pay the ancient money fine for manslaughter; a sinning wife was to suffer the loss of all her property and her ears and nose.[3] Certain

---

[1] On this subject the most important work is Steenstrup's *Danelag* (*Normannerne*, iv.); see especially pp. 75-76, 85-92, 175 ff.; also *Normannerne*, iii., 366-368.

[2] *II. Canute*, c. 30, 5.   [3] *Ibid.*, c. 50 ff.

institutions of Scandinavian origin took on a peculiar form during Canute's reign: for instance,
the guard of housecarles in its English and later
Danish form, and the office of staller or the King's
spokesman at the popular assemblies, which office
seems to have been introduced into England in
Canute's day.[1]

It is still more difficult to determine what results the union had for the institutional development of Denmark. On only one point have we
clear evidence: Canute was the first Danish King
to begin a systematic coinage of money. Coins
were stricken in Denmark before his day, but
there was no organised system of mints. Canute
supplied this need, using the English pattern. He
brought moneyers from his western kingdom and
located them in the chief cities of Denmark; coins
have come down to us that were stricken by these
moneyers in the cities of Roeskild, Ringsted,
Odense, Heathby (Sleswick), and Lund.[2]

On the other hand, Canute's Norwegian legislation shows clear traces of Anglo-Saxon influence.
Of his three kingdoms, Norway, doubtless, had the
least efficient constitution. In Norway there was
much liberty, but also much disorder; emphasis
was placed on personal rights, especially on those
of the aristocracy; but such emphasis is too
frequently subversive of good government. The
Dane was a believer in strong, orderly administra-

[1] Larson, *The King's Household in England*, c. 7.
[2] *Danmarks Riges Historie*, i., 404–405.

tion: it was his purpose to introduce European principles into the Norse constitution. Had he been personally in control he might have succeeded but his deputies at Nidaros were unequal to the task; discontent and rebellion were the result.

For the laws that the new regents proclaimed in Norway, the Norsemen were inclined to lay all blame on Sweyn's mother, Elgiva (Alfiva, the Northmen called her), Canute's mistress of olden time. But there can be little doubt that in this matter she and her son merely carried out the King's instructions. The laws fall into three classes: revenue legislation, police and military ordinances, and a new definition of penalties.[1]

A new tax that apparently affected the entire population was the demand that at Christmas time every hearth should contribute certain "gifts": a measure of malt, the leg of a full-grown ox, and as much unspun flax as could be held between the thumb and the middle finger. This reminds one somewhat of the English ferm, a contribution that was due from the various counties. It was also enacted that the franklins should assist in erecting buildings on the royal estates, and that merchants and fishermen and all who sailed to Iceland should pay certain dues to the King.

A law that was clearly aimed at the ancient practice of blood feud provided that murder should entail the loss of lands as well as of personal pro-

[1] Snorre, *Saga of Saint Olaf*, c. 239.

perty; also that the King alone should take inheritance after an outlaw. In those same years Canute decreed in England that whoever committed
a deed of outlawry should forfeit his lands to
the King. The new Norse laws also forbade any
subject to leave the land without permission, on
pain of outlawry. Parallel to this is the English
law that ordered forfeiture for leaving one's lord,
with the difference that in Norway the King himself was the lord. It was also decreed that the
testimony of a Dane should outweigh that of ten
Norsemen, the purpose of which was clearly to
secure the lives of Danish officials and soldiers.

It was further provided that every male above
the age of five years should be counted one of
seven to equip a soldier. It may be that this
provision was suggested by the Old English custom
of grouping five hides of land (originally the lands
of five households) for similar purposes. Snorre
believes that these laws were Danish in origin;
but it is more likely that they grew out of Canute's
experience with Anglo-Saxon custom and the
principles of Continental feudalism, though it is
possible that some of them had been introduced
into Denmark earlier in the reign and came to
Norway from the southern kingdom.

RUNIC MONUMENT FROM UPLAND, SWEDEN
(Shows blending of Celtic and Northern art.)

CHAPTER XIII

TO present an adequate discussion of the state of culture among Canute's subjects in the space of a single chapter would be impossible. So far as the western realm is concerned it would also be unnecessary, as the subject of Anglo-Saxon culture is an old study and discussions in English are readily accessible. This chapter will therefore be chiefly concerned with the civilisation of the Northern lands, and especially with the great transformations that came with the viking age and were becoming most evident toward its close.

The two controlling types of civilisation in the Anglo-Scandinavian Empire, the English and the Norse, were both fundamentally Germanic; but English culture had for centuries been permeated with Christian thought, while in the North the ideals of heathendom were still a force to be taken into account. It is difficult to characterise Northern society in the earlier decades of the eleventh century: all the various regions were not in the same stage of development; all were not subject to the same modifying influences. But it

285

was a growing organism, showing change in almost
every fibre.   Scandinavian civilisation was gradually approaching the European type.   There is
danger that we may place the Northman on a too
high plane of culture; but the error is more frequently on the other side.[1]   Measured by the
standards of his own age, the Northman was not
a barbarian.   He had great energy of mind and
much intellectual curiosity.   He sailed everywhere and frequently included European ideas in
his plunder or merchandise.

The population throughout Scandinavia was
overwhelmingly rural; cities were few and insigni-
ficant, when we consider the number of houses and
inhabitants, though it appears that the urban
element was rapidly developing in the eleventh
century.   As early as the ninth century we find
mention of Birca, an island city in Lake Maelar in
eastern Sweden; of Heathby near the modern city
of Sleswick on the southern border of Denmark;
and of Skiringshall in southern Norway.[2]   These
and other cities evidently originated in the need
of definite market places.   Roads were poor in the
middle ages and the sea was often a dangerous
highway; commerce was therefore largely limited
to the more favourable seasons of the year, and

---

[1] See Montelius, *Kulturgeschichte Schwedens*, 251–252.

[2] Birca is mentioned in an early life of Saint Ansgar (*ca*. 850);
Langebek, *Script. Rer. Danic.*, i., 444.   Heathby and Skiringshall are alluded to in King Alfred's *Orosius* (Journeys of Ottar
and Wulfstan).

hence the importance of periodic markets. These were often held in connection with the great sacrificial festivals and it is therefore not strange that the earlier cities grew up on or near the sites of the ancient sanctuaries.[1]

In such localities grew up Odense on the island of Funen, Wisby on the island of Gotland, and Skiringshall on the great Bay.[2] Nidaros (Throndhjem) is said to have been founded by the first King Olaf, but its great importance dates from the canonisation of Saint Olaf whose bones were buried there. Kingscrag (Konungahelle) at the mouth of the Gaut River, and Tunsberg on the western shore of Folden Bay seem to have had their origin as landing places for merchants and vikings. On the other hand, Sarpsborg across the inlet from Tunsberg evidently grew up around a stronghold established in the days of Saint Olaf. Urban developments can also be traced in the western colonies: old cities in England, especially in the Danelaw, passed into the control of the Northmen; new cities rose on the shores of the Irish Sea.

This commercial movement began to gather strength during the quiet decades of the tenth century but it must have progressed rapidly during the peaceful reign of Canute. From Novgorod in Russia to Bristol and Limerick in the British Isles

---

[1] Bugge, *Studier over de norske Byers Selvstyre og Handel,* 4-5.
[2] *Ibid.* The great Bay (Folden Bay) is the modern Christiania Firth.

the ships of the North sailed every summer laden
with the products of all Northern Europe: furs
from Norway and Russia; the teeth of the walrus
from the Arctic waters; cured fish from the Scandinavian seas; honey from the Baltic shores;
Norwegian hawks for the English sportsmen;
and numerous other products.   In return for these
the Northmen received the luxuries of the South,
especially wine, wheat, and silk; but numerous
thralls were also imported, particularly from the
Celtic lands.[1]

These foreign products were chiefly consumed
in the homes of the Scandinavian aristocracy.
In material comforts the Northmen were probably
not far behind the corresponding classes elsewhere
in Europe. When the god Righ came to the
chieftain's house,

> Then the housewife thought of her arms,
> Smoothened her linen, pleated her sleeves.
> Broad was her headgear, a brooch on her breast;
> She wore trailing sashes and a blue-dyed sark.

When her son was born, "she swaddled him in
silk"; and when her daughter-in-law came to the
hall as a bride, "she walked under the veil of fine
linen."[2]   The sudden consciousness of rare finery
was not limited to the women; rich and highly
coloured clothing also delighted the men.

[1] On the commerce of the viking age see Montelius. *Kulturgeschichte Schwedens*, 266 ff.; Olrik, *Nordisk Aandsliv*, 52–53;
Norges Historie, I., ii., 223 ff. (Bugge).

[2] *Corpus Poeticum Boreale*, i., 239–241: "The Lay of Righ."

The influence of alien culture was also shown in the entertainment provided for the visiting god:

Then took Mother a markéd[1] cover
Of bleached linen and laid upon the board.
Next she laid out the thinnest loaves
Of wheaten flour on the white cover.
She set the table with silver-mounted dishes
Heaped with roasted birds and ham.
The wine brightened the mounted beakers.
They drank and talked till the day was done.[2]

"The Lay of Righ" was composed, it is believed, in the days of Canute's grandfather; but the civilisation that it describes was not new; even a century earlier the ruling classes in the North had reached a high stage of culture, as we know from the large number of articles indicating a refined and cultivated taste that were found when the Oseberg ship was discovered and excavated a few years ago.[3]

As in early Saxon times before the clergy had monopolised learning, the higher forms of cultured life saw their finest fruitage in the halls of kings and chiefs. The old Scandinavian house was a wooden structure of rectangular shape, its length being considerably greater than the width. In its general lines it doubtless bore close resemblance to the Anglo-Saxon dwelling of the same period.

[1] Embroidered with colours.
[2] "The Lay of Righ," ll., 114–122.
[3] *Norges Historie*, I., ii., 56–60.

In the number and arrangement of the rooms
the individual houses showed some, though not
great, variety; but a large living-room seems to have
been characteristic of all. In the middle of this
room a long trough lined with stones was sunk
into the floor; this served as fireplace, the smoke
finding its way out through an opening in the
roof. On either side of this long fireplace ran a
row of pillars that served to support the roof;
these also gave opportunities for the carver's art.
Between the pillars and the wall stood the benches
where the feasters sat with portable tables before
them. The walls were ornamented with shields
and weapons and with the trophies of the chase.
At the middle of the long north wall, facing the
entrance door on the opposite side, stood the high-
seat of the lord of the hall. The size and splendour
of the room would depend on the wealth and
importance of the owner: some of the larger halls
were planned for the entertainment of several
hundred guests and henchmen.[1]

There were many other buildings besides the
hall, the number depending on the needs of the
estate. The king's garth probably differed very
little from those of the wealthier chiefs. In
England, too, even as late as the year 1000, the
palace architecture must have been of the same
modest type. In his homily on Saint Thomas,

[1] For brief descriptions of the Northern halls in the viking
age see Bugge, *Vikingerne*, ii., 156–157; Montelius, *Kulturgeschichte Schwedens*, 282–283; Olrik, *Nordisk Aandsliv*, 15–16.

ready for the following day; otherwise he should hang for his presumption in composing a short poem on King Canute. Thorarin added a refrain and eked the poem out with a few additional stanzas. The refrain, "Canute guards the land as the lord of Greekland [God] the kingdom of heaven," evidently pleased the King. The poet was forgiven and the poem rewarded with fifty marks of silver. Thorarin's poem came to be known as the Head Ransom.[1]

It is said that when Ottar came to the King's hall he asked permission to recite a poem, which the King granted.

And the poem was delivered to a great gathering at the next day's moot, and the King praised it, and took a Russian cap off his head, broidered with gold and with gold knobs to it, and bade the chamberlain fill it with silver and give it to the poet. He did so and reached it over men's shoulders, for there was a crowd, and the heaped-up silver tumbled out of the hood on the moot-stage. He was going to pick it up, but the King told him to let it be. "The poor shall have it, thou shalt not lose by it."[2]

Of the court poets of the time Sighvat was easily the chief. Canute recognised his importance and was anxious to enroll him among his henchmen. But Sighvat, who had already sworn fidelity to King Olaf, excused himself with the

---

[1] Snorre, *Saga of Saint Olaf*, c. 172.
[2] *Corpus Poeticum Boreale*, ii., 151.

Alfric (who wrote his sermons in the decade of Canute's birth) tells the story of how the Apostle went to India to build a palace for a king, and, by the way, used the money for building churches:

Then he examined the grounds where it was to be builded.
And Thomas went about measuring the place with a yardstick,
And said that he would build the hall first of all
At the east end of the grounds, and the other buildings
Behind the hall: bath house and kitchen
And winterhouse and summerhouse and winsome bowers,—
Twelve houses altogether with good arches—
But such it is not customary to build in England
And therefore we do not mention them particularly.[1]

During the reign of Canute, however, there must have been material advancement in the direction of greater magnificence in the royal garth. The sagas testify to a splendour at Winchester that was greater than what was to be seen anywhere else.[2]

The men of the viking age usually associated the royal hall with the thought of elaborate festivities. The greatest moment in such an occasion was when the scald rose to sing the praises and recite the exploits of his host. It has been thought that the activities of the court poet show Celtic

[1] Alfric's *Lives*, ii., 404.
[2] Snorre, *Saga of Saint Olaf*, c. 130.

influence,[1] and it may be that the scald had learned
freely from the bard; but the institution itself is
most probably of native origin.   Like the Irish
singer his chief theme was praise; but we need not
suppose that the scald confined himself wholly to
contemporary themes: the gleeman in Beowulf
sang of the great hero that sat beside the King;
but he also told the tales of the Volsungs and the
still older story of creation; before the onslaught
at Stiklestad one of Saint Olaf's scalds recited
the ancient Bjarkamál, the Old Norse version of
Beowulf's last fight.   The holy King seems to
have enjoyed the inspiriting strains of heathen
heroism; he thanked the poet, as did all the host.

Old Norse poetry had its beginnings in the
ninth century; but its greater bulk belongs to the
tenth and eleventh.   It begins with a wonderful
series of mythical poems, most of them belonging
to the period of lull in the viking activities (900–
980).   The series culminates in the Sibyl's Prophecy (Voluspá), one of the grandest monuments
of mediæval literary art and thought.   It tells the
story of the creation, the destruction, the regeneration of the world in heathen terms with heathen
gods, giants, and demons as the actors.   But it contains unmistakable Christian elements and the poet
must have had some acquaintance with the faith
that ruled in the Western Islands.   The poem
seems to have been composed a generation or two
before the days of Canute; but it was doubtless

[1] Bugge, *Vesterlandenes Indflydelse paa Nordboernes Kultur*, 65.

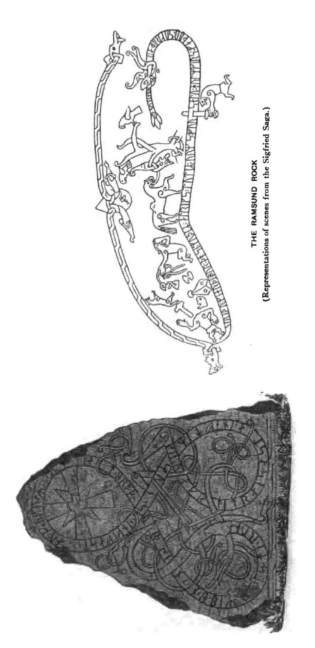

THE RAMSUND ROCK

(Representations of scenes from the Sigfried Saga.)

THE VIK STONE

(Illustrates the transition from heathendom to Christianity; shows a mixture of elements, the serpent and the cross.)

widely current during the years of his kingship. That the later scalds knew and appreciated the poem is evident from the fact that it was quoted by Christian poets in the following century.[1] No doubt it was an important number in their repertoire of song and story, and perhaps we may believe that it was gladly heard by Canute and his henchmen in the royal hall at Winchester.

The four decades that the Norns allotted to Canute (995?–1035) are a notable period in the history of Northern literature: it was the grand age of Old Norse poetry. The advance of Christianity had made the myths impossible as poetic materials, but new themes were found in the deeds and virtues of the old Teutonic heroes and of the mighty war lords of the viking age. The saga materials of the heroic age, the stories of Helgi and Sigrun, of Sigurd and Brunhild, of Gudrun's grief and Attila's fury, had long been treasured by the Northern peoples. Just when each individual tale was cast into the form that has come down to us is impossible to say; the probabilities are, however, that a considerable number of the heroic lays were composed in the age of Canute.

When we come to the court poetry we are on firmer ground: unlike the other poems, the dirges and praise-lays are not anonymous and their dates can be determined with some definiteness. The scald found the age great with possibilities. Those were the days of Hakon and Erik, of Sweyn and

[1] *Corpus Poeticum Boreale*, i., 193.

Canute, of Erling and Thurkil,—men who typified
in their warlike activities the deified valour of the
old faith.   It was also a period of famous battles:
Swald, Ringmere, Clontarf, Ashington, and Stiklestead, to mention only the more prominent.
About twenty scalds are known to have sung at
the courts of the viking princes, but the composi-
tions of some of them have been wholly lost or
exist in mere fragments only.   In the reign of
Canute three poets stood especially high in the
royal favour: Thorarin Praisetongue, Ottar the
Swart, and Sighvat the Scald.

The three were all Icelanders and were of a
roving disposition as the scalds usually were.
They all visited Canute's court, presumably at
Winchester.   Sighvat came to England on the
return from a trading journey to Rouen in 1027,
it seems, just after the King's return from his
Roman pilgrimage, which the poet alludes to in
his Stretch Song.   Ottar seems to have visited
Winchester the same year: his poem, the Canute's
Praise, closes with a reference to the Holy River
campaign in 1026.   Thorarin Praisetongue had
his opportunity to flatter the King a year or two
later, most likely in 1029: his Stretch Song deals
with the conquest of Norway in 1028.

Canute appears to have attached considerable
importance to the literary activities of these
Icelanders.   When he learned that Thorarin had
composed a short poem on himself, he became very
angry and ordered him to have a complete lay

ready for the following day; otherwise he should hang for his presumption in composing a short poem on King Canute. Thorarin added a refrain and eked the poem out with a few additional stanzas. The refrain, "Canute guards the land as the lord of Greekland [God] the kingdom of heaven," evidently pleased the King. The poet was forgiven and the poem rewarded with fifty marks of silver. Thorarin's poem came to be known as the Head Ransom.[1]

It is said that when Ottar came to the King's hall he asked permission to recite a poem, which the King granted.

And the poem was delivered to a great gathering at the next day's moot, and the King praised it, and took a Russian cap off his head, broidered with gold and with gold knobs to it, and bade the chamberlain fill it with silver and give it to the poet. He did so and reached it over men's shoulders, for there was a crowd, and the heaped-up silver tumbled out of the hood on the moot-stage. He was going to pick it up, but the King told him to let it be. "The poor shall have it, thou shalt not lose by it."[2]

Of the court poets of the time Sighvat was easily the chief. Canute recognised his importance and was anxious to enroll him among his henchmen. But Sighvat, who had already sworn fidelity to King Olaf, excused himself with the

[1] Snorre, *Saga of Saint Olaf*, c. 172.
[2] *Corpus Poeticum Boreale*, ii., 151.

remark that one lord at a time was sufficient. Canute did not press the matter but permitted the poet to depart with a golden arm-ring as the reward for his poem, the Stretch Song, whose ringing refrain, "Canute is the mightiest King under heaven," is high praise from one who had travelled so widely and had probably visited all the more important courts in northern and western Europe.

Did Canute also patronise Anglo-Saxon literature? We do not know, but the chances are that he did not, as during his reign very little was produced in the Old English idiom that could possibly appeal to him. The Anglo-Saxon spirit was crushed; and out of the consciousness of failure and humiliation can come no inspiration for literary effort. Even that fierce patriot, Archbishop Wulfstan, accepted the conquest and came down from York to assist at the dedication of the church at Ashington where Saxon rule had perished. After the appearance of the splendid poem that tells the story of Byrhtnoth's death at Maldon in 991, the voice of Anglo-Saxon poetry is almost silent for nearly two centuries. Early in the eleventh century Saxon prose, too, entered upon its decline. Alfric's best work was done before the close of the tenth century; he seems to have written his last important work, a pastoral letter, just before the accession of Canute to the English throne.[1] In the English cloisters the monks were still at work and valuable manu-

---

[1] *Cambridge History of English Literature*, i., 127.

scripts were produced; but Canute can hardly have taken much interest in grammars, glossaries, Biblical paraphrases, and pastoral letters. It seems evident that he did nothing to encourage the monastic annalist: the entries for Canute's reign in the *Anglo-Saxon Chronicle* are extremely meagre and disappointing; it seems probable that they were not written till after the King's death. The disappearance of Old English literature, both prose and poetic, dates from a time more than half a century earlier than the Norman conquest,— from the time when the Danish hosts filled the homes of Wessex with gloom and horror. The coming of the Normans did not put an end to literary production in the speech of the conquered English: it prevented its revival.

It is not to be inferred, however, from this lack of literary originality and productiveness, that the age had lost all appreciation of the poet's art. Two of the greatest monuments of Old English culture, the so-called Vercelli Book and the Exeter Codex, were apparently produced during the earlier decades of the eleventh century, possibly as late as the accession of Canute. In these manuscripts the Anglo-Saxon scribes have preserved to us some of the earliest literary productions of the English race. The Vercelli Book takes us back in the writings of Cynewulf to the eighth century; the Exeter manuscript looks back even farther and introduces us to the singers of heathen or semi-heathen times. Canute may not have shared the enthusiasm of the scribes for the Old English past; but he seems to have appreciated the work of a skilled copyist. In those days the exchange of presents was an essential part of diplomatic negotiations; and good manuscripts made very acceptable presents. Mention has already been made of the beautiful codex, written with golden letters, that made a part of the gift that Canute is said to have sent to Duke William of Aquitaine. As the Duke was renowned as a patron of the literary art, there can be no doubt that the present was properly appreciated. It will be remembered that Canute's gift to the church at Cologne was also in the form of manuscripts.

One of the most important contributions of the West to Northern civilisation was the written book. Writing was not a new art in the Scandinavian lands; but neither the symbols nor the materials in use were such as did service in the Christian lands. The men of the North wrote on wood and stone; they used characters that had to be chiseled into the tablet to be inscribed. These symbols were called runes; and graven into granite the runic inscriptions have defied the gnawing tooth of time. The large number of runic monuments that have come down to us would indicate that the art of writing was widely known, though it also seems likely that it was the peculiar possession of the "rune-masters," men of some education who knew the runes and were skilled in the art of inscribing.

The runes were of divine origin and were taught mankind by Woden himself. The term "run," which probably means "secret," reveals the attitude of the Germanic mind toward this ancient alphabet: thoughts were hidden in the graven lines, but that was not all: the characters were invested with magical properties. Graven on the sword hilt they were runes of victory; on the back of the hand, runes of love; on the palm, runes of help; the sailor cut sea runes into the rudder blade; the leech traced runes on "the bark and on the stock of a tree whose branches lean eastward."[1] There were also ale runes, speech runes, and mind runes, which "thou shalt know if thou wilt be wiser than all other men."[2]

The runic alphabet was originally a common Germanic possession; but among the Scandinavian peoples alone did its use become extensive and long-continued. Some of the Northern inscriptions are of a very early date, the earliest going back, perhaps, to the fourth century or possibly to the third.[3] They are of necessity terse and brief; but to the student of culture and civilisation they give some valuable information. These runes reveal a time when all the Northern tribes spoke the same language and were one people, though clearly not organised into a single state.[4] The inscriptions also show the rise of dialects and

[1] *Corpus Poeticum Boreale*, i., 40-41.   [2] *Ibid.*, 41.
[3] von Friesen, *Om runskriftens härkomst*, 10-12.
[4] Bugge, *Vikingerne*, i., 8.

the development of these into idioms, though this is a growth of the later centuries. Doubtless the changes in language bear some relation to a parallel political development, a grouping of tribes into states, until in the tenth century three dynasties claimed kingship in the North. In that century the monuments begin to have great value for narrative history. Members of the Knytling dynasty are mentioned on several important stones, as earlier pages of this volume have shown.

The runes that were in use in the tenth and eleventh centuries are the younger series, an alphabet of sixteen characters selected and developed from the older series of twenty-four. As the number of elementary sounds in the language was greater than the number of letters, several of the runes were used to represent more than one sound, a fact that has made reading and interpretation somewhat difficult. The runes were used especially for monumental purposes: a large number of the many hundred extant mediæval inscriptions (Sweden alone has more than fifteen hundred)[1] are epitaphs recording the death of some friend or kinsman. But the runes were also found useful for other purposes. They were used in making calendars; articles of value very often bore the owner's name in runic characters; in early Christian times we find runic characters traced on church bells and baptismal fonts; in later centuries attempts were even made to write books in the runic alphabet.

[1] Montelius, *Kulturgeschichte Schwedens*, 355.

PAINTED GABLE FROM URNES CHURCH
(Norse-Irish ornamentation.)

**CARVED PILLAR FROM
URNES CHURCH**
(Norse-Irish ornamentation.)

Wherever Northmen settled in the middle ages, inscriptions of this type are still to be found; some of the most interesting Scandinavian monuments were raised on the British Isles; even classic Piræus once had its runic inscription.

Sometimes the scribe did more than chisel the letters. Like the Christian monk who illumined his manuscript with elaborate initials and more or less successful miniatures, the rune-master would also try his hand at ornamentation. In the earlier middle ages, Northern art, if the term may be used, was usually a barbaric representation of animal forms, real and imaginary, the serpent and the dragon being favourite subjects. But in the western colonies the vikings were introduced to a new form of ornamentation, the Celtic style, which was based on the curving line or a combination of curved interlocking lines that seemed not to have been drawn in accordance with any law of regularity or symmetry, but traced sinuously in and out as the fancy of the artist might direct.[1] This form was adopted by the Norse colonists and soon found its way to the mother lands. In the North it suffered an important modification: the Norse artists added an element of their own; the old motives were not entirely abandoned for the winding body of the serpent or the dragon readily fitted into the new combinations. It was this modified form of Irish ornamentation that ruled among the Northmen in the days of Canute

[1] Olrik, *Nordisk Aandsliv*, 58.

and later. It appears wherever decoration was
desired: on runic monuments, on articles of personal adornment, and even on the painted walls
of the early Scandinavian churches.

While these early efforts at pictorial representation are frequently associated with runic inscriptions and incidental to them, such is not always the
case. The Northern countries possess a number of
"pictured rocks," on which the picture is the chief
and often the only matter of importance. As
many of these belong to the heathen period, the
themes are often mythological or suggestive of
warfare: the coming of the fallen warrior to
Walhalla on the Tjängvide Stone[1]; viking ships
on the Stenkyrka Stone. The comparatively new
sport of hawking is represented on a stone at
Alstad in Southern Norway.[2] Themes from the
heroic age seem to have attained an early popularity: especially do we find frequent pictorial
allusions to the story of Wayland Smith and
the adventures of the wonderful Sigfried. With
Christianity came a wealth of new subjects that
could be used in artistic efforts. One of Canute's
contemporaries, the Norwegian woman Gunvor,
raised (about 1050) a memorial rock bearing a
series of pictures from the story of Christ's
nativity.[3] The work rarely shows much original-

---

[1] The Tjängvide Stone probably dates from about the year
900. The warrior represented may be Woden on his eight-footed
horse. Bugge, *Vesterlandenes Indflydelse*, 323.

[2] Bugge, *Vikingerne*, ii., 234.   [3] *Norges Historie*, I., ii., 322, 323.

THE HUNNESTAD STONE   THE ALSTAD STONE

the development of these into idioms, though this is a growth of the later centuries. Doubtless the changes in language bear some relation to a parallel political development, a grouping of tribes into states, until in the tenth century three dynasties claimed kingship in the North. In that century the monuments begin to have great value for narrative history. Members of the Knytling dynasty are mentioned on several important stones, as earlier pages of this volume have shown.

The runes that were in use in the tenth and eleventh centuries are the younger series, an alphabet of sixteen characters selected and developed from the older series of twenty-four. As the number of elementary sounds in the language was greater than the number of letters, several of the runes were used to represent more than one sound, a fact that has made reading and interpretation somewhat difficult. The runes were used especially for monumental purposes: a large number of the many hundred extant mediæval inscriptions (Sweden alone has more than fifteen hundred)[1] are epitaphs recording the death of some friend or kinsman. But the runes were also found useful for other purposes. They were used in making calendars; articles of value very often bore the owner's name in runic characters; in early Christian times we find runic characters traced on church bells and baptismal fonts; in later centuries attempts were even made to write books in the runic alphabet.

[1] Montelius, *Kulturgeschichte Schwedens*, 355.

PAINTED GABLE FROM URNES CHURCH
(Norse-Irish ornamentation.)

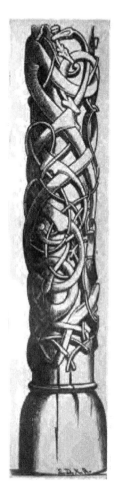

CARVED PILLAR FROM
URNES CHURCH
(Norse-Irish ornamentation.)

of rings, doubtless because of their ancient use for monetary purposes. Even in the days of Canute, the ring, especially the large arm-ring, was commonly used in rewarding the kingsmen. Saint Olaf once stroked the arm of a henchman above the elbow to determine whether Canute had bribed him.[1] Canute's officials procured the allegiance of Björn, Saint Olaf's spokesman, for English silver and two heavy gold rings.[2] Canute's ring gift to Sighvat has been noted elsewhere; Bersi, the poet's companion, received "a mark or more and a keen sword."[3]

Northern industrial art of the later heathen age found its best and highest expression in the ship-builder's trade. Merchant ships as well as ships for warfare were built, but the builder's pride was the ship that the King sailed when he sought the enemy. The ships that bore Canute's warriors to England were no doubt mainly of the so-called long ship type, a form that was developed during the second half of the tenth century. The long ship was built on the same general plan as the dragon ship of the century before, of which type we have a remarkably well-preserved example in the ship that was found in a burial-mound at Gokstad near Sandefjord in Southern Norway. The Gokstad ship is nearly eighty feet long from stem to stern, and a little less than one fourth as wide. The builders of the long ship increased the length

---

[1] Snorre, *Saga of Saint Olaf*, c. 165.   [2] *Ibid.*, c. 185.
[3] *Corpus Poeticum Boreale*, ii., 133.

of the dragon, but did not increase the width proportionally. Oak timbers and iron rivets were the materials used. It is likely that by the close of the viking age the shipbuilder's art was as highly developed in the North as anywhere else in Christian Europe.

The long ship was built with pointed prow and stern. The gunwales generally ran parallel to the water line, but in the prow the timbers curved sharply upward to join the stem, which projected above the body of the ship and frequently terminated in some carved image like those described by the Encomiast.[1] The stern was built in much the same fashion. The ribs were supported and held in place by strong cross-beams, which also served as supports for the deck. In the fore-end the deck was high; here stood the stem-men, the best warriors on board. From a similarly raised deck in the stern, the chief directed the movements of the ship and the men when battle was joined. But in the middle portion of the ship the deck was low; here the oarsmen sat, each on a chest containing his clothes and other belongings. The number of pairs of oars would usually indicate the size of the ship; fifteen or twenty pairs were the rule; but larger ships were sometimes built: the *Long Serpent* had thirty-four pairs. A rudder or "steering board" was fastened to the after-part of the vessel, on the side that has since been known as starboard.

[1] *Encomium Emmæ*, i., c. 4.

The long ship was also equipped with a mast and a sail. The mast was planted amidships, but in such a way that it could be lowered when not in use. The sails were generally made of coarse woollen stuff; they often bore stripes, blue, red, or green, and such striped sails were counted highly ornamental. The ship was painted and the gunwales frequently hung with shields, alternately yellow and red. An awning was provided to protect the vessel from rain and sunshine.[1] The average long ship had, perhaps, eighty or ninety men on board, the oarsmen included. The number varied, of course, with the size of the ship: the *Long Serpent* is said to have had a crew of three hundred men.[2]

In culture the later viking age was emphatically one of transition. The movement that transformed Northern into European civilisation culminated in the reign of Canute and was no doubt given great impetus by the fact of his imperial au-

---

[1] For brief descriptions of Northern ships of the viking age, see *Danmarks Riges Historie*, i., 256–257, 318–322; Montelius, *Kulturgeschichte Schwedens*, 260–264.

[2] English writers seem inclined to estimate a ship's crew at not more than 50 or 60 on the authority of Heremannus, who wrote the "Miracles of Saint Edmund" toward the close of the eleventh century (*Memorials of Saint Edmund's Abbey*, i., 72, 92). But on the question of viking ships and crews his statements cannot be used as evidence: his ships are merchant ships, not viking ships, and they are not Scandinavian. It should also be noted that one of the ships (c. 50) in addition to "nearly 60" passengers carried 36 beasts (heads of cattle?) and 16 horses heavily laden with merchandise.

ANGLO-SAXON TABLE SCENE
(From a manuscript in the British Museum reproduced in *Norges Historie*, i., ii.)

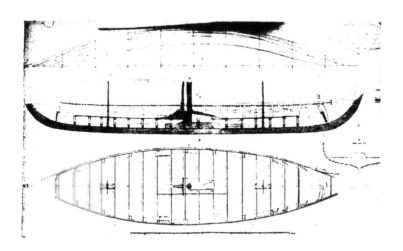

thority in the Christian West. The seeds of the new culture had been gathered long before and in many lands: the German, the Frank, the Celt, and the Saxon had all contributed to the new fruitage. But in the North as elsewhere in the middle ages, the mightiest of all the transforming forces was the mediæval Church. In one sense the poetic activities of the tenth century had made the transition to Christian worship easier than in other lands: the author of the Sibyl's Prophecy had, unintentionally, no doubt, bridged the gap between the contending faiths. The intelligent Northmen found in the teachings of Christianity conceptions very similar to those in the great poem, only in a different historical setting. In the outward symbolism, too, the Northman found similarities that made the step easier: he had already learned to pour water over the new-born infant; in the cross of Christ he may have seen a modification of Thor's hammer; the Christian tree of life reminded him of the ash Yggdrasil that symbolised the unity of the worlds; the Yule festival of midwinter tide was readily identified with the Christian celebration of the Nativity on December 25th. Too much importance must not be assigned to these considerations, but they doubtless had their effect.

But even the Church was not able to make its conquest of the North complete. The Scandinavian peoples never entirely severed their connection with the historic past. The bridge that was built by the Sibyl's Prophecy was never demol-

ished. The poet purged the old mythology of
much that was revolting and absurd and thus
made the old divinities and the old cosmic ideas
attractive and more easily acceptable. Even
when the new cult became compulsory and even
fashionable, it was hard for the Northman to
desert his gods. Hallfred Troublousscald, who
flourished in the years of Canute's childhood, gives
expression to this feeling in one of his poems:

> 'T is heavy to cherish hatred
> For Frigg's divine husband
> Now that Christ has our worship,
> For the scald delighted in Woden.

But Olaf Trygvesson has commanded that the old
faith be renounced and men have obeyed, though
unwillingly:

> Cast to the winds all men have
> The kindred of mighty Woden;
> Forced to renounce Njord's children
> I kneel to Christ in worship.

After several verses of regretful and half-hearted
renunciation the scald continues:

> I will call upon Christ with love words
> (I can bear the Son's wrath no longer;
> He rules the earth in glory)
> And God the Father in prayer.[1]

The gods continued to live in the popular imagination as great heroic figures that had flour-

[1] *Corpus Poeticum Boreale*, ii., 96–97.

THE LUNDAGÅRD STONE
(Shows types of ornamentation in Canute's day.)

ished in the earlier ages of the race. Much that belonged to the worship of the Anses was carried over into the Christian life. The Scandinavian Christians on the Isle of Man evidently found nothing incongruous in placing heathen ornamentations on the cross of Christ. Sometimes the attributes of the ancestral divinities were transferred to the Christian saints. The red beard with which Christian artists soon provided the strong and virile Saint Olaf was probably suggested by the flaming beard of the hammering Thor.

ᚠ ᚢ ᚦ ᚨ ᚱ ᚲ ᛬ ᚼ ᚾ ᛁ ᛆ ᛋ ᛬ ᛏ ᛒ ᛚ ᛘ ᛉ

f u th o r k   h n i a s   t b l m -r

RUNIC ALPHABET

CHAPTER XIV

THE LAST YEARS

1031–1035

AFTER the passing of the Norman war-cloud and the failure of the Norse reaction in 1030, Canute almost disappears from the stage of English history. The *Anglo-Saxon Chronicle* which gives us so much information on his earlier career in England has but little to tell of his activities as king; for the closing years of the reign the summaries are particularly meagre. Evidently the entries for this reign were written from memory some years after the death of the great King; and the scribe recalled but little. It is also likely that the closing years in Britain were peaceful and quiet, such as do not give the annalist much to record. Of the larger European movements, of the Norse secession, of movements on the Danish border, and of the renewed compact with the Emperor, the cloister was probably not well informed.

As the Chronicler thinks back upon the passing of a King who was still in his best and strongest

THE JURBY CROSS, ISLE OF MAN

THE GOSFORTH CROSS,
CUMBERLAND

years, there comes to him the memory of certain
strange natural phenomena which suddenly take
on meaning.   In 1033, two years before the
King's death, "appeared the wild fire," such as
none could remember the like of.   There could be
no doubt as to the interpretation: it was an omen
giving warnings of great changes to come, the end
of alien rule, even as a fiery heaven announced its
imminence in the days of the boy Ethelred.

Later writers report that during the last years
of his life Canute was afflicted with a long and
severe illness, and it has been inferred that this
may account for the uneventful character of this
period.   There may be an element of truth in this,
but he was not too ill to take an active interest in
political affairs.   His legislation evidently belongs
to one of these years.   In one of the manuscripts of
Canute's code he is spoken of as King of Angles,
Danes and Norwegians, a title that he could not
claim before 1028.   As he did not return from his
expedition to Norway before the following year,
the earliest possible date for the enactment of Canute's laws is Christmas, 1029.[1]   For they were
drawn up at a meeting of the national assembly
"at the holy midwinter tide in Winchester."

There are reasons for believing, however, that
the laws are of a still later date.   Little need there
was, it would seem, for extensive ecclesiastical
legislation in those years when paganism was in

[1] The author has discussed this subject further in the *American
Historical Review*, xv., 741-742.

full retreat and Christianity had become fashionable even among the vikings. Some condition
must have arisen that made it necessary for the
King to take a positive stand on the side of the
English Church. Such a condition may have
grown out of the canonisation of Saint Olaf in
1031. He was the first native saint of the North
and the young Scandinavian Church hailed him
with a joy that was ominous for those who had
pursued him to the grave. It may have been in
the hope of checking the spread of the new cult
in England that the witenagemot, the same that
ratified Canute's legislation, canonised the imperious Archbishop who had governed the English
Church two generations earlier. The method of
canonisation was probably new; but the nobles
and prelates of England were surely as competent
to act in such a matter as the youthful church at
Nidaros.

Canute showed an interest in the welfare of the
Church to the last months of his life. It was
apparently in this period that he initiated the
policy of advancing his own chapel priests to
episcopal appointments: in 1032 Elfwine became
Bishop of Winchester; the following year Duduc,
another chapel priest, was promoted in the same
manner.[1] The church of York was remembered
with a large gift of lands to Archbishop Alfric.[2]
Gifts to some of the larger monasteries are also

[1] Larson, *The King's Household in England*, 141.
[2] Kemble, *Codex Diplomaticus*, No. 749.

recorded for these same years: to Sherburne, Winchester, Abingdon, and Croyland.[1] These usually took the form of land, though ornaments and articles intended for use in the church service were also given. Abingdon received lands and bells and a case of gold and silver for the relics of "the most glorious martyr Vincent of Spain" whose resting place was in this church.[2] It is worth noting that Abbot Siward who ruled at Abingdon during the last few years of the reign bore a Danish name.

Canute's last recorded gift was to the Old Minster at Winchester in 1035, the year of his death. This comprised a landed estate, a bier for the relics of Saint Brice, a large image, two bells, and a silver candlestick with six branches.[3] It may be that he had premonitions of coming death, for in this abbey he chose to be buried.

We do not know what efforts Canute may have made to improve the material conditions in his Anglo-Saxon kingdom, but it appears that such undertakings were not wholly wanting. The King showed great favour to the religious establishments in the Fenlands and was evidently impressed

[1] Kemble, *Codex Diplomaticus*, Nos. 748, 750, 751, 1322. The Croyland charter is clearly a forgery, but Canute may have made the grant none the less as the forged charters frequently represent an attempt to replace a genuine document that has been lost or destroyed.

[2] *Chronicon Monasterii de Abingdon*, i., 443.

[3] *Annales Monastici*, ii., 16.

with the difficulty of travel from abbey to abbey. An attempt was made to remedy this:

and that same road through the marshes between Ramsey and the borough that is called King's Delf he caused to be improved that the danger of passing through the great swamps might be avoided. [1]

Matthew Paris, our authority for this statement, wrote nearly two centuries after Canute's day, but it is likely that he is reporting a correct tradition; if the work had been done at the instance of one of the later kings, it is not probable that it would have been associated with the name of the Danish ruler.

The Norwegian sources have little to say of Canute after the battle of Stiklestead; but they follow the troubles of the Norse regency in some detail. It was thought best, when Sweyn was sent to Norway, to give him the royal title; but as he was a mere youth, the actual power was in the hands of his mother, Elgiva, who was probably associated with Earl Harold of Jomburg, Harthacanute's minister and guardian in Denmark, who seems to have acted as Canute's personal representative in his eastern kingdoms. [2] Mention has already been made of the opposition that soon arose to the Danish régime. It was not long before the dissatisfied elements formed an alliance with the partisans of the old dynasty who were

[1] Matthew Paris, *Chronica Majora*, i., 509.
[2] Munch, *Det norske Folks Historie*, I., ii., 814.

assiduously disseminating the belief that the fallen Olaf was a saint.

All through the winter that followed the King's martyrdom stories were current of miracles performed by the holy relics: wounds had been healed and blindness removed by accidental contact with the royal blood. At the same time much ill-feeling developed against Bishop Sigurd who had shown such a partisan spirit on the eve of the tragedy at Stiklestead. Sigurd was a Dane who had served as chaplain at the English court[1] and had therefore a double reason for preferring Canute. Under the regency he had continued as chief of the Norwegian Church, but soon the murmur became so loud that the zealous prelate had to withdraw to England.

Einar Thongshaker now came forward to lead the opposition to the regents. He was the first of the chiefs to express his belief in Olaf's sanctity and many were ready to follow his lead. Bishop Grimkell, who since Olaf's flight in 1029 had remained in comparative quiet in the Uplands, was asked to come and investigate the current rumours of miraculous phenomena. The Bishop responded very promptly. On the way he visited Einar, by whom he was gladly welcomed. Later the prelate appeared at Nidaros and began extended investigations into the matter of the reported wonders. Einar was next summoned to conduct the negotia-

[1] Taranger, *Den angelsaksiske Kirkes Indflydelse paa den norske*, 176.

tions with the regency. The plans of the national faction seem to have been carefully laid; it was probably not accidental that the city suddenly was thronged by incoming Norsemen.

Having secured permission from King Sweyn to act in the matter, Einar and Grimkell, followed by the multitude, proceeded to the spot where Olaf's remains were said to have been buried. According to the legend that Snorre in part follows, the coffin was found to have risen toward the surface and looked new as if recently planed. No change was observed in the remains except that the hair and nails showed considerable growth; the cheeks were red as those of one who had just fallen asleep. But the Queen-mother was not easily convinced:

"Very slowly do bodies decay in sand; it would have been otherwise if he had lain in mould." Then the Bishop took a pair of shears and clipped off a part of the King's hair and beard,—he wore a long moustache, as custom was in those days. Then said the Bishop to the King and Alfiva: "Now is the King's hair and beard as long as when he died; but it has grown as much as you see I have cut off." Then replied Alfiva: "I believe hair to be sacred if it is not consumed in fire; often have we seen whole and uninjured the hair of men who have lain in the earth longer than this man." So the Bishop placed fire in a censer, blessed it, and added the incense. Then he laid Olaf's hair in the fire. But when the incense was consumed, the Bishop took the hair from the fire, and it was wholly

THE FALL OF SAINT OLAF
(Initial in the Flat-isle Book.)

unburnt. The Bishop showed it to the King and the other chiefs. Then Alfiva requested them to place the hair in unblessed fire; but Einar Tremblethong spoke up, bade her keep silence, and used many hard words. Then by the Bishop's decision, the King's consent, and the judgment of the entire assembly, it was decreed that King Olaf was in truth a holy man.[1]

Whatever the procedure employed, there can be no doubt that King Olaf was canonised in the summer of 1031 (August 3d is the date given) by popular act; nor can it be doubted that Elgiva resisted the act—she must have seen that the canonisation meant her own and her son's undoing. For she must surely have realised that political considerations were an important element in the devotion of the Norsemen to their new patron.

There was later a tradition among the monks of Nidaros that Canute at one time planned to establish a monastery in the northern capital.[2] If such an attempt was made, it evidently failed; but it would not be strange if the King should try to establish an institution where loyalty to the empire might be nursed and which might assist in uprooting nationalistic tendencies. If the attempt was made, it was probably soon after the canonisation, when it became important to divert attention from the new cult.

For the worship of Saint Olaf spread with

[1] Snorre, *Saga of Saint Olaf*, c. 244. For the preliminary steps see cc. 239–243.

[2] Matthew Paris, *Chronica Majora*, v., 42.

astonishing rapidity not only through Norway but through the entire North and even farther. The Church had saints in great number; but here was one from the very midst of the Scandinavian people. Moreover, Saint Olaf was a saint whom the men of the day could appreciate: he was of their own type, with the strength of Thor and the wisdom of Woden; they had seen him and felt the edge of his ax. So all along the shores that Olaf the Stout had plundered in his earlier heathen days churches arose dedicated to the virile saint of the North.[1]

There were other difficulties, too, that the regents had to contend with. Hunger stalked over the land. The Norwegian people had always been accustomed to hold their kings responsible for the state of the harvest; they were to secure the favour of the gods; a failure of crops meant that this duty had been shirked. The feeling lingered for some time after the disappearance of heathendom. Sweyn was only a youth and was not held responsible; the blame fell upon the hated Queen-mother and the hard years of her rule were known as the "Alfiva-time." The general discontent is expressed in a contemporary fragment attributed to Sighvat:

> Alfiva's time our sons will
> Long remember; then ate we
> Food more fit for oxen,
> Shavings the fare of he-goats.

[1] Daae, *Norges Helgener*, 48-60.

> It was not thus when the noble
> Olaf governed the Norsemen;
> Then could we all boast of
> Corn-filled barns and houses. [1]

And Thorarin Praise-tongue in the Shrine-song addressed to Sweyn the son of Canute urges the young regent to seek the favour of the new saint, "the mighty pillar of the book-language":

> Pray thou to Olaf that he grant thee
> (He is a man of God) all his land rights;
> For he can win from God himself
> Peace to men and good harvests. [2]

In 1033, a revolt broke out in Norway in the interest of one Trygve, a pretended son of Olaf Trygvesson and an English mother. The attempt failed; the Norse chiefs had other plans. In Russia was Magnus, the illegitimate son of the holy King, now about nine or ten years old; him had the chiefs determined upon as their future leader. Early the next year an embassy was sent to Russia led by the two magnates Einar and Kalf. Here oaths were sworn and plans were laid, and in the following spring (1035) Magnus Olafsson appeared in Norway as the foster son of Kalf who had led his father's banesmen at Stiklestead.

From the moment when Magnus set foot on his native soil Norway was lost to the empire. Sweyn

---

[1] *Corpus Poeticum Boreale*, ii., 144.　　　[2] *Ibid.*, 161.

was farther south in his kingdom when news came of revolt in the Throndelaw. He promptly summoned the yeomanry, but feeling that their devotion to him was a matter of grave doubt, he gave up his plans of resistance and fled to his brother Harthacanute in Denmark, where he died less than a year later.[1] His mother Elgiva evidently withdrew to England, where the death of Canute the following November doubtless gave her another opportunity to play the politician.

So far as we know, Canute made no effort to dislodge Magnus. It may be true that he was ill; or perhaps the power of the Church restrained him: Magnus was the son of a saint; would not the martyred King enlist the powers of heaven on the side of his son? But it was probably want of time and not lack of interest and purpose that prevented reconquest. There is an indication that Canute was preparing for important movements: at Whitsuntide, 1035, while the imperial court was at Bamberg, he was renewing his friendship with the Emperor and arranging for the marriage of his daughter Gunhild to the future Henry III.[2] Perhaps we should see in this a purpose to secure the southern frontier in anticipation of renewed hostilities in the North.

But whatever may have been Canute's plans, they were never carried out—the hand of death came in between. On Wednesday, November 12,

---

[1] Snorre, *Saga of Magnus the Good*, cc. 4, 5.
[2] Manitius, *Deutsche Geschichte*, 411–412.

1035, the great Dane saw the last of earth at
Shaftesbury, an old town on the Dorset border,
a day's journey from the capital. The remains
were brought to Winchester and interred in the
Old Minster,[1] an ancient abbey dedicated to the
chief of the Apostles, which Canute had remembered so liberally earlier in the year.

We have already noted the tradition reported
by both Norse and English writers that his death
was preceded by a long and serious illness; one
of the sagas states that the fatal disease was
jaundice.[2] There would be nothing incredible
in this, but the evidence is not of the best. The
fact that death came to him not in the residential
city but in the neighbouring town of Shaftesbury
seems to indicate that he was at the time making
one of his regular progresses through the country, as seems to have been his custom.[3] In that
case the illness could hardly have been a pro-
tracted one.

It is likely, however, that Canute was not phy-
sically robust; he died in the prime of manhood,
having scarcely passed the fortieth year; and he
seems not to have transmitted much virility to his
children. Three sons and a daughter were born
to him, but within seven years of his own death
they had all joined him in the grave. Sweyn, who
seems to have been the oldest, died a few months

[1] *Anglo-Saxon Chronicle*, 1035; *Encomium Emmæ*, iii., c. 1.
[2] *Knytlingasaga*, c. 18.
[3] *Historia Rameseiensis*, 135.

21

after his father, perhaps in the early part of 1036. Gunhild followed in 1038; Harold in 1040; and Harthacanute in 1042. With Harthacanute passed away the last male representative of the Knytling family; after a few years the crown of Denmark passed to the descendants of Canute's sister Estrid, to the son of the murdered Ulf.

None of Canute's children seems to have attained a real maturity: Harold and Harthacanute probably reached their twenty-fourth year; Sweyn died at the age of perhaps twenty-two; Gunhild could not have been more than eighteen when she laid down the earthly crown. There is no reason for thinking that any of them was degenerate with the exception of Harold Harefoot, and in his case we have hostile testimony only; at the same time, they were all surely lacking in bodily strength and vigour.

Nor is there any reason for thinking that these weaknesses were maternal inheritances, for the women that Canute consorted with were evidently strong and vigorous and both of them survived him. We know little of the concubine Elgiva except that she was proud and imperious, on fire with ambition for herself and her sons. Emma was a woman of a similar type. Canute apparently found it inconvenient to have the two in the same kingdom, and when the mistress returned to England after the Norse revolt, we seem to see her hand in the consequent intrigues. Queen Emma survived her husband more than sixteen years; "on March 14 [1052], died the Old Lady, the mother of King Edward and Harthacanute, named Imme, and her body lies in the Old Minster with King Canute."[1] At the time of her death she must have been in the neighbourhood of seventy years of age.

Of Canute's personality we know nothing. The portraits on his coins, if such rude drawings can be called portraits, give us no idea of his personal appearance. Nor is the picture in the *Liber Vitæ* likely to be more than an idealistic representation. Idealistic, too, no doubt, is the description of Canute in the *Knytlingasaga*, composed two centuries or more after his time:

Canute the King was large of build and very strong, a most handsome man in every respect except that his nose was thin and slightly aquiline with a high ridge. He was fair in complexion, had an abundance of fair hair, and eyes that surpassed those of most men both as to beauty and keenness of vision.[2]

The writer adds that he was liberal in dealing with men, brave in fight, favoured of fortune, but not wise. Except for the details as to the nose, which give the reader the feeling that the writer may, after all, have had some authentic source of information at his disposal, this picture would describe almost any one of the heroic figures of the time.

[1] *Anglo-Saxon Chronicle*, 1052.   [2] C. 20.

On his own contemporaries Canute made a profound impression which succeeding generations have shared. In Britain he was called the Great; in Scandinavia the Rich, the Mighty or the Powerful. The extent of his possessions, the splendour of his court, the size of his navy, his intimate relations with Pope and Emperor—all these things gave him a position and a prestige that was unheard of in the Northlands. And it was indeed a marvellous achievement for a pirate chief from a nation just emerging from heathendom to gather into his power the realms and territories that made up the Knytling empire.

To analyse a character such as that of Canute is a difficult task, as character analysis always must be. There was so much that was derived from a heathen time and ancestry, and also so much that had been acquired by contact with Christian culture and influences, that the result could be only a strange composite out of which traits and characteristics, often contradictory and hostile, would come to the surface as occasion would suggest. Canute was a Christian, probably baptised in his youth by some German ecclesiastic, as the Christian name Lambert, which in harmony with custom was added to the one that he already possessed, seems distinctly German. But the new name was evidently not much employed, except, perhaps, on occasions when the King wished to emphasise his Christian character. He seems to have entered into some sort of fraternal relations with the monks of Bremen: in the book of our brotherhood, says Adam the monk, he is named Lambert, King of the Danes.[1]

The historians of Old English times, both Saxon and Norman, were ecclesiastics and saw the reign of Canute from their peculiar view-point. To them the mighty Dane was the great Christian King, the founder of monasteries, the giver of costly gifts and valuable endowments to the houses of God. To the undisputed traits of Christian liberality, they added those of piety and humility, and told stories of the visit to the monks of Ely and of Canute's vain attempt to stem the tides and compel their obedience. The former is probably a true story; there is no reason why the King, who seems to have taken great interest in the abbeys of the Fenlands, should not have visited the cloisters of Ely, and he may have been attracted by the chants of the monks, which is more doubtful. But the tale of how Canute had to demonstrate his powerlessness before his admiring courtiers is a myth too patent to need discussion.[2] There was nothing of the Oriental spirit in the Northern courts.

That Canute was religious cannot be denied. Nor should we doubt that he was truly and honestly so, as religion passed among the rulers

[1] *Gesta*, schol. 38.

[2] The story must have arisen soon after the Danish period; it is first told by Henry of Huntingdon who wrote two generations later. *Historia Anglorum*, 189.

of the age. The time demanded defence and support of the priesthood, and this Canute granted, at least toward the close of his life. Perhaps in real piety, too, he was the equal of his contemporaries whom the Church has declared holy: Saint Stephen of Hungary, Saint Henry of Germany, and Saint Olaf of Norway. Still, it becomes evident as we follow his career that at no period of his life, unless it be in the closing years of which we know so little, did Canute permit consideration for the Church or the Christian faith to control his actions or determine his policies. The moving passion of Canute's life was not a fiery zeal for the exaltation of the Church, but a yearning for personal power and imperial honours.

In the Northern sources written by laymen, especially in the verses of the wandering scalds, we get a somewhat different picture of Canute from that which has been painted in the English cloisters. Little emphasis is here placed on Canute's fidelity to the new faith; here we have the conqueror, the diplomat, the politician whose goal is success, be the means what they may. The wholesale bribery that he employed to the ruin of Saint Olaf, the making and breaking of promises to the Norwegian chiefs, and the treatment of his sister's family suggest a sense of honour that was not delicate, a passion for truth that was not keen. In his preference for devious ways, in the deliberate use that he made of the lower passions of men, he shows a characteristic that is not Northern. All was not honest frankness in the Scandinavian lands; but the pirates and their successors, as a rule, did not prefer bribery and falsehood to open battle and honest fight.

Slavic ancestry, Christian culture, Anglo-Saxon ideas, and the responsibilities of a great monarchy did much to develop and modify a character which was fundamentally as much Slavic as Scandinavian. Still, deep in his strong soul lay unconquered the fierce passions that ruled the viking age —pitiless cruelty, craving for revenge, consuming hatred, and lust for power. As a rule he seems to have been humane and merciful; he believed in orderly government, in security for his subjects; but when an obstacle appeared in the path of his ambitions, he had little scruple as to the means to be employed in removing it. The mutilation of the hostages at Sandwich, the slaughter and outlawry of earls and ethelings in the early years of his rule in England, the assassination of Ulf in Roeskild church suggest a spirit that could be terrible when roused. Something can be said for Canute in all these instances: Ulf was probably a traitor; the hostages represented broken pledges; the ethelings were a menace to his rule. But why was the traitor permitted to live until he had helped the King in his sorest straits; and what was to be gained by the mutilation of innocent Englishmen; and was there no other way to make infants harmless than to decree their secret death in a foreign land?

fairly effectually the Baltic, the North, and the
Irish Seas together with the English Channel
to viking fleets; and the raven was thus forced
to fly for its prey to the distant shores beyond
Brittany. Piracy continued in a desultory way
throughout the eleventh century; but it showed
little vigour after Canute's accession to the Danish
kingship.

CHAPTER XV

THE COLLAPSE OF THE EMPIRE

1035–1042

KING CANUTE was dead, but the great king-thought that he lived for, the policy of his dynasty, their ambition to unite the Northern peoples in the old and new homes under one sceptre persisted after his death. Historians have generally believed that Canute had realised the impossibility of keeping long united the three crowns that he wore in his declining years, and had made preparation for a division of the empire among his three sons. In the year of his death one son is found in England, one in Denmark, and one in Norway; hence it is believed that like Charlemagne before him he had executed some sort of a partition, so as to secure something for each of the three. Such a conclusion, however, lacks the support of documentary authority and is based on a mistaken view of the situation in the empire in 1035.

We should remember in the first place that when Harthacanute and Sweyn received the royal title (in 1028 and 1030), Canute cannot have been more than thirty-five years old, and at that age rulers are not in the habit of transferring their dominions to mere boys. In the second place, these two sons were sent to the North, not to exercise an independent sovereignty, but to represent the royal authority that resided at Winchester. Finally, there is no evidence that Canute at any time intended to leave England or any other kingdom to his son Harold. The probabilities are that he hoped to make the empire a permanent creation; perhaps he expected it to become in time wholly Scandinavian, as it already was to a large extent, except in the comparatively small area of Wessex.

Canute's policy is revealed in the act at Nidaros, discussed in an earlier chapter, when in the presence of lords from all his realms, he led Harthacanute to the high seat and thus proclaimed him a king of his own rank. That Denmark was intended for the young King is undisputed. England was to be added later. The Encomiast tells us that when Harthacanute had grown up (evidently toward the close of Canute's reign) all England was bound by oath to the sovereignty of Harthacanute.[1] The early promise that Canute made to Queen Emma was apparently to be kept. Most likely, the loyalty that Godwin and other West Saxon magnates showed to the King's legitimate heir is to be explained, not by assuming

[1] *Encomium Emmæ*, ii., c. 19.

a pro-Danish sentiment, but by this oath, surely taken in England, perhaps earlier at Nidaros.

The situation in Norway, however, made it difficult to carry out Canute's wishes. On the high seat in the Throndelaw sat Magnus the son of Saint Olaf. To be the son of a saint was a great asset in the middle ages; in addition Magnus had certain native qualities of the kingly type and soon developed into a great warrior. Knowing that war was inevitable, Magnus began hostilities and carried the warfare into Danish waters.[1] It was this difficulty that prevented Harthacanute from appearing promptly in England in the winter of 1035–1036, when Harold Harefoot was planning to seize the throne.

After the flight of her son Sweyn in the summer of 1035, Elgiva is almost lost to history. Apparently she retired to England, where she played the part of Queen-mother during the reign of her son Harold: in a will of Bishop Alfric we find the testator giving two marks of gold to King Harold and one mark to my lady.[2] As we do not find that the King had either wife or children the presumption is that the lady was his mother, the woman from Northampton.

We may then conjecture that the struggle for the English crown in the winter following Canute's death was at bottom a fight between the two women who bore Canute's children, each with a

[1] Snorre, *Saga of Magnus the Good*, c. 6.
[2] Kemble, *Codex Diplomaticus*, No. 759.

son to place in the high seat; each with a party
devoted to her cause, each with a section of the
country ready to follow her lead.   Elgiva had her
strength in the Danelaw; there were her kinsmen,
and there her family had once been prominent.
Queen Emma was strongest in the south; on her
side were Earl Godwin and the housecarles.[1]

The sources that relate the events of these
months are anything but satisfactory and their
statements are sometimes vague or ambiguous.
But it is clear that soon after the throne became
vacant (thirteen days, if the Chronicler is accurate)[2]
a meeting of the "wise men" was held at Oxford,
the border city where Danes and Saxons had so
frequently met in common assembly.   At this
meeting, as the *Chronicle* has it, the northern
magnates led by Leofric, Earl of Mercia, and
supported by the Danes in London, "chose
Harold to hold all England, him and his brother
Harthacanute who was in Denmark."   To this
arrangement Godwin opposed all his influence and
eloquence; but though he was supported by the
lords of Wessex, "he was able to accomplish
nothing."   It was finally agreed that Queen
Emma and the royal guard should continue to
hold Wessex for Harthacanute.[3]   The north was
evidently turned over to Harold.

[1] *Anglo-Saxon Chronicle*, 1035.

[2] The *Chronicle* (Ann. 1039 [1040]) states that Harold died
March 17, 1040, and that he ruled four years and sixteen weeks.
This would date his accession as November 25, 1035.

[3] *Anglo-Saxon Chronicle*, 1036 [1035].

The decision reached at Oxford has been variously interpreted. At first glance it looks as if the kingdom was again divided along the line of the Thames valley. The statement of the Chronicler that Harold "was full King over all England" seems not to have been strictly contemporary but written after the King had seized the whole. What was done at Oxford was probably to establish an under-kingship of the sort that Canute had provided for Norway and Denmark. The overlordship of Harthacanute may have been recognised, but the administration was divided. This did not necessarily mean to the Scandinavian mind that the realm was divided; in the history of the North various forms of joint kingship are quite common.

For one year this arrangement was permitted to stand; but in 1037, Harold was taken to king over all England—the nation forsook Harthacanute because he tarried too long in Denmark.[1] Emma was driven from the land, perhaps to satisfy the jealousy of her rival Elgiva. The cause for the revolution of 1037 is unknown; but we may conjecture that intrigue was at work on both sides. Possibly the appearance of Emma's son Alfred in England the year before may have roused a sense of fear in the English mind and may have hastened the movement.

Sorrows now began to fall heavily upon England. In 1039, the Welsh made inroads and slew several

[1] *Anglo-Saxon Chronicle,* 1037.

of the Mercian lords. A "great wind" scattered destruction over the land. A remarkable mortality appeared among the bishops, four dying in 1038 and one more in 1039. The following year died Harold, whose unkingly and un-Christian behaviour was no doubt regarded as the cause of these calamities. He died at Oxford and was buried at Westminster. The same year Harthacanute joined his mother at Bruges, whither she had fled when exiled from England.[1]

It was neither listless choice nor lack of kinglike interest that had detained Harthacanute in Denmark; it was the danger that threatened from Norway. Hostilities seem to have begun in the spring of 1036 and to have continued for about two years. The war was finally closed with an agreement at the Brenn-isles near the mouth of the Gaut River in south-western Sweden. According to this the two young kings became sworn brothers, and it was stipulated that if the one should die leaving no heirs, the other should succeed him.[2] It was not so much of a treaty on the part of the kings as of the chief men of the kingdoms, as both peoples were evidently tiring of the warfare.

Perhaps that which most of all determined the Danes to seek peace was the news that Harold had seized the government of all England the previous year. This must have happened late

[1] *Anglo-Saxon Chronicle*, 1039 [1040].
[2] Snorre, *Saga of Magnus the Good*, c. 6.

in the year, as the Chronicler tells us that Queen
Emma was driven out of England "without pity
toward the stormy winter." In Norway there
was no party that still favoured the Knytlings;
the situation in England looked more favourable.
Evidently Harthacanute's counsellors had concluded that his inherited rights in Britain should
be claimed and defended.

Harthacanute came to Bruges with a small
force only; but it was probably the plan to use
Flanders as a base from which to descend upon
England. Nothing seems to have been done in
1039, however, except, perhaps, to prepare for a
campaign in the coming spring. But for this
there was no need: before the winter was past,
Harold lay dead at Oxford. History knows little
about the fleet-footed Prince; but from what has
been recorded we get the impression of a violent,
ambitious youth, one to whom power was sweet
and revenge sweeter. So far as we know, government in his day was poor both in state and church.
Oxford, it seems, was his residential city.

After Harold's death messengers came from
England to Bruges to summon Harthacanute.
The succession was evidently not settled without
some negotiations, for Harthacanute must have
waited two months or more before he left Flanders.
No doubt the chiefs who had placed his half-brother
on the throne were unwilling to submit without
guarantees; their behaviour had not been such as
to render their future secure. Just before mid-

22

summer Harthacanute finally arrived in England with sixty ships; he was crowned probably on June 18th.[1] For two years he ruled the country but "he did nothing kinglike."[2] Partly as a punishment, perhaps, he made England pay for the expedition that he had just fitted out, and consequently forfeited what favour he had at the very beginning.

Harthacanute is described as a sickly youth, and a Norman historian assures us that on account of his ill-health he kept God before his mind and reflected much on the brevity of human life.[3] He seems to have been of a kindly disposition, as appears from his dealings with his half-brother Edward. His sudden death at a henchman's wedding is not to be attributed to excesses but to the ailment from which he suffered. But the drunken laugh of the bystanders[4] indicates that the world did not fully appreciate that with Harthacanute perished the dynasty of Gorm.

Three men now stood forth as possible candidates for the throne of Alfred: Magnus the Good, now King of Denmark and Norway, Harthacanute's heir by oath and adoption; Sweyn, the son of Canute's sister Estrid, his nearest male relative and the ranking member of the Danish house, a prince who was probably an Englishman by birth,

[1] Steenstrup, *Normannerne*, iii., 421.
[2] *Anglo-Saxon Chronicle*, 1040.
[3] Duchesne, *Scriptores*, 179 (William of Poitiers).
[4] *Anglo-Saxon Chronicle*, 1042.

and whose aunt was the wife of Earl Godwin; and Edward, later known as the Confessor, who strangely enough represented what national feeling there might be in England, though of such feeling he himself was probably guiltless. It may be remarked in passing that all these candidates were sons of men whom Canute had deeply wronged, men whom he had deprived of life or hounded to death.

There is no good evidence that Edward was ever formally elected King of England. Harthacanute died at Lambeth, only a few miles from London. "And before the King was buried all the folk chose Edward to be King in London," says one manuscript of the *Chronicle*. If this be true, there could have been no regular meeting of the magnates. The circumstances seem to have been somewhat in the nature of a revolution headed no doubt by the anti-Danish faction in London.

That Edward was enabled to retain the crown was due largely, we are told, to the efforts of Canute's two old friends, Earl Godwin and Bishop Lifing.[1] The situation was anything but simple. The election of Magnus would restore Canute's empire, but it might also mean English and Danish revolts. To elect Sweyn would mean war with Magnus, Sweyn claiming Denmark and Magnus England. At the time the Danish claimant was making most trouble, for Sweyn seems to have arrived in England soon after Edward was pro-

[1] Florence of Worcester, *Chronicon*, i., 196-197.

claimed. All that he secured, however, was the promise that he should be regarded as Edward's successor.[1] It was doubtless well known among the English lords that the new King was inclined to, and probably pledged to a celibate life. We do not know whether Englishmen were at this time informed of the ethelings in Hungary. To most men it must have seemed likely that Alfred's line would expire with Edward; under the circumstances Sweyn was the likeliest heir.

With the accession of Edward, the Empire of the North was definitely dissolved. Fundamentally it was based on the union of England and Denmark, a union that was now repudiated. Still, the hope of restoring it lingered for nearly half a century. Three times the kings of the North made plans to reconquer England, but in each instance circumstances made successful operations impossible. After the death of Magnus in 1047, the three old dynasties once more controlled their respective kingdoms, though in the case of both Denmark and Norway the direct lines had perished. The Danish high seat alone remained to the Knytlings, now represented by Sweyn, the son of Estrid and the violent Ulf for whose tragic death the nation had now atoned.

[1] Adamus, *Gesta*, ii., c. 74.

APPENDICES

I.—CANUTE'S PROCLAMATION OF 1020[1]

1. Canute the King sends friendly greetings to his archbishops and suffragan bishops and to Thurkil the Earl and all his earls and to all his subjects in England, nobles and freemen, clerks and laymen.

2. And I make known to you that I will be a kind lord and loyal to the rights of the Church and to right secular law.

3. I have taken to heart the word and the writing that Archbishop Lifing brought from Rome from the Pope, that I should everywhere extol the praise of God, put away injustice, and promote full security and peace by the strength that God should give me.

4. Now I did not spare my treasures while unpeace was threatening to come upon you; with the help of God I have warded this off by the use of my treasures.

5. Then I was informed that there threatened us a danger that was greater than was well pleasing to us; and then I myself with the men who went with me departed for Denmark, whence came to you the greatest danger; and that I have with God's help forestalled, so that henceforth no unpeace shall come

---

[1] Liebermann, *Gesetze der Angelsachsen*, i., 273-275. For an earlier translation see Stubbs, *Select Charters*, 75-76.

to you from that country, so long as you stand by me as the law commands, and my life lasts.

6. Now I give thanks to God Almighty for His aid and His mercy in that I have averted the great evil that threatened us; so that from thence we need fear no evil, but may hope for full aid and deliverance if need be.

7. Now I will that we all humbly thank Almighty God for the mercy that He has done to our help.

8. Now I command my archbishops and all my suffragan bishops that they take due care as to the rights of the Church, each one in the district that is committed to him; and also my ealdormen I command, that they help the bishops to the rights of the Church and to the rights of my kingship and to the behoof of all the people.

9. Should any one prove so rash, clerk or layman, Dane or Angle, as to violate the laws of the Church or the rights of my kingship, or any secular statute, and refuse to do penance according to the instruction of my bishops, or to desist from his evil, then I request Thurkil the Earl, yea, even command him, to bend the offender to right, if he is able to do so.

10. If he is not able, then will I that he with the strength of us both destroy him in the land or drive him out of the land, be he of high rank or low.

11. And I also command my reeves, by my friendship and by all that they own and by their own lives, that they everywhere govern my people justly and give right judgments by the witness of the shire bishop and do such mercy therein as the shire bishop thinks right and the community can allow.

12. And if any one harbour a thief or hinder the

pursuit, he shall be liable to punishment equal to that of the thief, unless he shall clear himself before me with full purgation.

13. And I will that all the people, clerks and lay-men, hold fast the laws of Edgar which all men have chosen and sworn to at Oxford;

14. for all the bishops say that the Church demands a deep atonement for the breaking of oaths and pledges.

15. And they further teach us that we should with all our might and strength fervently seek, love, and worship the eternal merciful God and shun all un-righteousness, that is, slaying of kinsmen and murder, perjury, familiarity with witches and sorceresses, and adultery and incest.

16. And further, we command in the name of Almighty God and of all His saints, that no man be so bold as to marry a nun or a consecrated woman;

17. and if any one has done so, let him be an out-law before God and excommunicated from all Christendom, and let him forfeit all his possessions to the King, unless he quickly desist from sin and do deep penance before God.

18. And further still we admonish all men to keep the Sunday festival with all their might and observe it from Saturday's noon to Monday's dawning; and let no man be so bold as to buy or sell or to seek any court on that holy day.

19. And let all men, poor and rich, seek their church and ask forgiveness for their sins and earnestly keep every ordained fast and gladly honour the saints, as the mass priest shall bid us,

20. that we may all be able and permitted, through

the mercy of the everlasting God and the intercession
of His saints, to share the joys of the heavenly kingdom
and dwell with Him who liveth and reigneth for ever
without end. Amen.

II.—CANUTE'S CHARTER OF 1027[1]

Canute, King of all England and Denmark and of
the Norwegians and of part of the Slavic peoples,[2]
to Ethelnoth the Metropolitan and Alfric of York,
and to all bishops and primates, and to the whole
nation of the English, both nobles and freemen, wishes
health.

I make known to you that I have lately been to
Rome, to pray for the redemption of my sins, and for
the prosperity of the kingdoms and peoples subject
to my rule. This journey I had long ago vowed to
God, though, through affairs of state and other impedi-
ments, I had hitherto been unable to perform it; but
now I humbly return thanks to God Almighty for
having in my life granted to me to yearn after the
blessed apostles, Peter and Paul, and every sacred
place within and without the city of Rome, which I
could learn of, and according to my desire, personally
to venerate and adore. And this I have executed
chiefly because I had learned from wise men that the
holy apostle Peter had received from the Lord the
great power of binding and loosing, and was key-
bearer of the celestial kingdom; and I, therefore,

---

[1] This translation (with slight changes) is that of Benjamin
Thorpe: Lappenberg, *History of England*, ii., 212–215.

[2] The original has Swedes; but see above p. 152. The statement that Canute was King of the Norwegians is doubtless an
addition by the chronicler; Norway was not conquered before 1028.

deemed it extremely useful to desire his patronage before God.

Be it now known to you, that there was a great assembly of nobles at the Easter celebration, with the Lord Pope John, and the Emperor Conrad, to wit, all the princes of the nations from Mount Gargano to the nearest sea, who all received me honourably, and honoured me with magnificent presents. But I have been chiefly honoured by the Emperor with divers costly gifts, as well in golden and silver vessels as in mantles and vestments exceedingly precious.

I have therefore spoken with the Emperor and the Lord Pope, and the princes who were there, concerning the wants of all my people, both Angles and Danes, that a more equitable law and greater security might be granted to them in their journeys to Rome, and that they might not be hindered by so many barriers, nor harassed by unjust tolls; and the Emperor and King Rudolf, who has the greater number of those barriers in his dominions, have agreed to my demands; and all the princes have engaged by their edict, that my men, whether merchants or other travellers for objects of devotion, should go and return in security . and peace, without any constraint of barriers or tolls.

I then complained to the Lord Pope, and said that it greatly displeased me, that from my archbishops such immense sums of money were exacted, when, according to usage, they visited the apostolic see to receive the pall; and it was agreed that such exactions should not thenceforth be made. And all that I have demanded for the benefit of my people from the Lord Pope, from the Emperor, from King Rudolf, and from the other princes, through whose territories our way lies to

Rome, they have freely granted, and also confirmed their cessions by oath, with the witness of four archbishops and twenty bishops, and an innumerable multitude of dukes and nobles, who were present.

I therefore render great thanks to God Almighty that I have successfully accomplished all that I desired, as I had proposed in my mind, and satisfied to the utmost the wishes of my people. Now then, be it known to you, that I have vowed, as a suppliant, from henceforth to justify in all things my whole life to God, and to rule the kingdoms and peoples subjected to me justly and piously, to maintain equal justice among all; and if, through the intemperance of my youth, or through negligence, I have done aught hitherto contrary to what is just, I intend with the aid of God to amend all.

I therefore conjure and enjoin my counsellors, to whom I have intrusted the counsels of the kingdom, that from henceforth they in no wise, neither through fear of me nor favour to any powerful person, consent to, or suffer to increase any injustice in my whole kingdom; I enjoin also all sheriffs and reeves of my entire kingdom, as they would enjoy my friendship or their own security, that they use no unjust violence. to any man, either rich or poor, but that every one, both noble and freeman, enjoy just law, from which let them in no way swerve, neither for equal favour, nor for any powerful person, nor for the sake of collecting money for me, for I have no need that money should be collected for me by iniquitous exactions.

I, therefore, wish it to be made known to you, that, returning by the same way that I departed, I am going to Denmark, for the purpose of settling, with the counsel of all the Danes, firm and lasting peace with those nations, which, had it been in their power, would have deprived us of our life and kingdoms; but were unable, God having deprived them of strength, who in His loving-kindness preserves us in our kingdoms and honour, and renders naught the power of our enemies. Having made peace with the nations round us, and regulated and tranquillised all our kingdom here in the East, so that on no side we may have to fear war or enmities, I propose this summer, as soon as I can have a number of ships ready, to proceed to England; but I have sent this letter beforehand, that all the people of my kingdom may rejoice at my prosperity; for, as you yourselves know, I have never shrunk from labouring, nor will I shrink therefrom, for the necessary benefit of all my people.

I therefore conjure all my bishops and ealdormen, by the fealty which they owe to me and to God, so to order that, before I come to England, the debts of all, which we owe according to the old law, be paid; to wit, plough-alms, and a tithe of animals brought forth during the year, and the pence which ye owe to Saint Peter at Rome, both from the cities and villages; and in the middle of August, a tithe of fruits, and at the feast of Saint Martin, the first-fruits of things sown, to the church of the parish, in which each one dwells, which is in English called church-scot. If, when I come, these and others are not paid, he who is in fault shall be punished by the royal power severely and without any remission. Farewell.

BIBLIOGRAPHY

Aarböger for nordisk Oldkyndighed og Historie, udg. af det Kongelige Nordiske Oldskriftsselskab. 1866–1885. 2. Række, 1886–. Copenhagen. Continuation of *Annaler*.

Ælfric's Lives of Saints, ed. W. W. Skeat. 2 vols. London, 1881–1900. (Early English Text Society.)

Anglo-Saxon Chronicle, ed. Benjamin Thorpe. 2 vols. London, 1861. Rolls Series, No. 23.

Annaler for nordisk Oldkyndighed og Historie, udg. af det Kongelige. Nordiske Oldskriftsselskab. 1836–1863. Copenhagen, 1836–1865.

These volumes and the *Aarböger* are of great value for the study of Scandinavian culture in the Middle Ages; for the career of Canute, however, they are of slight importance.

Annales Cambriæ, ed. J. W. ab Ithel. London, 1860. Rolls Series, No. 20.

Annales Monastici, ed. H. R. Luard. 5 vols. London, 1864–1869. Rolls Series, No. 36.

Baltische Studien, herausgegeben von der Gesellschaft für pommersche Geschichte und Alterthumskunde. 1835–1892. Stettin.

Especially important are Nos. 7, 13, and 25: articles on the early relations of the Danes and the Wends.

Bibliothek der Angelsächsischen Poesie, ed. C. W. M. Grein (revised edition by R. P. Wülker). 3 vols. Cassel, 1883–1898.

Björkman, Erik, *Nordische Personennamen in England in alt- und frühmittel-englischer Zeit*. Halle, 1910. (Morsbach's *Studien zur englischen Philologie*, xxxvii.)

Bremen, Adam of, *Gesta Hammenburgensis Ecclesiæ Pontificum*, ed. J. M. Lappenberg. Hanover, 1846. (Mon. Ger. Hist., Scriptores, vii.)

349

Bresslau, H., *Jahrbücher des Deutschen Reichs unter Konrad II.* Leipsic, 1879-1884.

Bugge, Alexander, et al., *Norges Historie fremstillet for det norske Folk.* To be published in 6 volumes. Vol. i., part ii. (Christiania, 1910) deals with Norwegian history to 1030.

——*Studier over de norske Byers Selvstyre og Handel.* Christiania, 1899.

——*Vesterlandenes Indflydelse paa Nordboernes og särlig Nordmændenes ydre Kultur, Levesæt, og Samfundsforhold i Vikingetiden.* Christiania, 1905.

——*Vikingerne.* 2 vols. Copenhagen, 1904-1906. A series of brilliant essays on Scandinavian colonisation and culture in the western islands (Britain).

Cambridge History of English Literature. Edited by A. W. Ward and A. R. Waller. (In process of publication.) I. Cambridge, 1907.

Canterbury, Gervase of, *The Historical Works of Gervase of Canterbury*, ed. William Stubbs. 2 vols. London, 1879-1880. Rolls Series, No. 73.

Chabannes, Adémar de, *Historiarum Libri iii*, ed. G. Waitz. Hanover, 1841. (Mon. Ger. Hist., Scriptores, iv.)

Chronicon Abbatiæ de Evesham ad Annum 1418, ed. W. D. Macray. London, 1863. Rolls Series, No. 29.

Chronicon Abbatiæ Rameseiensis, ed. W. D. Macray. London, 1886. Rolls Series, No. 83.

Chronicon Monasterii de Abingdon, ed. Joseph Stevenson. 2 vols. London, 1858. Rolls Series, No. 2.

Cirencester, Richard of, *Speculum Historiale de Gestis Regum Angliæ*, ed. J. E. B. Mayor. 2 vols. London, 1863-1869. Rolls Series, No. 30.

Cnutonis Regis Gesta sive Encomium Emmæ, ed. G. H. Pertz. Hanover, 1866. (Mon. Ger. Hist., Scriptores, xix.)

Collingwood, W. G., *Scandinavian Britain.* London, 1908.

Corpus Poeticum Boreale. Edited by Gudbrand Vigfusson and F. York Powell. 2 vols. Oxford, 1883.

Daae, Ludvig, *Norges Helgener.* Christiania, 1879.

Diceto, Ralph of, *Opera Historica*, ed. William Stubbs. 2 vols. London, 1876. Rolls Series, No. 68.

Duchesne, André (editor), *Historiæ Normannorum Scriptores Antiqui.* Paris, 1619.

DURHAM, SIMEON OF, *Opera Omnia*, ed. Thomas Arnold. 2 vols. London, 1882–1885. Rolls Series, No. 75.

Encomium Emmæ. See *Cnutonus Regis Gesta.*

Eulogium Historiarum, ed. F. S. Haydon. 3 vols. London, 1858–1863. Rolls Series, No. 9.

Fagrskinna, ed. Finnur Jónsson. Copenhagen, 1902–1903. Brief saga of the Norwegian kings. Earlier edition by P. A. Munch and C. R. Unger (Christiania, 1847).

Flateyarbók. Edited by Gudbrand Vigfusson and C. R. Unger. Christiania, 1860. The Flat-isle Book is a late and not very reliable collection of sagas, but it cannot be wholly ignored.

FLOM, GEORGE T., *Scandinavian Influence on Southern Lowland Scotch.* New York, 1900. (Columbia University Germanic studies, i., No. 1.)

FREEMAN, E. A., *History of the Norman Conquest of England.* 6 vols. New York, 1873.

FRIESEN, OTTO VON, *Historiska Runskrifter.* (Fornvännen, 1909.)

——*Om Runskriftens Härkomst.* (Sprokvetenskapliga Sällskapets Förhandlinger, 1904–1906.)

GIESEBRECHT, W. VON, *Geschichte der Deutschen Kaiserzeit.* 3 vols. Brunswick and Leipsic, 1855–1868.

HILDEBRAND, B. E., *Anglosachsiska Mynt i svenska Kongliga Myntkabinettet funna i Sveriges Jord.* Stockholm, 1881.

HILDEBRAND, HANS O. H., *Svenska Folket under Hednatiden.* Stockholm, 1886.

Historians of the Church of York and its Archbishops, ed. James Raine. 3 vols. London, 1879–1894. Rolls Series, No. 71.

HODGKIN, THOMAS, *The History of England from the Earliest Times to the Norman Conquest.* London, 1906. (Hunt-Poole, *Political History of England*, i.)

HUNT, WILLIAM, *The English Church, A.D. 597–1066.* London, 1899. (Stephens-Hunt, *A History of the English Church*, i.)

HUNTINGDON, HENRY OF, *Historia Anglorum*, ed. Thomas Arnold. London, 1879. Rolls Series, No. 74.

Jómsvíkingasaga ok Knytlinga, ed. C. C. Rafn. Copenhagen, 1828.

Jumièges, William of, *Historiæ Nomannorum Libri viii*, ed. André Duchesne. Paris, 1619. (Hist. Norm. Scriptores.)

KEMBLE, J. M., *Codex Diplomaticus Ævi Saxonici.* 6 vols. London, 1839–1848. (Eng. Hist. Soc.)

Knytlingasaga. See *Jómsvíkingasaga.*

KÖBKE, P., *Om Runerne i Norden.* Copenhagen, 1890. A brief popular account of the runes; valuable for its translation of important inscriptions.

LANG, ANDREW, *A History of Scotland.* 4 vols. Edinburgh, 1903–1907.

Langebek, Jacob (editor), *Scriptores Rerum Danicarum Medii Ævi.* 9 vols. Copenhagen, 1772–1878.

LAPPENBERG, J. M., *History of England under the Anglo-Saxon Kings.* Translated by Benjamin Thorpe. 2 vols. London, 1845.

LARSON, LAURENCE M., *The King's Household in England before the Norman Conquest.* Madison, 1904. (Bulletin of the University of Wisconsin.)

——*The Political Policies of Cnut as King of England.* American Historical Review, xv., No. 4 (July, 1910).

LAVISSE, ERNEST, *Histoire de France depuis les origines jusqu'à. la révolution.* 9 vols. Paris, 1903–1911.

LIEBERMANN, F., *Die Gesetze der Angelsachsen.* 2 vols. Halle, 1898–1899.

——*Ungedrückte anglo-normannische Geschichtsquellen.* Strasburg, 1879.

Liber Monasterii de Hyda, ed. Edward Edwards. London, 1866. Rolls Series, No. 45.

Liber Vitæ: Register and Martyrology of New Minster and Hyde Abbey, ed. W. de Gray Birch. London, 1892. (Hampshire Record Society.)

Lives of Edward the Confessor, ed. H. R. Luard. London, 1858. Rolls Series, No. 3.

MALMESBURY, WILLIAM OF, *De Gestis Pontificum Anglorum Libri Quinque,* ed. N. E. S. A. Hamilton. London, 1870. Rolls Series, No. 52.

——*De Gestis Regum Anglorum Libri Quinque,* ed. William Stubbs. 2 vols. London, 1887–1889. Rolls Series, No. 90.

MANITIUS, M., *Deutsche Geschichte unter den sächsischen und salischen Kaisern.* Stuttgart, 1889. (Bibliothek deutscher Geschichte.)

Memorials of Saint Edmund's Abbey, ed. Thomas Arnold. 3 vols. London, 1890–1896. Rolls Series, No. 96.

MERSEBURG, THIETMAR OF, *Chronicon*, ed. J. M. Lappenberg. Hanover, 1839. (Mon. Ger. Hist., Scriptores, iii.)

MIGNE, J. P., *Patrologiæ Cursus Completus. Series Latina.* 221 vols. Paris, 1844–1864. Vol. cxli. contains the sermons of Adémar and the letters of Fulbert.

MONTELIUS, OSCAR, *Kulturgeschichte Schwedens von den ältesten Zeiten bis zum elften Jahrhundert nach Christus.* Leipsic, 1906. An excellent account of Northern antiquity based largely on archeological evidence.

MORRIS, WILLIAM A., *The Frankpledge System.* New York, 1910. (Harvard Historical Series, xiv.)

MUNCH, P. A., *Det norske Folks Historie.* 8 vols. Christiania, 1852–1863.

Napier, A. S., and Stevenson, W. H. (editors), *The Crawford Collection of Early Charters and Documents.* Oxford, 1895.

Olafs Saga hins Helga. Edited by R. Keyser and C. R. Unger. Christiania, 1849. A saga of Saint Olaf; largely legendary.

OLRIK, AXEL, *Nordisk Aandsliv i Vikingetid og tidlig Middelalder.* Copenhagen, 1907. An excellent popular discussion of medieval culture in Scandinavia.

OMAN, C. W. C., *England Before the Norman Conquest.* New York, 1910. (Oman, *History of England in Seven Volumes*, i.)

Origines Islandicæ. Edited by Gudbrand Vigfusson and F. York Powell. 2 vols. Oxford, 1905.

PALGRAVE, FRANCIS, *History of Normandy and England.* 4 vols. London, 1851–1864.

PARIS, MATTHEW, *Chronica Majora*, ed. H. R. Luard. 7 vols. London, 1872–1883. Rolls Series, No. 57.

Pertz, G. H., et al. (editors), *Monumenta Germaniæ Historica, Scriptores.* 30 vols. Hanover, 1826–1896.

POITIERS, WILLIAM OF, *Gesta Willelmi Ducis Normannorum et Regis Angliæ*, ed. André Duchesne. Paris, 1619. (Hist. Norm. Scriptores.)

POLLOCK, F., and MAITLAND, F. W., *The History of the English Law Before the Time of Edward I.* 2 vols. Cambridge, 1895.

RAMSAY, J. H., *The Foundations of England.* 2 vols. London, 1898.

RAOUL GLABER, *Les cinq livres de ses histoires*, ed. M. Prou. Paris, 1886. (Collection de Textes, No. 1.)

23

Saga Book of the Viking Club, vi., part i. London. January, 1909.

Saga Olafs Konungs ens Helga. Edited by P. A. Munch and C. R. Unger. Christiania, 1853. The so-called "Historical Saga" of Saint Olaf.

ST. JOHN, JAMES A., *History of the Four Conquests of England.* 2 vols. London, 1862. Extremely uncritical.

SAXO GRAMMATICUS, *Gesta Danorum*, ed. A. Holder. Strasburg, 1886.

SCHÜCK, HENRIK, *Studier i nordisk Litteratur- och Religionshistoria.* 2 vols. Stockholm, 1904.

SNORRE. See Sturlason.

Sproglige og historiske Afhandlinger viede Sophus Bugges Minde. Christiania, 1908. Historical and philological essays by various authors. Cited as Afhandlinger, etc.

STEENSTRUP, JOHANNES C. H. R., et al., *Danmarks Riges Historie.* 6 vols. Copenhagen, 1896–1906. The great co-operative history of Denmark. Vol. i. is by Steenstrup.

——*Normannerne.* 4 vols. Copenhagen, 1876–1882. (See Foreword.)

——*Venderne og de Danske för Valdemar den Stores Tid.* Copenhagen, 1900. A study of Danish expansion on the south Baltic shores.

STEPHENS, GEORGE, *The Old-Northern Runic Monuments of Scandinavia and England.* 4 vols. London and Copenhagen, 1866–1901. Of great value for the inscriptions that the author has collected and reproduced; the interpretations, however, are not always reliable. Vol. iv. is by S. O. M. Söderberg and J. S. F. Stephens.

STUBBS, WILLIAM, *Registrum Sacrum Anglicanum.* Oxford, 1897.

STURLASON, SNORRE, *Heimskringla: Nóregs Konunga Sogur*, ed. Finnur Jónsson. 4 vols. Copenhagen, 1893–1901. Samfundet til Udgivelse af Gammel Nordisk Litteratur. Cited as Snorre. This is the chief source of information as to Canute's ambitions for empire in the North.

SVENO AGGONIS, *Historia Legum Castrensium Regis Canuti Magni*, ed. Jacob Langebek. Copenhagen, 1774. (Script. Rer. Danic., iii.)

TARANGER, A., *Den angelsaksiske Kirkes Indflydelse paa den norske.* Christiania, 1890. (Norske Historiske Forening.)

DA
.T 952
181°

TURNER, SHARON, *History of the Anglo-Saxons.* 3 vols. London, 1823.

VITALIS, ORDERICUS, *Historia Ecclesiastica*, ed. Auguste le Prévost. 5 vols. Paris, 1838–1855. (Société de l'Histoire de France.)

Wharton, Henry (editor), *Anglia Sacra.* 2 vols. London, 1691.

WIMMER, LUDVIG F. A., *De danske Runemindesmærker.* 4 vols. Copenhagen, 1895–1908.

——*Die Runenschrift.* Übersetzt von Dr. F. Holthausen. Berlin, 1887.

WIPO, *Vita Chuonradi Regis.* Hanover, 1854. (Mon. Ger. Hist., Scriptores, xi.)

WORCESTER, FLORENCE OF, *Chronicon ex Chronicis*, ed. Benjamin Thorpe. 2 vols. London, 1848–1849. (Eng. Hist. Soc.)

WORSAAE, J. J. A., *Minder om de Danske og Nordmændene i England, Skotland, og Irland.* Copenhagen, 1851. Translation: *An Account of the Danes and Norwegians in England, Scotland, and Ireland.* London, 1852.

INDEX

A

Abingdon, monastery of, 176, 193, 313
Adam of Bremen cited, 14, 35 n., 154, 161, 185, 193, 194, 272, 273, 325 *et passim*
Adémar de Chabannes cited, 165 n., 264, 265
Agdir, district in southern Norway, 238
Alain, Duke of Brittany, 254
Aldgyth, wife of Edmund Ironside, 71, 125
Alfiva, 316–318; *see* Elgiva
Alfred, King of England, 23, 24, 45, 79, 85, 105, 126, 158, 181, 338–340
Alfred, son of Ethelred, 53, 127, 253–256, 335
Alfric, Archbishop of York, 312, 344
Alfric, Bishop, 333
Alfric, English ealdorman, 95
Alfric, ealdorman, and naval commander, 27 n.
Alfric, old English author, 291, 296
Algar, English magnate, 88
Ali, housecarle, 135
Almar Darling, English magnate, 88
Alphabet, runic, 299, 300
Alphege, Archbishop, 29, 44, 147, 172, 173, 176
Alstad Stone, the, 302
America, discovery of, 17 and n.

Andover, 29
Anglo-Saxon Chronicle cited, 27, 29, 79, 80, 92 n., 128, 211, 215, 220, 221, 232, 297, 310, 334–339 *et passim*
Anglo-Saxon kingdom, 16, 21–24, 58, 84, 85
Anglo-Saxon legal system, the, 281
Anglo-Saxon literature, 296, 297
Anses, the, old Northern divinities, 163, 182, 183, 198, 309
Anund Jacob, King of Sweden, 207, 208, 213, 216–220, 225
Aquitaine, 74, 264, 265, 298
Arne, Norwegian magnate, 200, 245
Arngrim, magnate in the Danelaw, 70
Arnungs, Norwegian noble family, 199, 200, 245
Art, Celtic and Northern, 301 ff.
Asbjörn, Norwegian warrior, 199, 200
Ashington, battle of, 89, 93–96, 99–101, 109, 115, 117, 294; dedication at, 111, 169, 296
Asia Minor, 266
Aslak Erlingsson, Norwegian chieftain, 207
Attila, 293
Avon River, 191
Aylesford, 92

357

Heroes of the Nations

A SERIES of biographical studies of the lives and work of a number of representative historical characters about whom have gathered the great traditions of the Nations to which they belonged, and who have been accepted, in many instances, as types of the several National ideals. With the life of each typical character is presented a picture of the National conditions surrounding him during his career.

The narratives are the work of writers who are recognized authorities on their several subjects, and while thoroughly trustworthy as history, present picturesque and dramatic "stories" of the Men and of the events connected with them.

To the Life of each "Hero" is given one duodecimo volume, handsomely printed in large type, provided with maps and adequately illustrated according to the special requirements of the several subjects.

For full list of volumes see next page.

HEROES OF THE NATIONS

Ingram Content Group UK Ltd.
Milton Keynes UK
UKHW020020190423
420401UK00005B/76